I keep a weblog so that I can breathe in this suffocating air ... In a society where one is taken to history's abattoir for the mere crime of thinking, I write so as not to be lost in my despair ... so that I feel that I am somewhere where my calls for justice can be uttered ... I write a weblog so that I can shout, cry and laugh, and do the things that they have taken away from me in Iran today...

Email: lolivashe@yahoo.com
www.lolivashaneh.blogspot.com

WE ARE IRAN

Edited and translated from the Farsi by
NASRIN ALAVI

Soft Skull Press

An imprint of Counterpoint | Berkeley

ISBN-10: 1-933368-05-5
ISBN-13: 978-1-933368-05-4

Library of Congress Cataloging-in-Publication Data
Alavi, Nasrin.
  We are Iran / Nasrin Alavi.
    p. cm.
ISBN-13: 978-1-933368-05-4
1. Internet--Social aspects--Iran. 2. Weblogs--Iran. 3. Government, Resistance
to--Iran. 4.
Censorship--Iran. I. Title.

HN670.2.Z9I56 2005
323'.044'0955090511--dc22

2005019657

Cover design byTeresa Bubela
Text design by Lindsay Nash
Printed in the United States of America

Soft Skull Press
An Imprint of Counterpoint LLC
1919 Fifth Street
Berkeley, CA 94710
www.softskull.com
www.counterpointpress.com

Printed in the United States of America
Distributed by Publishers Group West

10 9 8 7 6 5 4 3

CONTENTS

I A VIRTUAL COMMUNITY

In September 2001 Hossein Derakhshan, a young Iranian journalist who had recently moved to Canada, set up one of the very first weblogs in Farsi, his native language. (For the uninitiated, a weblog or blog is a kind of diary or journal posted on the Internet.) In response to a request from a reader, Hossein created a simple how-to-blog guide in Farsi. With the modest aim of giving other Iranians a voice, he set free an entire community.

Today Farsi is the fourth most frequently used language for keeping on-line journals. There are more Iranian blogs than there are Spanish, German, Italian, Chinese or Russian. According to the 2004 NITLE Blog Census,[1] there are more than 64,000 blogs written in Farsi. A phenomenal figure, given that in neighboring countries such as Iraq there are fewer than 50 known bloggers.

Blogging in Iran has grown so fast because it meets the needs no longer met by the print media; it provides a safe space in which people may write freely on a wide variety of topics, from the most serious and urgent to the most frivolous. Some prominent writers use their blogs to bypass strict state censorship and to publish their work on-line; established journalists can post uncensored reports on their blogs; expatriate Iranians worldwide use their blogs to communicate with those back home; ordinary citizens record their thoughts and deeds in daily journals; and student groups and NGOs utilize their blogs as a means of co-ordinating their activities.

17 November 2004

I keep a weblog so that I can breathe in this suffocating air ... In a
society where one is taken to history's abattoir for the mere crime of
thinking, I write so as not to be lost in my despair ... so that I feel
that I am somewhere where my calls for justice can be uttered ... I
write a weblog so that I can shout, cry and laugh, and do the things
that they have taken away from me in Iran today ...

Email: lolivashe@yahoo.com
www.lolivashaneh.blogspot.com

The worst that could happen to a blogger in the West is that they might be
looked upon as self-absorbed 'cyber-geeks' or 'anoraks', but in Iran – a country
that Reporters sans Frontières called 'the biggest prison for journalists in the
Middle East' – honest self-expression carries a heavy price. In the last six years as
many as 100 print publications, including 41 daily newspapers, have been closed
by Iran's hardline judiciary.

In April 2003 Iran became the first government to take direct action against
bloggers. Sina Motallebi, a journalist behind a popular weblog (www.roozne-
gar.com), was imprisoned. His arrest was just the beginning and many more
bloggers and on-line journalists have been arrested since. As Reporters sans
Frontières put it: 'In a country where the independent press has to fight for its
survival on a daily basis, on-line publications and weblogs are the last media to
fall into the authorities' clutches.' They add that through arrests and intimidation, 'the Iranian authorities are now trying to spread terror among on-line journalists' (16 October 2004).

Intimidation such as the arrest of Sina Motallebi's elderly father or the
accusations of adultery against on-line journalist Fershteh Ghazi. According
to Reporters sans Frontières, five other imprisoned web journalists, 'Javad
Gholam Tamayomi, Omid Memarian, Shahram Rafihzadeh, Hanif Mazroi and
Rozbeh Mir Ebrahimi are expected to be accused of having sex with her. Some of
them are said to have been forced to sign confessions. Such accusations by the

authorities are common against political prisoners in Iran' (29 October 2004). Adultery is a crime punishable by stoning.

In October 2004, while several Internet journalists and bloggers were held in undisclosed locations awaiting trial, Ayatollah Shahrudi, the head of the judiciary, announced new laws expressly covering 'cyber crimes': anyone 'propagating against the regime, acting against national security, disturbing the public mind and insulting religious sanctities through computer systems or telecommunications would be punished'. This announcement was accompanied by a number of articles in state propaganda newspapers such the *Keyhan* daily, which 'exposed' the Iranian blogosphere as a 'network led by the CIA conspiring to overthrow the regime'.

The crackdowns suggest that the regime is determined to curtail freedom of speech in cyberspace. Yet faced with a judiciary prepared to stone someone to death to silence them, an increasing number of blogs are now written

Photo © Hossein Derakhshan www.vagrantly.com

SINA MOTALLEBI (*RIGHT OF PICTURE*) – THE FIRST BLOGGER IN THE WORLD TO BE IMPRISONED FOR THE CONTENTS OF HIS BLOG – IN THE SUMMER OF 2002 WITH COLLEAGUES AT THE *HAYAT-E NOU* NEWSPAPER. SOON AFTERWARDS THE NEWSPAPER WAS CLOSED DOWN, ALONG WITH MORE THAN 100 OTHER PUBLICATIONS. SINA HAS LEFT IRAN AND LIVES IN EUROPE WITH HIS WIFE AND SON. HOWEVER, ACCORDING TO REPORTERS SANS FRONTIÈRES, THE AUTHORITIES ARRESTED HIS FATHER IN SEPTEMBER 2004 IN AN ATTEMPT TO SILENCE THE NOW-EXILED BLOGGER.

anonymously. Additionally, many political Internet sites have gone underground, making them even more radical and critical.

Yet despite the very real risks, there are some bloggers who still write under their own names. Bijan Safsari was editor-in-chief and publisher of several independent pro-democracy newspapers – all of them shut down by the regime. Each time one of his newspapers was closed down, it quickly resurfaced under a new name. Eventually, this game of cat and mouse got Bijan thrown into jail and now that there are no other venues where he can write or publish, he keeps a blog.

---

18 February 2004

There are those such as [Muhammad-Ali] Abtahi [the Iranian Parliamentary ex-Vice President] who have called our virtual community too political and have said that we should use weblogs for their intended use ... that is to say, for clichéd daily diaries ... So what if we use our blogs in ways not intended for or defined during the distant conception of this medium?

At a time when our society is deprived of its rightful free means of communication, and our newspapers are being closed down one by one — with writers and journalists crowding the corners of our jails ... the only realm that can safeguard and shoulder the responsibility of free speech is the blogosphere.

Email: safsari@bijan-safsari.com
http://bijan-safsari.com

According to data from the World Bank (2001), Iran has more personal computers per 1,000 people than the regional average. Estimates of the number of on-line users range from four million to seven million and growing. However, experts maintain that these figures do not reflect the current reality, because every month thousands more Iranians buy computers and go on-line. The number of Iranians on-line is likely to more than double again in the next five years, in a country where two-thirds of the population are under 30 and many are already technologically savvy.

Interestingly – even ironically – thanks to the education policies of the Islamic Republic, those who enter further education tend to be from a wide cross-section of Iranian society; and many of these students throughout Iran, all of them from very different social and regional backgrounds, have access to the Internet at their place of study.

---

20 July 2003

Has everyone noticed the spooky absence of graffiti in our public toilets since the arrival of weblogs? Remember the toilets at university we used to call our 'Freedom Columns'?

Email: pythonir@yahoo.com
http://python.persianblog.com

---

1 May 2003

My blog is an opportunity for me to be heard ... a free microphone that doesn't need speakers ... a blank page ...
   Sometimes I stretch out on this page in the nude ... now and again I hide behind it. Occasionally I dance on it ... Once in a while I tear it up ... and from time to time I draw a picture of my childhood on it ... I think ... I live ... I blog ... therefore I ... exist.

Email: deltangestan@yahoo.com
http://deltangestan.com

---

12 January 2004

This is a personal note of gratitude to Hossein Derakhshan, the 'Godfather' of Iranian blogs, who opened up the world to a society ... proving that even a 30-year-old Iranian, with merely the aid of a notebook and a connection to the Internet, can make a difference ... So much so that according to a *Guardian* newspaper report [18

December 2003] he is deemed one of the top 15 international figures 'whose weblogs have caused the biggest stir both in and outside the blogosphere'.

Within only a two-year period his tireless efforts have led to tens of thousands of Farsi blogs ... a phenomenon that I believe will eventually influence our awareness, our personas and our lives ...

Email: silence1355@yahoo.com
http://shortcut.persianblog.com

In recent decades analysts, academics and journalists have had little or no real access to Iran. So they have at times relied unduly on partial inquiry and the images presented by State propaganda. Dan De Luce, the *Guardian*'s correspondent in Iran for more than a year, was expelled from the country by the Iranian government in May 2004. As he puts it: 'Stifling the flow of information means that the nuances of Iranian society are often obscured to the outside world. Any foreigner who visits Iran is struck by the gap between the reality of Iranian society and the image cultivated by the regime.' (*Guardian*, 24 May 2004)

Yet through the anonymity that blogs can provide, those who once lacked voices are at last speaking up and discussing issues that have never been aired in any other media in the Islamic world.

30 October 2003

Islam is compatible with democracy*

*Subject to terms and conditions

Email: weblog@ksajadi.com
www.ksajadi.com/fblog

Iran's burgeoning on-line communities have been able to evade the cultural and political restraints regarding speech, appearance and relations between the sexes; restraints which are strictly enforced in public. As researchers such as Babak Rahimi[2] have revealed, websites and blogs have made it possible for young Iranians to express themselves freely and anonymously – especially young women. The Internet, 'as an advancing new means of communication, has played an important role in the ongoing struggle for democracy in Iran', says Rahimi, and 'has opened a new virtual space for political dissent'.

VOTING AGAINST 'GOD'S REPRESENTATIVE ON EARTH'

In recent years the Iranian people have demonstrated their desire for change by overwhelmingly voting for those parliamentary candidates who promise democracy. The Islamic hardliners have a single campaign theme: the principles of the 1979 Islamic Revolution will receive a fatal blow if the reformers are victorious.

In the 1997 election campaign Ali Akbar Nateq-Nouri, the Speaker of Parliament, enjoyed the implicit endorsement of the Supreme Leader, who is deemed by the ruling clergy to be 'God's representative on earth'. Nearly 80 per cent of eligible voters participate and a massive 70 per cent of them voted for the little-known cleric Muhammad Khatami, giving his reform agenda enormous backing, while at the same time voting against Ali Akbar Nateq-Nouri, ignoring the endorsement of God's representative on earth.

Ex-President Khatami had gained the overwhelming support of the Iranian people because of the consistent message of his speeches: 'There are those ... who concede no change ... Their God is their meagre and dim perceptions, which fight all the people's demands in the name of religion ... God forbid that one day our people will feel the authorities are not meeting their real demands and that dirty hands have succeeded in disappointing them and thus alienating them. Then, no military, security or judicial power will be able to save the country.' In two subsequent presidential elections, ex-President Khatami had won 77 per cent and 70 per cent of the vote, with approximately 20 million votes cast. He succeeded everywhere, in every demographic group – he even carried Qom, the religious bastion of Iran.

But change has been totally blocked by the hardliners who keep hold of the real power through the judiciary and the Guardian Council (a conservative supervisory body). They have demonstrated their formidable power by abolishing the reformist press, vetoing parliamentary and election candidates, and arresting, torturing and assassinating many liberals and student activists.

---

8 January 2004

You have heard the story of my generation many times. A generation that grew up with bombs, rockets, war and revolutionary slogans ... A generation that had battle-green grenade-shaped piggy banks ...

The girls of my generation will never forget their head teachers tugging hard at tiny strands of hair that somehow fell out of their veils to teach them a lesson. The boys of my generation will never forget being slapped five times in the face for wearing shirts with Western labels on them ... all of us have hundreds of similar memories ...

My generation is the damaged generation. We were constantly chastised that we were duty-bound to safeguard and uphold the sacred blood that was shed for us during a revolution and a war. Any kind of happiness was forbidden for us ...

My generation would be beaten up outside cinema queues or pizza restaurants ... punished in the public parks; kicked and punched in the centres of town by the regime's militia ... I will never forget the militia's Toyota vans and the loudspeaker announcements in Vali'Asr Square: 'We will fight against all boys and girls!' – shouting those exact words!

Who can forget? For my generation talking to a member of the opposite sex (something quite ordinary for the new generation) was akin to adultery and its punishments are better left unsaid. These are just partial moments in all of our bitter lives: each and every one of us could write a book about them.

But I also remember the start of the reform movement. This same generation would distribute election pamphlets and posters for Khatami. And even for this we were reprimanded and beaten, but we stood up for him so that one day hope might come. It's unfair to say he did nothing ... we got concerts, poetry readings, carefree chats in coffee shops and tight Manteaus. But is this all that my generation wanted?

It was also during this time that student activists were thrown in prison, newspapers were shut down – and yet Khatami was silent ... it was at this time that the students of my generation were labeled hooligans and Western lackeys ... and again Khatami appeared to agree through his silence ...

Even the subsequent parliamentary elections of reformists did not bring any benefits for my generation. Under the almighty shadow of the Guardian Council, sometimes hearing the words of the enemy from the mouths of those you considered friends has been even harder to bear ...

Email: arareza@Gmail.com
dentist.blogspot.com

EX-PRESIDENT KHATAMI

© Hadi Heidary www.haditoons.com

HADI HEIDARI

The unelected Supreme Leader Ayatollah Ali Khamenei and the conservative clerics and lawyers control the courts, the army, the media, political councils and the powerful Islamic foundations (bonyads) that very nearly run the economy. In February 2004 the conservatives banned more than 2,000 candidates from running in parliamentary elections, dropping any pretence at democracy and reasserting full control over the State.

---

13 February 2004

One of the greatest blessings of the Islamic Republic has been that we no longer hold anything sacred …

In 1935 the monarch Reza Shah, a secular modernizer, issued an edict that declared the wearing of traditional dress (for both women and men) an offence punishable by a prison term … As hard as Reza Shah tried, he could not have done what the ayatollahs have recently achieved … it has gone so far that today's burgeoning youth, supposedly ruled by the 'representative of God on earth', now even deny the existence of God himself.

http://weblog.omila.com

THE CHILDREN OF THE REVOLUTION

Those who lived through the Islamic Revolution almost a quarter of a century ago are now a minority. More than 70 per cent of the nation is under 30, and for this population, literacy rates for young men and women stand well over 90 per cent, even in rural areas. Notably, more than half of those graduating from university in Iran today are women.

Iran's younger generation has been completely transformed through the Islamic Republic's education policies of free education and national literacy campaigns. Paradoxically, this has created an educated and politicized youth with voting rights at 16 – and they are ready and willing to express their frustration.

Yet today, just as Muslim women elsewhere in the Islamic world are once

Photos © Yalda Moaiery www.kargah.com

YOUNG IRANIANS AT A SHOPPING CENTRE

again taking up the veil, it is the norm in Iran to see young women trying to keep their covering to a 'legal' minimum. They have turned the veil into a mark of protest. Twenty-five years after the Revolution, its boldest and most vocal opponents are the children of the Revolution. The Iranian authorities want to shield young people from the 'cultural onslaught' of the West, but this has only made them more curious about – and almost fixated upon – the foreign culture they are being denied.

'Many Iranians, even those on very limited incomes, own illegal satellite dishes that give them instant access to American television,' explains the veteran journalist and writer Elaine Sciolino (*Persian Mirrors*, 2000). 'CDs, videos, and computer programs are pirated and sold on the streets for a fraction of their price in the United States. E-mail is more widely available in Iran than in many other Middle Eastern countries.'

---

19 July 2003

There will come a day when every single thing will be put right ...
There will be no censors filtering blogs ... If they show a veiled
woman on TV ... They will chequer the TV screen ... Then you and I
... will walk the streets till dawn, with a bottle of Champagne ...
That is, if your mum lets us!

Email: farshiid@gmail.com
http://acetaminophen.persianblog.com

For a quarter of a century Iran has been a laboratory of political and social experimentation. It has also experienced what no other Muslim state has experienced in the twentieth century, namely two decades during which ideological, revolutionary Islam co-existed with what could be called a more 'secular' dimension.

IRANIAN GIRLS DISCUSSING HAPPENINGS
IN THE BLOGOSPHERE

Cartoon © Hamidreza Nasiry

In this mixed public space debates, inquiries and even some reforms proved possible. By exposing Islam to public criticism, the Iranian Revolution has made possible discussions about religion, values and the relationship between religion and society.

---

8 August 2002

What have the likes of me learned after 12 years of formal religious education? What is the outcome of being consistently bombarded with sacred information in this Islamic Republic of ours?

1. When you talk about your religion for over 20 years, its problems will be highlighted.

2. Religious education is the best way to create agnostics in the modern world. Just look around at the people you personally know who went to the infamously strict Islamic schools, like Haghani, Kamal, Moofid, etc.

3. Even those most addicted to religion will at some stage overdose.

4. The problem is not with Islam but with a few of our radical fellow Muslims.

The other day I saw a construction worker fast asleep next to a cement mixer; he appeared to have developed a deaf ear to all that noise. After so many years of being bombarded with religious facts you just stop hearing them.

Email: lbahram@yahoo.com
http://lbahram.blogspot.com

After a visit to Iran in 2002, Professor Jürgen Habermas said of future social developments there: 'Nobody knows ... You would, for example, have to have a greater insight into the thoughts of young women, above all those with an academic background. Women already comprise over half the student population. How many of them would take off their headscarves in public if they could?

Do these heads contain a powder keg that the regime of the old ayatollahs has to fear more than anything else?'[3]

---

16 June 2003

At last it's over. I've spent the last five years in the nasty hell-hole of May'boad.* But it's over ... I've packed my things and moved back home.

I remember when I started my course at that so-called university ... we must have been the first group of single girls entering that God-forsaken place and setting up on our own ... so many times coming home and washing the spit of passers-by off my clothes ... they just could not tolerate our shameful headscarves ... without exception then, all the native women used to wear chadors ... They say that things are changing and extremists are getting more tolerant ... a friend of mine even thinks that we started a revolution here ...

It's been just five years, but the same shopkeepers who would refuse to serve us if we were not wearing a chador now have teenage daughters who dress more provocatively than we ever dared to ... Looking around this tiny town, only five years later you see that many of the local young girls have shed their black chadors.

We did not start a revolution here. Our 'allegedly Reformist President' did not bring about a more tolerant society ... Societies evolve and change and it's the ordinary people that change them ... 70 per cent of our population is under 30 and many just don't want to live like their parents used to ... Eventually they will have to ... not just tolerate us ... but also live by our rules ...

* May'boad is a tiny desert town; as part of the realization of the Islamic Republic's policy of 'higher education for the masses', universities have been set up throughout Iran

By Borderline

---

21 September 2003

When most of our people are fed up and, according to the
Government's own figures, 11 per cent have no income at all ... And
we still don't know anything about the state of the students they
arrested after last term's mass demonstrations and ... then to be
treated with contempt during my registration at Shahid Beheshty
University ...

The first thing they noticed was my make-up!!! Scrolled across
my Conduct Form: HEAVY MAKE-UP!!! And started telling me that I
would be answerable for this in the after-life!!! Is wearing make-up
cannibalism or something?!!!

What about all our corrupt government officials? Will they ever
be answerable to anyone?!!!

They're saying our veils are getting too small. 10 cm is too small?
Why don't they make the boys with long hair cover their heads!!?
Hair is hair!!! Anyway we have to burn these veils!! So don't bother
wasting your money buying the stuff ...

By Water Lily

20 November 2003

Yesterday I bought a turquoise ring ... They say it brings you
happiness ... I didn't let my boyfriend buy it ... I bought it myself.

I wanted to be the creator of my own happiness, beauty and
freedom ... The era of fairy-tale heroes has come to an end.

Email: myownsroom@yahoo.com
http://myownsroom.blogspot.com

3 June 2003

Do you have a fantasy that can never fade away?

I want to be with a man who would talk to me rapidly in Italian
... While not understanding a word of it, to know what he means in

the depths of his eyes ... and to just nod my head in agreement ...
Farsi words have become so shallow for me.

I want someone who speaks a different language. I want us to be
able to use our hands, eyes and our heat, as words can be very
treacherous. Very.

Email: khanoomigoli@yahoo.com
http://khanoomgol.blogspot.com

One of the major attractions of blogging in Iran is that it enables young people
to bypass many of the strict social codes imposed on them by the theocratic
regime. The Internet makes it easy to socialize, flirt, tell irreverent jokes, arrange
dates and keep in touch. Popular young bloggers such as 'acetaminophen' (see
below) offer us a snapshot of the underground landscape of their lives.

---

7 December 2002

Eid-e Fetr at the end of Ramadan is the only Eid when everyone's
happy. For those who have been fasting for a month and those of
you who have been having secret tortuous lunches, Happy Eid!

22 March 2003

– Darling you look beautiful tonight ...
– But you're still the same trash that I've had to put up with for a
lifetime ...

I prefer it when my beloved parents at least communicate, as it's
so boring when they totally ignore each other ...

24 March 2003

Do you have a boyfriend? No I write a weblog instead ...

2 October 2003

I dreamt I was Cinderella, everything was going really well until the

king's envoy appeared and announced to my wicked stepmother:
'We must see all the girls in this household, the prince has been
assassinated and the only piece of evidence left by the assassin is
this glass slipper.'

7 December 2003

Sin or whatever …

I've fallen in love with myself … but I can't work out whether it's
the real thing or I'll end up taking advantage of myself …

Email: farshiid@gmail.com
http://acetaminophen.persianblog.com

---

21 July 2002

This is my situation.
For my love a suitor has come via her family.
But so that no one can know about our love
She is forced to see him a while before rejecting him.
A forced relationship with my hateful rival.
And I who am privy to all her secrets and the soothers of all her
pains
Am burning in my lover's fire.

Email: fiftypercentnormal@yahoo.com
http://www.goldoon.com

---

8 March 2003

My good deed of the day:
I came across a cockroach in the kitchen today (I don't want any
of you out there thinking we have cockroaches in our house,
because we don't – it must have got in through a window or
something), but out of the total kindness of my heart I ignored it
and let it escape …
I'm glad Mum wasn't in the kitchen to see this as she would have

said: 'What? Have you fallen in love again?!!!' Mum thinks the only
people on earth who don't kill cockroaches ... are those who have
just fallen in love!

Email: z8unak@z8un.com

http://z8un.com

CULTURAL INVASION

In recent years social scientists have observed that young Iranians are caught in
the conflict between globalization and tradition. Their formal education and the
state media try to keep them in line, but Islamic revolutionary values are being
challenged by a 'Western cultural onslaught': the Internet and satellite television
have opened the world to Iranians. Twenty-five years after the Revolution, Iran
has a young, educated population – in particular an assertive generation of educated women who are entering previously forbidden domains.

The Morality Police have enforced the rules of the regime: no alcohol, no
dancing and no pop music – bans that are still in force today. The intention was
to create 'soldiers for Islam', but now groups of young people who aspire to a
more Western lifestyle have turned such culturally alien events as St Valentine's
Day into a local festival. According to one report on 14 February 2003: 'Tehran's
traders were rubbing their hands on Thursday after seeing sales of perfume and
other gifts soar ahead of St Valentine's Day, the new cause for celebration for
young lovers in Islamic Iran.' Meanwhile, Iranians such as the blogger Massoud
Borjian have made the day their own.

14 February 2004

For us Iranians who rarely have moments for real tranquillity and
calm free from turmoil, 14th of February, Saint Valentine's Day has
become the best excuse to remember our beloveds ...

As Hafez [Persian poet [1326–1389]] has
said:
Truthfully I admit, with much joy and
such glee
Enslaved to love, from both worlds I am
free
Congratulation on the Eid of lovers

Email: borjian@gmail.com
http://borjian.blogspot.com

MASSOUD BORJIAN

© Amirali Ghasemi 2005 amiralighasmi.com

AT HOME IN TEHRAN

Scanning through the Iranian blogs on 14 February, one comes across numerous
references to Valentine's Day. Iran has been overwhelmed by the rapid growth of
this alien tradition and it has been hotly debated in the Press. In the *Sharg* newspaper on 14 February 2004, Davood Penhani writes that 'Valentine Day or as they
say the Day of Lovers, a totally Western tradition, is gradually entering the hearts
of the youth of the East. Just glance at the shops scattered around town selling
presents for this European celebration and you can grasp the reality.' What has
happened to a society that at one time was 'willing to go to battle for its cultural
identity', but is now so 'receptive to the traditions and customs of strangers' that

it shows 'no fear of forgetting its own national and religious customs'? This is the key question for Iran: is this healthy or is it dangerous for Iranian society and culture?

VALENTINE'S DAY IN IRAN

While many within the establishment regard such trends as a crisis, others take a more pragmatic approach – among them the Iranian reformist ex-Vice President and mid-ranking cleric Muhammad-Ali Abtahi, to judge by his own blog.

---

12 February 2004

It has become a custom of ours to have a day that represents love and life ... this custom like many other traditions has been imported to our country. Even though many have raised objections to this ... we cannot deny the reality.

Nonetheless, friendship and love are entwined with our history and literature ... and the Islam that I know encourages life and love.

http://www.webneveshteha.com

---

14 February 2003

These days on every street you are confronted by many shops laden
with countless varieties of cuddly toys piled up in their windows ...
everything plastered with an 'I love you' message for Valentine's Day
... with flocks of young girls and boys huddled around these shops
breathlessly consulting about what to get ...

But what has this Valentine got to do with us? However hard I
look into our history I can't find a tradition, date or anything that is
similar to this ... We have countless lovers in our stories and poetry,
but no day like Valentine's Day when we express love ... So because
we don't have such a thing must we borrow from those nearby? Like
all other things? Like the way we dress, our behaviour, dances and
music?

This culture of ours is so totally mixed up that I don't know
where it will end ... In direct opposition to those in charge, people
are now readier and readier to distance themselves from their own
culture, no matter what ...

Email: awat_hiva@yahoo.com
http://awathiva.persianblog.com

Science tells us to be detached and objective, but sometimes the truth is subjective
and fully involved in the issues that matter. When so much of the attention
directed at the Islamic world is focused on violence and terrorism, blogs offer
outsiders a fresh perspective on the lives of ordinary men and women, relaying
their experiences – their fears, dreams, disappointments and insecurities – while
allowing others to eavesdrop on the clandestine conversations of a closed society.

29 October 2003

My daughter wanted to get her nose pierced. I resisted and told
her that she was bound to regret it and that she should wait until

she was a bit older and then decide for herself. She looked at me then and said: 'Piercing your nose is no big deal. Maybe I will in the end regret it ... but that's not the whole world. It is a small wish. By banning me ... you're turning a small wish into my ultimate dream. Why do you want me to have such insignificant dreams? If I can fulfil these small wishes and not grow up with such trivial dreams, don't you think I will have a better life waiting for me?'

*

We too had such insignificant wishes and even when we grew up they didn't come true ... There were so many times we wanted to go somewhere and they wouldn't let us and it became a dream. So many times they even stopped us from running. It came to the point that we weren't even allowed to take small steps ...

This is Iran. You hear my voice from the land of the most compassionate mothers ... mothers who break your legs for fear that you may hurt your ankle walking on our very hard pavements ... Mothers who are more terrified than you are. They bring you up as cowards and riddled with guilt ... This is Iran, where all our 'mothers are destined to the heavens'* ... and every single one of us ... when we become mothers, we turn into the most compassionate mothers the like of which no one has ever encountered anywhere else on earth ... monumental dams ...In the name of compassion, worry, future outlook ...

This is Iran. When a mother says 'Don't', you don't leave; and when she says 'Die', you die.

This is Iran and when you don't ever [experience life fully] there is not a whiff of shame or humanity about you ...

This is Iran. Mothers have to worry ... they have to be anxious ... and they have to break your legs.

* A quote attributed to the prophet Muhammad.

Email: faeze_am@yahoo.com

http://faeze.blogspot.com

© Atieh Noori www.kargah.com

PORTRAIT OF MY GRANDMOTHER (2003) BY ATIEH NOORI

21 August 2003

At times it's been hard getting used to being a widow, with the
children all away … My grandchildren come over as much as they
can …

Yet at last he's back – the two years he's been away have been
hard. Still, he has experienced national service and being away from
home … now I'm no longer alone and there is someone that I can
discuss many things with. There is a lot of happiness in having a
young person at home. Your fridge has to be full … You have to
think about cooking, and get to have the sound of the washing
machine in the background all day long.

Nothing is under your control any longer and you have found a
powerful contender ...
And when you say, 'Give me some peace to write my blog.' He
says: 'Look at you, the trendy young rebel, keeping a blog ...'
Siavash, my dear son, welcome home.

Email: badrivahidi@yahoo.com
http://hamneshinedel.persianblog.com

Upholding Iran's Morality

Much to the disappointment of the regime, 25 years of revolutionary rule have
still not created those model citizens who were supposed to adhere slavishly to
strict moral laws, dress codes and the rules governing contact between the sexes.
In fact, the laws have to be enforced by the Morality Police who roam the streets
of Iran. In the summer of 2002 this force was strengthened with the creation of
Special Units (Yeganeh Vizhe), the newest group among an already large number
of volunteer, semi-official and regular police organizations that concern themselves with enforcing public morality. These Special Units are a startling spectacle: armed men in shiny black four-wheel-drive vehicles all dressed up with smart
black berets to match their cars. Their arrival was hailed in the local press as a
means of combating what is referred to as 'social corruption among the young'.

22 April 2003

The patrol cars that put fear in the hearts of our youth ... the militia
forces that are there to safeguard national morality ... the effect has
been the total opposite and today our youth hold nothing sacred ...
For 24 years our youth have lived dual lives ... the way they have
to behave in schools and official places in stark contrast to their
home life ... private lives are the total antithesis of the dictates of
the ruling clergy ...

This has created dual personalities for many people ... with the improvements in modes of communications like video and Internet ... our awareness and our identity crisis has only intensified ...

National security in ideological and totalitarian regimes can be endangered even by dressing in a way that is not in harmony with the rules ...

In a system where the leaders do not have the people's backing and keep power by force ... these leaders are terrified of the smallest things ...

We are all painfully aware of the manifestations of this totalitarian system ... its absolute need to influence every aspect of the life of its individual subjects, and to produce people of uniform thoughts, while opposing free thought and democracy ...

Blogger Sina Motallebi was arrested and charged with jeopardizing national security! You have to pity a regime whose national security can be jeopardized by the writings of a blogger! Or perhaps laugh ... Jeopardizing national security by writing about art and literature!

Email: ranginkamaan2000@yahoo.com
http://ranginkamaan.persianblog.com

Soon after the Iranian Revolution, observing the hejab (Islamic dress) and wearing the veil became mandatory for all Iranian women. But laws are regularly updated. The Martyr Godousi Judicial Centre's 1997 dress-code guidelines called for prison terms from three months to a year – or fines and up to 74 lashes with a whip – for wearing 'stylish outfits, such as suits or a skirt without a long overcoat on top'. The regulations ban mini or short-sleeved overcoats and the wearing of any 'depraved, ostentatious or sparkly object on hats, necklaces, earrings, belts, bracelets, glasses, headbands, rings, neck scarfs and ties'.

Here is Atash (Fire) describing her encounter with the Morality Police.

25 May 2003

I could feel the searing sun like a piece of burning coal on my veil ... My veil and my long robes make me smell like a corpse ... I walk on the street but can't see the end ... Far, far away, a group of trees are doing a choreographed dance ...

And I, on the street, I'm walking ... Passers-by, those in cars, can't see me, as if I'm here but I'm not ... Far, far away, I can see a mirror that has taken up the width of the street ... And the nearer I get to it the more distant I become ... I'm walking in a scorching heat that rips the breath out of you ...

I catch a glimpse of myself, lighter, lighter and lighter ... With each step in my mind's eye, I no longer feel the burden of my walk.

I'm wearing a white short-sleeved top, green shorts and a scented straw hat ... I no longer smell like a corpse or like my grandmother's damp basement.

I walk freely and am spreading my fragrant sweet dreams among people who cannot see me ... They're running to get away from the harsh, searing sun ... What ecstasy ...

There is a hand on my shoulder that abruptly swallows my world

... The toxic street voice with rage barks: 'Pull your veil forward!' I hear it, but I don't want to hear it.

The street filth put his hand in his back pocket to show that he's searching for something ... His mime does not frighten me. He pulls out a transmitter from his putrid shirt pocket and this time pointing at his black patrol van, with fury, hollers: 'What do you say now?'

As I was stranded between two worlds ... at high noon ... I was hungry and thirsty ... in an endless street where right at the end the trees were doing a choreographed dance ... My veil moved and came forward ... A few steps away my veil moved back again.

Email: at_857@hotmail.com
http://atash3.blogspot.com

The enforced dress codes for men and women are a symbol of the will of the regime. Iranians are fully aware of these laws, but look around any city centre in Iran at random you will see that many disregard the regulations and use their appearance to make a protest, despite the serious consequences. Girls mock the strict guidelines by wearing their compulsory headscarves way back over their head to reveal as much (illicit) hair as possible; meanwhile the obligatory

© Yalda Moaiery www.kargah.com

GIRLS BUYING SHOES

manteau gowns are getting shorter and tighter, to the point that they are no longer the black cloaks considered the ideal revolutionary hejab.

The morality laws also permit judges to mete out discretionary punishments to those who, among other gross infractions such as being found in possession of alcoholic drinks or lying to the authorities, hold hands or kiss publicly ...

---

28 October 2003

Do you have 'the Heart'?

This game of theirs started when they were first married ... Mum and Dad were making their way home one winter's night ... They didn't have a car then and had to wait a long time by the roadside for a taxi. Apparently, my dad on impulse had kissed Mum on the lips ... anyhow, a car had stopped and picked them up ... Once inside they'd noticed that the driver was staring at them in his rear-view mirror and laughing to himself. Well, this had really irritated my dad, so he'd asked the man what he found so amusing. Evidently he had seen them kissing and was full of admiration for them ... According to Mum, the whole journey home he praised Dad so much, telling him he was a true lionheart ... 'You really have heart.' He told Dad that he was the bravest man in the whole of Iran and had gone on about it so much that for a long time Dad really felt as though he was the bravest man ever ...

Now for years whenever Mum is in a playful mood in the oddest of places she fixes her eyes on Dad and asks, 'Do you have the heart?' They giggle, look around, weigh up the situation, then they kiss and then they have a good laugh. My dad always seems to have 'the heart' ...

Recently we were standing in a long bustling queue outside Cinema Savaz in Karaj ... Mum was sure that she would get the better of Dad and he would not have 'the heart' this time ... She turned to him and teasingly asked, 'Do you have the heart?' Even though Dad at first seemed hesitant, he paused a few seconds, had a good look around … but he eventually turned to her and kissed her on the lips … suddenly a couple of people in the crowd started clapping and whistling and soon pretty much the whole queue were applauding …

My brother, of course, was fuming (this game of Mum and Dad's always annoys him), but it doesn't bother me and I'm happy that my dad always has 'the heart'!

I wish more men had his 'heart'!

Email: z8unak@z8un.com
http://z8un.com

© Ehsan Shahin Sefat www.ehsanshahin.tripod.com

A YOUNG COUPLE HOLDING HANDS IN SHIRAZ, IRAN, 2002

Although the Morality Police are still very much out in force, in recent years there has been a dramatic relaxation of the regime's strict official codes of dress and conduct. The morality laws have come a long way since the early days when women's lips were cut with razors in public view to deter others from wearing lipstick.

18 October 2003

I don't like to think back to my childhood days ... there are some things that happened back then that I am still dodging ... Still, some memories always stay with you ... Between the ages of four and eleven I had a favourite tree ... Its sturdy trunk and powerful branches were the place for my childhood solace ... It was from the top of this tree that I first set eyes on the girl next door, in her summery outfit and short skirt.

Bygone memories of my childhood friend, the scent of jasmine, Grandfather, Grandmother ...

At the age of six I started school ... My Mother would always clean all the make-up from her face, pull on thick black tights and cover herself completely from head to toe in black before leaving the house ... I would complain: 'Why are you doing this to yourself, it's embarrassing, why can't you go out as you are at home?'

She would always laugh and say, 'They will arrest us ...'

© Nafise Motlagh www.nafisegallery.com

I found out later, that everyone feared being arrested ... I even
understood this better when a woman jumped out of a muddy-
coloured car and with a razor took off the lipstick from the lips of a
girl ... a girl who looked a lot like the girl next door ...

During those first days we were being transformed ...

Now years have passed and my father and mother's generation
are called the 'burnt generation', while we are now referred to as the
'rebellious generation'.

By Underground

Hezbollah: the 'Party of God'

Ayatollah Khomeini set up Hezbollah or the 'Party of God' a quarter of a century
ago as the only official party of the ideological state. Ironically the 'defenders of
the faith' that control Iran often complain of being marginalized by the 'immoral
masses' and appear consistently disturbed by the country's changing society.

A 2004 editorial in Yal'Saratal-Hussein (an official publication of Iran's
Hezbollah) is typical of this hysteria. It is addressed to the security forces, the
Interior Ministry and the head of the judiciary, and warns that, 'at this speed, in
a few years, this country will overtake Turkey in the immorality stakes and in the
percentage of women unveiled. Be warned that today we are confronted with the
prospect of drowning in the quagmire of corruption and vice.' It continues:

If you still believe that the veil is the prerequisite of Islamic honour, but
you can no longer deal with the sleazy law-breakers, announce this to the
devout so they can go out and defend the laws of God. Believe us when
we tell you that those that we see disobeying God's rules do so
intentionally as a fight against a religious government. Believe us that
what American warships cannot even imagine creating in Iran – the
control of this country and our youth – the bare arms, the nude legs, the
immoral made-up faces and bare heads – is already happening here. We

ask you in the name of everything that you hold sacred to safeguard the
honour of this nation. Deal with this colossal tidal wave of immorality!
Don't keep saying that it's impossible! Stop saying that we do not have
the resources! All it requires is to hold on to our honour dearly and to do
a bit of thinking.

Today many believe it is impossible to hold back the burgeoning youth culture,
so the Iranian regime has been forced to grant young people a limited degree of
social freedom. While activities such as holding hands on the street or wearing
make-up are still classed as crimes, the authorities sometimes turn a blind eye.
Yet the introduction of armed Special Units in their black berets in the summer
of 2002 shows that the ruling clerics remain determined to combat 'social corruption among the young' whenever they can.

---

16 October 2003

I was about to be picked up by the Basij [a volunteer force of
religious vigilantes] today ... a couple of puny guys ... couldn't have
been older than 17 ... One flashed his Basij card and told me that I
was a shameful spectacle ... that I either take off my make-up and
tighten my headscarf or he was taking me in ...

I? A spectacle? A vision of loveliness ... Absolutely ... But you
know what the Basij are like ... they see beauty in other bearded
men ...

Fine, I'll admit it ... I was a bit scared ... But I remembered what
a friend of mine had done a few weeks ago. She had started
protesting and people had come to her rescue ... and I also thought
there is no way I am taking notice of two smelly rats, especially as I
was meeting some friends later on and my make-up was just too
perfect for words today ... (I'm not being big-headed or anything ...
it's just that I can never spend longer than five minutes putting on
my make-up and I usually get it wrong ... but today I looked good.)

Mirdamad Street was pretty busy. I wasn't the odd person out … they were … So I just started screaming … Within seconds, a crowd had gathered … The great thing is that no one looked scared and everyone was poking fun at them … a middle-aged couple that I have never met even claimed me as their daughter and started telling them off. The man was really good and kept saying, 'How dare you even address my daughter, you dishonourable rogues?'

At first they kept threatening that they were going to call for back-up and the whole crowd would be taken away … but the crowd just got bigger and bigger … so they told my lovely new mum and dad to take their daughter and go home … So, it ended well … but I wish some gorgeous man would have claimed me as his wife for the day … well, that's life …

Moral of the story: next time you get stopped, do as I did today … the less we give in the more likely they are to leave us alone …

(But don't be stupid either … make sure they are not armed or the Special Units … as it's just not worth it.)

By Arched Brows

2 REVOLUTION, WAR AND DISSENT

Under the rule of the conservative clerics in Iran, the cult of personality has tended to make the leader and the State synonymous. The 'Representative of God on Earth', Ayatollah Khamenei, has his portrait hung in all public buildings, while artists, poets and the State-controlled media glorify him repeatedly. Yet the Supreme Leader of Iran – as is typical in dictatorships – is usually represented as humble and modest. His vast and elaborate personality cult is portrayed as nothing more than a spontaneous manifestation of the nation's love for their leader. Nevertheless, dictators give birth to anti-establishment heroes. In Iran they thrive in the sanctuary of cyberspace. Revelling in the forbidden, many writers use their blogs to honour men and women who are loathed by the regime.

The bloggers pay tribute to anti-establishment heroes like Dr Muhammed Mossadegh, whose democratically-elected government was toppled in a joint American-British coup in 1953. He remains highly regarded by many Iranians, who see him as an uncorrupted modernizer and democrat who defied the imperialists. But as far as the ruling clergy are concerned, Mossadegh is to be disparaged as a secular liberal and given no state memorial.

In December 2000 the New York Times published the CIA's official history of its intervention in 1953. It discussed in detail America's role in this regime change, thereby revealing to a western public what most Iranians had known for

decades. This coup earned the United States and Britain the lasting hatred of
large sectors of Iranian public opinion, uniting communists, nationalists and
Shia clerics in their enmity toward meddling foreigners. William O. Douglas, a
former US Supreme Court Justice, has said of Mossadegh after the coup:

> When Mossadegh in Persia started basic reforms, we became alarmed.
> That man, whom I am proud to call my friend, was a democrat in the La
> Follette-Norris sense of the term. We united with the British to destroy
> him; we succeeded; and ever since our name has not been an honoured
> one in the Middle East.

Iranian bloggers have a strong historical awareness. They tend to reel off dates
and minute details about historical events with a striking frequency and ease.
Some blogs are fastidiously accurate; others are littered with 'what-ifs' and conspiracy theories – Iranians can sometimes feel as if they have been conspired
against throughout their history. Nevertheless, for many bloggers the past
haunts the present and sowed the seeds of Iran's current dilemmas.

Half a century on from the toppling of Mossadegh, there are numerous com-
memorative occasions on which bloggers write. There is Oil Nationalization
Day (20 March) or the date of the CIA coup (19 August). There are even those who
commemorate 7 April 1951: the date of Mossadegh's first decree as the then
newly-elected Prime Minister of Iran, instituting a free press – a nostalgic time
before such historical setbacks as the abolition of Mossadegh's Free Press Law.
As Stephen Kinzer[1] has pointed out: 'During the spring and summer of 1953,
not a day passed without at least one CIA-subsidized mullah, news commentator or politician denouncing Prime Minister Mossadegh. The prime minister,
who had great respect for the sanctity of free press, refused to suppress this
campaign.'

Dr Mossadegh still looms large in the Iranian blogosphere. Sometimes one
finds nothing more than a picture of him posted on a website on a significant
date.

MOSSADEGH AS A LAW STUDENT AT NEUCHÂTEL
UNIVERSITY, SWITZERLAND 1910S

5 March 2003

The most influential democratic leader in
Iranian modern history died on this day ...
At a time when America is telling the world
its aims are to bring democracy to the
whole planet, the Mossadegh era proves all
of America's protestations to be a long lie.
In honour of Dr Mossadegh, a man who
never betrayed his own people, ...

Email: shabah@shabah.org
http://www.shabah.org

Elsewhere bloggers lament what Iran lost when Mossadegh was ousted; and
sometimes we find short tributes written on the anniversary of his death. Here
is one by the ex-journalist and publisher Bijan Safsari.

5 March 2004

What is there to be done ... when we are faced with a futile century-
old struggle for change and today all we possess are volumes of
history books so that those who come after us can take heed and

tell apart a mirage and a spring of water?

It is a pitiable time, now that the seventh parliamentary
elections are over and reform has failed, there is a prevailing
silence and despair that engulfs us in shadows ...

Today is the anniversary of Mossadegh's passing: his love for
this land and his good name will forever be honoured in our
ancient history ... yet after so many years we are back where we
started ... now that our victors are dancing at our downfall, I want
to revisit an anecdote about Mossadegh's trial – as it may be
comforting to us all ...

After the coup, in one of the court sessions when an old and frail
Dr Mossadegh was defending his record, a well-known monarchist
Malekeh Etamadi had interrupted him, shouting out: 'Old man,

© Ehsan Shahin Sefat www.ehsanshahin.tripod.com

* MENAR JUMBAN IS A 600-YEAR-OLD STRUCTURE WITH TWIN TOWERS AND MECHANICALLY
REVOLVING MINARETS IN ISFAHAN, IRAN.

you took our country to the edge of the abyss and now you shake
as you defend your tyranny.'

Dr Mossadegh, who knew her well, turned and said: 'Menar
Jumban has been shaking for many years but it still stands
resolute.'

Email: safsari@bijan-safsari.com

http://bijan-safsari.com

Decimation of Non-violent Dissidents

In the intermittently benign post-war era of the 1950s – when the rise to power
of the likes of Ayatollah Khomeini could not even be imagined – Mossadegh,
a Swiss-educated lawyer, was viewed as a dangerous threat to Western
interests in the Middle East. As a *Time* magazine article put it, having chosen
Mossadegh as its 'Man of the Year' for 1951, the only democratically-elected
leader of his era in the Middle East was helping to create a 'fanatical state of
mind' in the region:

> The Iranian George Washington was probably born in 1879 (he fibs
> about his age). His mother was a princess of the Kajar dynasty then
> ruling Persia; his father was for 30 years Finance Minister of the country.
> Mohammed Mossadegh entered politics in 1906 [in the pro-democracy
> Constitutional Revolution]. An obstinate oppositionist, he was usually
> out of favour and several times exiled. In 1919, horrified by a colonial-
> style treaty between Britain and Persia, he hardened his policy into a
> simple Persia-for-the-Persians slogan. While the rest of the world went
> through Versailles, Manchuria, the Reichstag fire, Spain, Ethiopia and a
> World War, Mossadegh kept hammering away at his single note. Nobody
> in the West heard him.
>
> Since Mossadegh's rise, US correspondents have been swarming over
> the Near and Middle East. Their general consensus is that the British
> position in the whole area is hopeless. They are hated and distrusted

almost everywhere. The old colonial relationship is finished, and no other power can replace Britain.

There were millions inside and outside of Iran whom Mossadegh symbolized and spoke for, and whose fanatical state of mind he had helped to create. They would rather see their own nations fall apart than continue their present relations with the West.

Time (7 January 1952)

The CIA-backed coup came as a total shock to many Iranians – including Mossadegh, who had always regarded the Americans as allies. He had visited the United States and had many friends and supporters in the American administration. He had the backing of President Harry S. Truman, who had stood up to the British when they wanted to force Mossadegh from office. But with the election of Eisenhower in 1953 the mood in Washington had changed.

Before the coup the Americans had been extremely popular in Iran. In fact, two unlikely heroes of Iran's experiment with democracy at the turn of the twentieth century were Americans.

In 1909 Howard Baskerville, just out of Princeton University, arrived at a mission school in Tabriz. A young idealist, he found himself championing the Iranian people's right to self-rule and their struggle against the imperial powers that ruled Iran through a puppet monarchy.

He soon resigned from the mission school and joined the pro-democracy constitutionalists. Baskerville lost his life aged 24 leading 150 soldiers in battle. He had been killed trying to get food supplies to the starving inhabitants of Tabriz, which was under siege from the monarchist forces. Baskerville had fought under the direct command of Sattar Khan, who is to Iranians what General Washington is to many Americans. Thousands of mourners turned up as Baskerville's funeral procession made its way through the streets of Tabriz to the American churchyard.

Professor Thomas M. Ricks served as a Peace Corps volunteer in Iran during the 1960s. He reports that on his visits to Baskerville's grave in Tabriz during the 1980s and 1990s – when anti-American feeling was at its height in Iran – 'the tomb was always covered with yellow roses. Given the political climate, no one

A BOOKLET ENTITLED *THE STORY OF AN AMERICAN WHO DIED IN THE CAUSE OF IRANIAN FREEDOM AND INDEPENDENCE* (KAYHAN PRESS, 1959). IT WAS WRITTEN AND PUBLISHED IN IRAN BY DR S. R. SHAFAGH (A PRO-DEMOCRACY ACTIVIST) TO MARK THE FIFTIETH ANNIVERSARY OF HOWARD BASKERVILLE'S DEATH.

claimed any knowledge of who had placed the flowers on any particular day, but there was general agreement that the tomb always had fresh flowers on it."

Another American hero in Iran was Morgan Shuster. In 1906 the Constitutional Movement had given impetus to the Iranian people's struggle for democracy and freedom. It established a Western-style cabinet government with an appointed prime minister and a bicameral legislature composed of an elected lower house and appointed upper house.

The Iranian parliament turned to the US government for help. Clearly, at the turn of the twentieth century, the United States was not then the world's sole superpower, but a young democracy, albeit a powerful one. Morgan Shuster was invited to Iran to reorganize the national finances – which is how a lawyer from Washington became the Treasurer-General of Persia.

By all accounts Shuster wholeheartedly supported the Iranian cause and maintained his faith in the future of a liberal democracy embodied in the country's constitution. His reforms strengthened Iran, but they threatened Russian and British interests. Parliament was dissolved after a coup orchestrated by the puppet monarchy and Shuster was dismissed. When the Russian army invaded northern Iran and demanded that Shuster be expelled, he was so popular that the Iranian parliament unanimously voted to take a stand against their mighty imperial neighbour to the north, just to keep him.

Schuster reluctantly left Iran. In his poignant memoir *The Strangling of Persia* (1912) he recounts how Britain and Russia strangled the early aspirations of Iranians for democratic change. From then until the coup of 1953, the Americans were still regarded as the heroes of the pro-democracy movement in Iran, with Britain assuming the role of exploitative imperial power.

As Ali Ansari – an 'Iran expert' at London's Royal Institute of International Affairs – explains[3], the British succeeded in demolishing any hopes of

Image courtesy of Wilfrid M. de Freitas books, Canada

MORGAN SCHUSTER, 1912

democratic governance in Iran after the 1906 Constitutional Revolution (which sought to institute a constitution based on the Belgian one of 1831), just as a joint American-British *coup* would later bring to an end the democratically elected government of Mossadegh.

Oil had been of vital importance to Britain ever since the Royal Navy switched from coal in the early years of the century, notes Ansari. As Lord Curzon once declared, in the First World War the Allies had 'floated to victory on a wave of oil', and Britain was even more dependent on it in the Second World War. The post-war government of Prime Minister Clement Attlee was against sharing control of the Anglo-Persian (later Anglo-Iranian) Oil Company with Iran. Iran in those days was the world's fourth-biggest oil exporter, supplying Europe with 90 per cent of its petroleum. Hence, the British government was reluctant to make any concessions to the democratic aspirations of Iranians.

Ali Ansari believes that the 1953 coup 'brought to an end a period of political pluralism and social dynamism which, while occasionally chaotic, had undoubtedly left its mark on the political consciousness of the nation'.

Some observers (such as veteran *New York Times* correspondent Stephen Kinzer in his reconstruction of the hour-by-hour events that led to Mossadegh's downfall)[4] have even argued that in 1953 the US sowed the first seeds of anti-Americanism by putting a stop to democratic movements in the Middle East. 'It is not far-fetched,' says Kinzer, 'to draw a line from Operation Ajax [the *coup*] through the Shah's repressive regime and the Islamic Revolution to the fireballs that engulfed the World Trade Centre in New York.' He adds that 'but for the *coup*, Iran would probably have become a mature democracy. So traumatic was the *coup*'s legacy that when the Shah was overthrown in a popular uprising in 1979, many Iranians feared a repetition of the 1953 *coup*, which was one of the motivations for the student seizure of the US embassy.'

By bringing down a democratically elected government, the United States also empowered key radical Islamic groups in Iran. According to disclosed CIA files, Kermit Roosevelt, the then CIA chief of operations in Tehran, gave $10,000 to Ayatollah Kashani on 18 August 1953, a day before the coup. Meanwhile the violent Islamic fundamentalist group Fadayee'an Islam (the forerunners of

Khomeini's Hezbollah) was mobilized by the CIA during the orchestrated street demonstrations that led to the coup.

In the post-Mossadegh era, some of Iran's younger generation, having witnessed the elimination of non-violent dissidents, chose the path of armed rebellion against the dictatorial monarchy. Like most Islamic countries, the absence of democracy created a void that Islamic militants alone seemed able to fill. While governments brutally crushed all dissident groups, Islam enjoyed the safe use of the sanctified space of the mosque.

Come the revolution of 1979, the new breed of mutant Islamists were better equipped to take control. To this day Iran's supreme leader Ayatollah Ali Khamenei justifies the regime's extremism by saying: 'We are not liberals like [Salvador] Allende [in Chile] and Mossadegh, whom the CIA can throw out.'

The social and political commentator Masoud Kazemzadeh[5] is not alone in believing that 'ever since the Iranian revolution of 1979, in which a group of fundamentalist Shia clerics outmaneuvered liberals, socialists and non-fundamentalist Islamists, Islamic fundamentalism has become the dominant force in much of the Islamic world.'

The Struggle for Power

Activated by a number of political, social and economic factors, the Revolution began as a pro-democracy movement, but developed into something that was no more democratic than the monarchy it replaced. Revolutionary leader Ayatollah Khomeini spoke of 'freedom' and 'democracy', and initially his government was dominated by liberal figures. But just two years later Iran was a theocracy governed by severe Islamic law, with Ayatollah Khomeini established as supreme leader and 'God's Representative on Earth'. Iranians had traded one unaccountable regime for another. Here's the Iranian journalist and blogger Ibrahim Nabavi on the subject.

---

6 February 2004

We had a revolution so that a regime that from 1957 to 1975 had at most killed hundreds of Iranians ... could be overthrown, and we brought in a regime that would kill thousands during its first days alone ...

Email: nabavionline@hotmail.com

http://khabarnameh.gooya.com/nabavi

In *Tortured Confessions*,[6] Ervand Abrahamian, a professor of history at the City University of New York, describes the widespread abuse and torture deployed against political prisoners under the Shah. Most Iranians thought that the 1978–9 revolution promised an end to this culture of political repression, but only days after the fall of the Shah a different group of Iranians began to suffer brutal treatment at the hands of their new rulers. For more than two years, Iran's new regime hurriedly established revolutionary tribunals where many figures from the previous regime were executed after summary trials for 'sowing corruption on earth'.

9 August 2003

How I learned not to hang my father

As your average five-year-old boy, I was crazy about toy cars of all varieties and colours. During an ordinary outing to the shops, my father refused to buy me a toy car; I threw your average run-of-the-mill temper tantrum and I was carried kicking and screaming into a taxi ...

But I guess you could say it was an incomparable time in our history, those early days of the Revolution.

The streets were full of people with complete mayhem all around. I hated my father and I wanted him hanged like all the people that they were executing on our television screens. There were no children's programmes, everything was suspended and we would sit and watch as they hanged and hanged.

Even at the tender age of five I knew who Khalkhali [the hanging

Judge] and the Savakis [the Shah's secret service] were. I believed
every guilty person was a Savaki and at that moment in time that
included my father.

I started talking to the taxi driver, who acknowledged me with a
smile.

'Hey, Mister.'

'What is it?'

'Hey Uncle, my dad is a Savaki!'

The driver abruptly placed his foot on the brakes and started
cursing my dad. Thank God my father could (and still can) talk to
people, and soon they were both laughing at me ...

How many Savakis do you know? When will we stop hanging
people who don't give us the toy cars we want?

Email: daftaresepid@yahoo.com
http://daftaresepid.blogspot.com

On 1 February 1979, reporting the arrival of Ayatollah Khomeini in Iran after the
fall of the monarchy, Agence France Presse described 'a reception committee at
the airport to greet the Ayatollah, consisting of representatives of the country's
religious and secular opposition forces. Turbaned clerics jostled with suit-clad
liberals and Marxist opponents, struggling to get close to the stern-looking
cleric, now the most powerful man in Iran.'

Ayatollah Khomeini was hailed by many leading Iranian political activists as
Iran's Gandhi, though in reality he was an unknown entity, having spent many
years in exile. He was a blank canvas who could be all things to all people. No one
had any reason to doubt the statements Khomeini gave to the world's press while
exiled in Paris:

I have repeatedly said that neither my desire nor my age nor my position
allow me to govern. (United Press, 8 November 1978)

In Iran's Islamic government the media have the freedom to express all

Iran's realities and events, and people have the freedom to form any form
of political party and gathering that they like. (*Paese Sera*, 2 November
1978)

Women are free in the Islamic Republic in the selection of their activities,
future and their clothing. (*Guardian*, 6 November 1978)

Perhaps it is not so astounding that in 1979 Maryam Firouz, a female executive
member of the communist Tudeh Party (and a secular feminist activist since the
1940s), hailed Ayatollah Khomeini as the 'leading advocate of women's rights in
our history'. After all, when he seized power in Iran, US President Jimmy Carter's
UN Ambassador Andrew Young speculated that, if successful, Khomeini would
'eventually be hailed as a saint'. Communism was regarded as the real threat
facing the West, not 'political Islam' – which even seemed like a safeguard against
Communism.

Yet it wasn't long before Khomeini started singing from a totally different
songsheet.

Those who are trying to bring corruption and destruction to our country
in the name of democracy will be broken ... they must be hanged. We will
oppress them by God's order and God's call to prayer. (Qom, 30 August
1979)

---

5 December 2002

Yoghurt, cucumbers and fresh herbs ...
For as long as I can remember my parents' home was the centre of
gatherings for the whole family. It was impossible to imagine a
Friday without lots of people: aunts and uncles, my brothers, sisters
and cousins, their spouses, and me.

The cooker would be in use all day. And my father's vodkas in the
freezer he called 'the Pharaoh's grave'. They would always start
drinking their vodka at the sight of the first sparkling star in
the sky.

We, the youngsters, used to help out with preparing the food ... Sitting around chatting, peeling and chopping up vegetables and fresh herbs; creamy yoghurt with diced cucumbers; spinach and yoghurt with fresh mint, tarragon, red basil and walnuts; olives mixed with ruby-red juicy pomegranates, walnuts, garlic, lime and fresh herbs; slabs of sturgeon seasoned with garlic, fresh dill, lime and saffron for the barbeque ... Father and Uncle were the only ones drinking vodka, but the food was for the rest of us. Not forgetting the first-rate Persian caviar that we used to pay a negligible sum for then (it came out of our own seas in abundance) ...

During the days of the Revolution, Mother was so hopeful. She used to say things like: 'Things are changing. The Army will join the people ... It's obvious, the religious groups are not capable of running a country; the Left will take control ... The Shah will go and then it will be our turn for a government of our choice ...' My father had always been a liberal, but mother was a Communist ...

Two of my aunt's kids had become Mojahedins; my other cousin was a staunch supporter of the Islamic movement (while his own father didn't even know the direction of Mecca to pray to); the sister of this born-again Muslim was a monarchist; my grandmother, around whom everyone else gravitated, was a modern Muslim who believed in social equality, women's education and emancipation. And our born-again Muslim cousin was now suddenly a direct 'descendant of the Prophet' ...

It used to make you dizzy ... I used to think we are just practising democracy ... despite our differences we still love each other. You can't abandon humanity and compassion ...

After a month of Ayatollah Khomeini entering Iran, everyone still used to come, except my born-again Muslim cousin. He completely cut off ties with everyone. Today he has a position in the system ... the alarm bells had rung for us. Kindness and humanity had gone astray ...

Email: bamdadz@yahoo.com
http://bambad.blogspot.com

During the early days of the Revolution a range of political groups – from the far Left to the far Right, from secular to ultra-Islamic – were vying for political power and pushing rival agendas. Although inconceivable today, one prominent candidate in the 1979 presidential race of the Islamic Republic was Hassan Habibi, a member of the communist Tudeh Party, and in the first parliamentary elections several politically diverse candidates were successful.

30 March 2004

Twenty-five years ago on a day like this, the first happy day of a New Year without a dictator, our parents said 'yes' to something they had no understanding of: to an Islamic Republic.

A regime in which 'Marxism would be taught at university by a Marxist lecturer' (a quote from Islamic Republic, a publication by Ayatollah Motahari [one of the founding theologians of the revolutionary state, President of the Constitutional Council of the Islamic Republic of Iran and a member of the Revolutionary Council. He was assassinated soon after the Revolution]).

A regime in which 'a Zoroastrian woman would have identical legal rights to a Muslim man' (a quote from a documentary shown nationwide on 11 January 2004 on State television. On the programme, a Zoroastrian woman – a lawyer, incidentally – on camera 25 years ago, gave this statement as her reason and guarantee in voting for an Islamic Republic).

But today I can't stop wondering why my mother didn't ask: 'What exactly is this Islamic Republic?' Why didn't she ask: 'How do you guarantee what you are promising us today?'

The only (repeated) answer that I always come up with is this: that all our parents knew for certain was that they no longer wanted a Shah. That's all.

Email: sanaz5674@yahoo.com
http://khojaste.persianblog.com

Those first months were a time of tension and power struggles. The provisional Prime Minister Mehdi Bazargan and his allies such as Ayatollah Talaghani, together with other liberal politicians and intellectuals all objected to the killings and violations of law. Bazargan had been deputy prime minister to Mossadegh in the 1950s. Although he had spent many years in prison under the previous regime, he objected to the execution and torture of the very same people who had tortured him.

He was driven to resign several months later, because radical clerics were undermining him over issues such as the mass executions or the enforcement of Islamic dress for women. He finally handed in his resignation 24 hours after the taking of the American embassy hostages. The same America that had toppled the Government he had been a part of in 1953.

'TREACHEROUS' LEGACIES OF THE 'ENEMIES WITHIN'

Liberal figures like Bazargan were branded as traitors. The cry of the mutant Islamists was to 'destroy the enemies within'. There were many merciless and even farcical episodes, such as the seizure of Bazargan's personal correspondence with the French philosopher Michel Foucault as evidence of his collaboration with foreign intelligence agents. In one such letter Foucault had written to Bazargan, that

> For weeks now you have tried to stop the unauthorized courts and their speedy executions. Justice and injustice are the sensitive points of every revolution. Revolutions are born from these points, and it is from these that they go astray and die ...'

Soon many of Bazargan's cabinet were arrested, while his spokesman in the Provisional Government, Abbas Amir-Entezam, remains in captivity today after 25 years in prison. Amir-Entezam has been hailed as the Islamic world's equivalent of Nelson Mandela by the people who campaign for his release. In 1995 in a letter from prison to Renate Schmidt, a German MP, Amir-Entezam wrote:

> I am just one of the millions of victims of the arrogant, tyrannical and uncivilized rulers of the Islamic Republic of Iran. They don't dare try me publicly. For the past 16 years, against all laws, they have refused to give me a public trial because they know that I do not care if I die. And that, for as long as I live, I will defend my fellow countrymen, whose rights, as well as my own, have been violated.

Photos Nehzate Azadi

ABBAS AMIR-ENTEZAM (*ABOVE*) FACING A REVOLUTIONARY COURT CHARGED WITH TREASON (1979)

Photos courtesy of Iran-amirentezam.com

AMIR-ENTEZAM, THE SO-CALLED 'IRANIAN MANDELA', ON A BRIEF MEDICAL FURLOGH, VISITING A NEWPAPER OFFICE IN TEHRAN.

Every time they release Amir-Entezam from jail on medical grounds, believing him to be either at death's door or too weak to be able to do much, he dons the same 30-year-old suit and tie and preaches his lifelong message of democracy and accountability to anyone willing to listen. Now his plan to force the regime to accept constitutional change through a popular referendum has been taken up by Iran's largest nationwide student group, Tahkim Vahdat, and it unites many pro-democracy groups in Iran as their main hope of effecting non-violent change.

---

3 May 2003

I detest hero-worship ... but cannot help but feel like a lesser man when compared to the likes of Abbas Amir-Entezam ... A devotee of Dr Mossadegh ... a graduate of a top American university (so he didn't even need to live among us) ... He came to Iran after the Revolution to serve this country ... Like Mossadegh and Bazargan he was against any sort of armed struggle ... But today he is one of our oldest-serving political prisoners having spent the last 24 years in Evin [prison] ... Throughout these years he has steadfastly refused to ask for a pardon and passes his time teaching English to his fellow inmates ...

Now imagine that you are Amir-Entezam ... and they free you from jail at 70 years of age ... Would you not leave the country that has treated you so ruthlessly? Or perhaps go and retire in a peaceful town near the Caspian Sea? Not our hero ... he goes to Tehran University at the invitation of Tahkim Vahdat [Iran's national student union] and calls for a national referendum on whether Iran should remain under a religious regime ... according to an AFP report, he's in dire need of medical help, but instead has been sent back to jail ...

Muhammad-Ali Safari
I can never think of Amir-Entezam without remembering Muhammad-Ali Safari. He passed away on the morning of

Wednesday, 18 February 2002, having suffered a heart attack on his
return from a brutal interrogation. A political journalist during the
Mossadegh era, he became a lawyer after the Revolution and
tirelessly defended many of our political prisoners in recent years,
including Amir-Entezam.

Like many of my students and university colleagues, I attended
his funeral. The place was packed with some of the leading pro-
democracy activists ... some had been defended by Muhammed-Ali
Safari during their time in prison, when no one else had dared take
their cases on ...

Yet, as anticipated, the authorities forbade anyone from saying a
few words or offering a eulogy ... As if that will ever make his life
and existence perish from our hearts ...

It only makes us more resolute to create a society that honours
the sacrifices of such blessed men who offer us a glimpse of
decency and courage in our darkest hours ...

By Godfather

In July 1999, Iran saw the largest student riots since the beginning of the
Revolution. Yet this time the students were chanting the names of liberal
leaders such as Mossadegh and Bazargan during these demonstrations and
rallies. Some even called for the release of Amir-Entezam.

Thousands of students took part in a demonstration entitled The Anti-dicta-
torship Student Gathering at Tehran University on Saturday, 7 December 2002.
Many were photographed holding posters (printed by Tahkim Vahdat) of
former Prime Minister Mossadegh.

The ruling clerics appeared startled when a leaked survey commissioned by
the Intelligence Ministry in 2000 revealed that Sahabi was the most popular
political figure among students. Taken aback by this phenomenon, in March
2001 the authorities arrested 40 elderly members and supporters of the Iran
Freedom Movement (IFM), which was founded by Bazargan. The previously
imprisoned Ali Afshari – the elected head of the student group Tahkim Vahdat

– was also charged with conspiring to overthrow the regime with the aid of a 76-year-old accomplice and IFM member, Ezataloh Sahabi.

---

7 February 2005

By Hossein Derakhshan
My ultimate wish for presidential elections (although at present out of reach) would be the candidacies of Shirin Ebadi and Ezataloh Sahabi. They would create real hope amongst the frustrated electorate and put the highest popular pressure on the establishment.

I know that we have a guardian council [that would veto them]. I am not stupid. I am just saying that they would get more votes than anyone else and they would also get the backing of the world community.

Email: hoder@hoder.com
http://www.i.hoder.com

After spending five months isolated in solitary confinement, Ali Afshari's 'confession' – that he had plotted to overthrow the Islamic Republic with the help of IFM members – was broadcast on state television. However, he later apologized to the 'Iranian people' for implicating others in his televized confession and for not standing up to the pressure put on him by the authorities during his confinement.

In recent years student groups have voiced their concerns by writing open letters to the ruling clergy, routinely quoting the late Bazargan when he stood trial in 1963, during the rule of the ousted monarch: 'We are the last generation who will continue to struggle politically within the legal framework of the constitution.' The ruling clerics seem to have been bewildered by this vast swell of student support for the dissidents of the past.

Decades after the Revolution, an elderly group of liberals – previously tolerated because dismissed as impotent – suddenly became the greatest threat to

(*ABOVE LEFT*) A YOUNG MEHDI BAZARGAN AND (*RIGHT*) WITH YADOLAH SAHABI DURING THEIR
STUDENT DAYS IN 1930S PARIS. LIKE MANY OF THEIR EDUCATED PEERS THEY WERE PART OF A
GENERATION THAT SUPPORTED AND FOUGHT FOR A DEMOCRATIC IRAN. SAHABI AND BAZARGAN
LATER BECAME KEY FIGURES IN THE GOVERNMENT OF PRIME MINISTER MOSSADEGH AND CO-
FOUNDED THE IRAN FREEDOM MOVEMENT.

THE FIRST REVOLUTIONARY PARLIAMENT IN 1979 (*ABOVE*) WAS LED BY KEY
LIBERAL FIGURES. YADOLAH SAHABI (*LEFT*) AND PRIME MINSTER MEHDI
BAZARGAN (*CENTRE*). IMMEDIATELY BEHIND BAZARGAN SITS A YOUNG CLERIC
ALI KHAMANEI WHO WOULD LATER BECOME THE 'REPRESENTATIVE OF GOD
ON EARTH'.

© Nehzate Azadi

Dr Yadollah Sahabi passed away aged 96 on 12 April 2002. His funeral procession was attended by an estimated crowd of between 30 and 50 thousand people (predominantly those under 30). His funeral swiftly turned into an anti-regime protest, with the crowd chanting slogans such as 'Political prisoners must go free!'. The large crowd turned up despite the fact that many of Sahabi's political colleagues were facing charges of treason and conspiring to overthrow the regime. In 2001 his son Ezatollah Sahabi, an IFM member, was imprisoned for over a year in solitary confinement and in an undisclosed location by the regime at the age of seventy-three.

© Hadi Heidary

Yadollah Sahabi as seen by one of Iran's top young cartoonists (April 2002)

national security and were accused of manipulating student groups.

November 2001 saw the biggest political trial since the establishment of the Islamic regime in 1979 – the eldest defendant being 84-year-old Ahmad Sadr. The Justice Ministry announced that the trial would be held behind closed doors, because the 'accusations in this case fall into the category of actions against national security ... Publicizing the hearings of the court would disrupt security and public order in the country.'

Many of the dissidents on trial had been active half a century before, when the CIA instigated a coup that overthrew a democratic government and reinstated the monarchy. Disenchanted by the Revolution when it turned to oppression in the name of Islam, they rebuffed former allies, writing and speaking out in the cause of freedom and even being arrested from time to time. Some have paid a heavy price. Take Ezatollah Sahabi: he has had to endure solitary confinement for well over a year at the grand old age of 73. He was accused of plotting with student leaders to overthrow the regime. Others have paid with their lives.

One such was 70-year-old Daryoush Forouhar, who was murdered in 1998 alongside his wife, the political activist and writer Parvaneh Eskandari. The dissident couple were found dead in their home, having been stabbed, their bodies left facing Mecca. The killings were among several horrific murders of anti-regime activists.

Ex-President Khatami eventually blamed the murders on 'rogue agents' from the Intelligence Ministry, but in a cruel irony the only person imprisoned for the crime was Nasser Zarafshan, the lawyer of the murdered couple. Accused of being in possession of alcohol and a firearm in his office, he was sentenced to 70 lashes and five years in prison. One of Iran's leading human rights lawyers, Zarafshan has maintained throughout that the evidence against him was planted in his office while he was in detention.

---

24 November 2003

The fifth anniversary memorials to mark the assassinations of the Forouhars took place ... There were many speakers at the podium ... I tried to take notes but gave up and thought you can probably

check out reputable news sources on the Internet for who said
what ...

Parastou [a daughter of the Forouhars] was the last speaker ...
the most moving bit of her speech was when she described
discovering the bodies of her parents ... And being confronted with
two wounds that represented her father's struggle ...

One was an old cut on his forehead, an injury he had received on
19 August [the date of the CIA coup in 1953] and the other a stab to
the heart one autumn five years ago ...

After the end of the memorial, security forces dispersed the
crowds, although I was not involved ... but I heard there were a few
arrests ...

By Golnaz

A quarter of a century after the Iranian Revolution there appears to be general consensus among most political commentators that Islamic militancy has proved a colossal failure at the level of Iran's population. The people have demonstrated their disenchantment through the ballot box.

Yet it has at times been said that no democratic change will come about in Iran, as the people do not have a Lech Walesa or a Nelson Mandela. Such statements are often made by armchair academics and journalists who have had little or no real access to Iran. So they have at times relied unduly on the images presented by official state organs or long-exiled groups that push their own political agendas.

16 June 2003

The wind will carry us

I deeply believe that there are no short cuts to democracy. There are
no other paths but those which Ghandi or Mandela took or
Mossadegh and Bazargan tried to take. The student movement can
be a catalyst for reform but only for reform and not a revolution. We

should not have to pay such a high price or end up again with the
destruction and extinction of the best children of this nation ...

Sudden overnight change would be like an earthquake,
destroying what shelter we have over our heads ... Reform was not
invented by Khatami, nor is it dependent on him ... Believe me, if
we again choose a revolution and violent change: the wind will carry
us.

Email: daftaresepid@yahoo.com
daftaresepid.blogspot.com

Iran has gone through monumental social changes in the last 50 years and pro-
democracy activists in Iran can be reassured that 80 per cent of the population
voted for reform. They are the people who have actually lived under an ideological regime and have endured years of war, hardship and international sanctions.
Still they have managed to raise their children to be the best-educated population in the Middle East. In a state that tolerates no opposition, talk of an Iranian
Lech Walesa or Nelson Mandela is best left to the gossip of cyberspace.

The regime has done its best to eliminate Iran's diehard pro-democracy
activists. In September 2004 the head of a parliamentary commission
announced that the political heirs of the likes of Mossadegh and Bazargan were
now 'dead and finished'. Abdolah Momeni, a spokesperson for Tahkim Vahdat,
replied that 'No one can proclaim a political movement dead.' Especially when
that movement 'has paid the heaviest price in its striving for democracy throughout Iran's recent history and is seen by the youth and people as honest – holding
a special place in people's hearts.'

16 February 2005

The union of Shah and Sheik [cleric] shattered the government of
Mossadegh and the legacy of the constitutional movement ... The
Revolution finally brought the clerics on the scene; stripping them
bare so that they could perform their magic shows ... and this same

Revolution will kick the clerics out once and for all from the political scene ...

Europe struggled for five centuries to banish religion and superstition from political and social life, making a lot of sacrifices along the way. Our country will be the first country in the Middle East to go on this journey in a relatively short time frame. We must make this hard and hazardous journey ourselves. There are no chains harder and stronger than the chains of religion and tradition ...

The Revolution is unstoppable until it reaches its final destination: the rebirth of a humanitarian culture and a democracy. Towards the end of the Revolution, no cleric will be able to go to a village and tell the people: 'They didn't allow us to have Islam.' Believe me, defending religious rule will be impossible then. This rebirth has to happen in our country.

Our people have not been very politically aware throughout their history. Today they know what they want and what they don't want. They have felt a religious regime and its decomposed cultural traditions with their flesh and skin. There are not many families in Iran that have not paid a sacrifice on this journey.

Yes. The Revolution is alive and will go forward. The Revolution is growing in the daily concerns of the nation – women, workers, teachers, student protestors, writers and journalists, on the Internet and in blogs and in the daily lives of ordinary people. They all call to account those thieves of the Revolution responsible for this brutal tyranny.

Have you not heard the voices?

Email: siprisk@gmail.com
http://siprisk.blogspot.com

Photo courtesy of Ms Fariba Amini

DARYOUSH FOROUHAR AND PARVANEH
ESKANDARI SPENT MANY YEARS COMPILING
HUMAN RIGHTS ABUSES IN IRAN BEFORE
THEY WERE BRUTALLY ASSASSINATED IN
THEIR HOME IN TEHRAN, THEIR BODIES LEFT
FACING MECCA.

THE ELIMINATION OF DISSENTERS: MASS EXECUTIONS AND TORTURE

Daryoush Forouhar was the Minister of Labour, but had resigned in 1979 alongside Bazargan and the rest of his cabinet after only nine months in office. Nevertheless, it was thanks to Bazargan and his cabinet that elements of republicanism were introduced into the constitution – such as bringing in a constitutional law whereby religious minorities like Iranian Christians and Jews must have representatives in Parliament. This is something which the ruling radical clerics take credit for today, despite their opposition to it at the time. When questioned about religious discrimination in Iran, Iranian officials routinely respond that 'France has four million Muslims but no Muslim representatives in Parliament, while 40,000 Jews in Iran are guaranteed representation according to Iran's constitution.'

Bazargan and his colleagues resigned when faced with a constitution that was being shaped around a supreme religious leader (Ayatollah Khomeini); the near-absolutist powers vested in him recalling an age when sovereigns were considered executors of the divine will. Although extremist Islamic groups (and most leftist and communist groups) initially called for more and speedier executions of former officials, by 1982 many of these same groups had been outlawed, with all known members tried by semi-military tribunals and imprisoned or executed.

Yet even in the midst of the brutal excesses of the Revolution, a majority of Iranians chose Dr Bani-Sadr, a prominent liberal figure, as the first President of the Islamic Republic of Iran, in a landslide victory in January 1980. Unfortunately ultimate power remained in the hands of Khomeini, the Supreme Leader. In due course, like Bazargan before him, Bani-Sadr was driven out by the extremist clerics and, fearful for his life, he escaped to France dressed as a woman.

The arrests and the executions continued ceaselessly throughout the 1980s. According to Professor Ervand Abrahamian, the victims came from a variety of groups: mojahedin, Marxist, Maoist, socialist and liberal. Abrahamian's thorough research reveals that the overwhelming majority of those executed in the 1980s were high-school and university students or recent graduates. Women constituted some 12 per cent of the victims.

---

18 September 2003

Khomeini killed my aunt!
The eighteenth of September 1988 is inscribed on that stone as the date of death. It makes no difference to me what it says, as I doubt that under that rubble sleeps the person I only used to see from behind glass. That stone is only good for Mother and my aunt ... to sit and stare at and slowly weep and curse her murderers. Every few weeks or so at Mother's insistence we go there ...

I still remember her humming voice from behind the glass asking about the mulberry tree, the sunflowers, the cats and birds in Grandfather's garden.

The images from those visits are still a part of my ceaseless nightmares; especially the time when my sister and I, and my cousin (her son) were to be permitted a visit. My cousin was allowed to see her, but they took us to another room. A small room with three angry cruel Revolutionary Guards, who had no patience for our screams and sobs and kept barking at us ... the shameful body searches ... I six and my sister five ... hostages in a room ...

Panicked, I pressed so hard on the bunch of flowers that I'd picked from Grandfather's garden that my hand bled …

I have never known why on that day they said: 'We have sent her to the same place as her husband.' We were expecting her to be released … my grandmother had even arranged for a doctor to give her a general check-up!

I will never forget that sunny day they came to pick me up from school. I had just started primary school. I could tell from the exchanges between Mother, Dad and my aunt that I would never see her again or hear her humming voice asking me about my cats. We had no rights to a funeral, so we had a small gathering at the home of my mother's great-uncle.

All I remember is the stunned look on my father's face; my grandmother and aunt screaming and howling; my mother silent and strong …

The next day at school I told my teacher, weeping, that Khomeini had killed my aunt! She later asked to see my mother at school … the same teacher who today is one of our closest family friends.

In memory of all those killed in the 1980s especially the summer of 1988 …

By Golnaz

Women's Prison, Iran (2003)

Photo © Zahrah Ranjbar www.kargah.com

12 September 2003

Thousands of women were executed during the massacre of
30,000 political prisoners in 1988 after summary trials.

According to official orders, the detained teenage girls later
executed for crimes against the Islamic Republic were first raped, thus
denying them the 'automatic entry to heaven granted to virgins'.

A young Revolutionary Guard who had been given the mission
of raping a very young girl, fell in love with her and refused to do
so. In reference to this evil episode in our history, Shamlou wrote
the poem that starts with the verse:

A butcher stood weeping
He had lost his heart to a little canary ...

By Red Rose

At the beginning of the Iranian Revolution, Iran's leading Grand Ayatollah was
Sharitamadary, and like many other traditional clergy he believed in keeping
politics separate from religion. As Khomeini had also consistently announced in
exile that he had 'no desire to personally take up a political role', many believed
that his beliefs on governance were similar to those held historically by other
clerics. Yet Sharitamadary was soon arrested, stripped of his religious credentials, and charged with treason.

Like many wealthy religious Christian organizations in the West, ayatollahs in
Iran are often bequeathed property and money under charitable trusts. According to Shia tenets, Muslims are required to give a fifth of their disposable
income to charity and traditionally many voluntarily donate such sums to the
ayatollahs to redistribute.

Just as petrodollars made the historically obscure Wahabi Islamic sect so
potent that it sprouted the likes of al-Qaeda – in Iran even the traditionally mar-
ginal radical clerics were now enjoying unprecedented financial clout as a result
of the oil boom.

As Grand Ayatollah, Sharitamadary held unrivalled financial assets that were then seized by Ayatollah Khomeini. Ironically, when Khomeini had faced possible execution by the monarchy in 1965, Sharitamadary had hastily arranged for his ordination as Ayatollah, to save the life of the dissident cleric – knowing that the Shah could not execute an ayatollah.

The front cover of a leading publication, *The Hope of Iran*, during the early months of the Revolution, depicts a triumphant Dr Mossadegh and his Foreign Minister Hussein Fatemi. After the *coup* that overthrew Mossadegh's democratic government, he remained under house arrest until his death. Fatemi was convicted of treason and executed in 1954.

Prior to the Revolution, while many of those who opposed the monarchy languished in jail, most clerics would end their sermons by offering up prayers for the Shah, referring to him as 'God's shadow on earth'. Today's clerics offer up prayers for the supreme religious guide, 'God's representative on earth'.

Photo courtesy of Saber

AFTER THE FALL OF MOSSADEGH, AT THE DAWN OF THE REVOLUTION, MANY BELIEVED THEY WERE FINALLY ABOUT TO SEE AN EGALITARIAN IRAN COME INTO EXISTENCE. IN THE TOP-LEFT CORNER IS A SMALL PICTURE OF GRAND AYATOLLAH SHARITAMADARY, DESCRIBED AS THE 'SANCTUARY OF ALL FREEDOM LOVERS'.

THE 1980–88 WAR: CONSOLIDATION OF POWER BY THE STATE CLERICS

As if imitating the French and Russian revolutions, domestic anarchy and oppression were followed by foreign quarrels and intervention. On 22

September 1980, Iraq attacked western Iran, launching the longest conventional war (1980–88) of the twentieth century, in which more than a million people were killed on both sides. Hundreds of thousands of Iranians were used as cannon fodder in 'human wave' attacks on Iraqi artillery positions.

---

12 July 2003

Our youth were either in Evin [prison] or at war. The best of that generation ended up in our cemeteries ... There was no one left to fight the regime ... until now and this new generation.

By Godfather

Saddam's Iraq had the backing of many Western powers during the war. Equally, several Arab monarchies – such as Kuwait – fearful of their own potential demise in a domino-effect Iran-style revolution, offered the Iraqi regime financial assistance. That the United States gave considerable assistance to Iraq during the war is well documented. According to such evidence,[8] the United States wanted to see Iran overpowered, fearing it would overrun or inflame other oil-producing states and export its Islamic revolution. Saddam Hussein's grip on power in Iraq was supplemented by German dual-use technology and French weaponry, which experts say ended up underpinning Iraq's chemical and biological warfare programmes.

Kenneth Pollack, an ex-member of the US National Security Council and at one time a principal working-level official responsible for implementing US policy on Iraq, has set out in detail what happened:[9] 'Washington began passing high-value military intelligence to Iraq to help it fight the war, including information from US satellites that helped fix key flaws in the fortifications protecting al-Basrah that proved important in Iran's defeat.' He adds that, 'By 1982, Iraq accounted for 40 per cent of French arms exports,' while 'Paris sold Baghdad a wide range of weapons, including armoured vehicles, air defence radars, surface-to-air missiles, Mirage fighters and Exocet anti-ship missiles.' Pollack additionally points out that 'German firms also rushed in without much compunction, not only selling Iraq large numbers of trucks and automobiles but also building vast complexes for Iraq's chemical warfare, biological warfare and ballistic missile programmes.'

The West sponsored Saddam's regime, despite clear evidence as early as mid-1983 that Iraq was using chemical weapons on Iranian forces. Today, paradoxically, many political commentators maintain that the war against Iran was crucial in strengthening the power base of the radical clerics, because even those Iranians who opposed the Islamic Republic moved to Khomeini's camp in defence against foreign aggression.

During the war the radical clerics took further steps to consolidate and to institutionalize the achievements of the Revolution and dissenters were put down with more force than ever before.

---

15 April 2004

When the most ruthless are the victors and not the wise ... the story is truly of a bloody vicious struggle ... The ruthless killings at the dawn of the Revolution ... the assassinations ... eight years of devastation and war ... the bombing of towns ... the dastardly killings of prisoners en masse in the 1980s ... These are all the bloody roots of our story ...

Yet today these blood feuds are fading from the minds of a new generation ... a generation that was created to fight for God ... a generation that was created for martyrdom is suddenly aware of its predicament and the world around ... and no longer believes in the endless wars of his forefathers ...

A new generation is pressing forward to destroy the old formula.

Email: baba@eparizi.com
http://baba.eparizi.com

---

22 September 2003

What an era we were born in ... Remember all those piggy banks

shaped like tanks and all the windows taped up? The rush to get to a
shelter, the terrorizing sound of sirens and then total darkness ...?

The best of our kind were disabled, maimed or died in the war
and the worst of our kind rule us now. May God protect us and
bring an end to this madness.

By Temptation

ABANDONED HOMES IN IRAN'S ETHNICALLY ARAB PROVINCE OF
KHUZESTAN STILL BEAR THE MARKS OF WAR IN 2002. (THERE ARE
AROUND 2.07 MILLION ETHNIC ARABS IN IRAN; 3 PER CENT OF
THE TOTAL POPULATION OF 69 MILLION IRANIANS ARE ARABS.)

23 September 2003

When I was a kid, war to me was Ali-Reza's dad, who was carried
home in a coffin on people's shoulders. When they were burying
him, I tried to go forward to see his face again, but I couldn't. I
found out later that even if I'd succeeded I wouldn't have seen him
anyway, as he was burnt, completely burnt ... When I was a kid every
time I remembered Ali-Reza's dad I couldn't control my tears. Even
now, when I remember him my eyes well up, because I miss him
and feel sorry for Ali-Reza ...

Now I get depressed because I see that this country is no longer
the country he died for ...

They are draining our people's blood. I also get sad when I

remember that Ali-Reza's dad died when he was as young as I am today.

By Human

Nearly 16 years after the war ended, in a weekly press briefing on 10 July 2004, Abdolah Ramezanzadeh, the government spokesman for ex-President Khatami, stated that there were still 240,000 victims of Saddam's chemical attacks living in Iran.

After Saddam's 1988 attacks on Halabja, which killed around 5,000 Kurdish civilians in northern Iraq, US officials initially blamed Iran for the atrocity. Then suddenly, in 2003, the British and US governments repeatedly cited Iraq's use of chemical weapons during the Iran–Iraq war as a major justification for invading Iraq. Yet credible journalists[10] have revealed extensive evidence that there was a covert US military initiative to assist Iraq in its war with Iran, supporting Saddam's plans to use chemical weapons in several battles. This programme was carried out under the Reagan administration, at a time when the White House was publicly condemning Iraq for its use of lethal gas.

In Iran today, so many years after the war ended, there are still hundreds of thousands of terminally ill casualties of chemical warfare. Many of them are

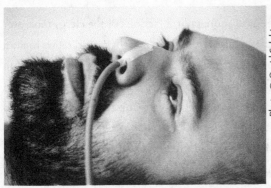

Photo © Omid Salehi, 2003
www.silkroadphoto.com

THIS MAN WAS SERIOUSLY INJURED AS A 17-YEAR-OLD
SOLDIER IN THE IRAN–IRAQ WAR. HE HAS BEEN IN A COMA
EVER SINCE AND IS CARED FOR ROUND-THE-CLOCK BY HIS
ELDERLY PARENTS IN THEIR HOME IN ISFAHAN.

civilians, some just children at the time of attacks. They suffer from chronic respiratory, eye and skin diseases and disabilities, and have a very low resistance to many viruses – even the common cold could prove debilitating or worse. And their communities have been as devastated as their immune systems.

---

12 November 2003

The Americans fight and go to war to prove to the world that they are cheerful, beautiful and sophisticated humanitarians ...

The Palestinians fight, as this is all they can do to defend their homes; sometimes I think 'Where do they get all those stones from?' ...

We fought so that men who represent God ... will have more chance of racketeering ... we fought against another Muslim country to defend this Islam ...

Email: myownsroom@yahoo.com
http://myownsroom.blogspot.com

THE KOMITEH, WAR AND YOUR DAUGHTER'S WEDDING

During the early days of the Revolution, radical factions of the clergy took over the mosques – evicting countless clerics from their 'parishes' – and set up komiteh (committees) throughout Iran. What ensued was chaotic looting and destruction – much as in Iraq after the fall of Saddam, because all political parties had been ruthlessly suppressed for decades – and the only organizations in any shape to coordinate a response were the mosques.

The Komiteh were the Morality Police: they would verify your devoutness before you were offered a job or they could have you dismissed from your post for any perceived shortcomings – and this applied to anyone from the dean of a university to the local postman.

The Komiteh could pay for your hospital bills or your daughter's wedding and it could also act as judge, jury and assassin when dealing with neighbourhood infidels. The *Komiteh* pretty much controlled every facet of life. But they became even more powerful during the Iran–Iraq War, when all alternative opposition was silenced. The *Komiteh* was granted its own paramilitary units, the *basij*, which acted as recruiting bases for the frontline and were responsible for distributing wartime food rations.

---

19 September 2003

The Story of 'Karam-the-Ass', as told by my taxi-driver on a ride through town today

Before the Revolution we had a guy at the factory called Karam, who used to insist that everyone should call him by his nickname 'Karam-the-Ass'! I mean, even if an engineer or one of the bosses were on the factory floor he wouldn't respond unless they called out his full title: Karam-the-Ass. During the war, the Islamic Revolutionary Union was trying to get our workers to volunteer for the Front. I dragged Karam along to the union office to discuss volunteering.

Karam asked: 'Sir, if I go to the Front, what will happen to my family?'

They explained to him that he could designate one other factory worker to be responsible for his legal affairs and the administrator of his will. His chosen colleague would also look after his family while he was away – or if he reached the 'honourable heights of martyrdom'.

His immediate response was: 'Well I don't care about the rest of the stuff, but I know that as soon as I become a martyr, that guy will be "doing" my wife.' Naturally the 'brothers' were furious …

Karam, totally unmoved, turned to them and said: 'It's not that I have any objections … anyhow he would indeed be performing a holy deed … but my point is altogether different. If I become a martyr, I want to make a will and request certain things for my funeral and you have to take an oath, that what I ask will be carried out.'

The 'brothers', suddenly overjoyed, said: 'Brother, that's what we are here for' and 'Inshallah [if Allah wills it] when you reach the sacred heights of martyrdom your will and testament shall be done.'

Karam turned to me and asked: 'How many years have you known me?'

I said: 'Ten, fifteen years?'

He said: 'In the factory, everyone from the managing director down to the floor manager and even you, what does everyone call me?'

'Karam-the-Ass!'

He said: 'Well done, and may God bless your forefathers.'

And then he faced the 'brothers' and said: 'My will is that when I become a martyr, while the crowd carry my coffin on their shoulders, they chant "This de-petalled flower" [a famous slogan of martyrs], but add to it the verse "was Karam but is now truly an ass!"'

The 'brothers' were predictably infuriated and, assuming he was deranged, threw him out. Later on, he told me: 'I am an ass, but I'm not so insane as to want to go to the Front.'

Well, we all ended up on the frontline except for Karam-the-Ass, who proved to be the wisest of all!

Email: shabah@shabah.org
http://www.shabah.org

LOOMING CONFLICT

A long costly war has undoubtedly left permanent scars on Iranian society. Yet the post-9/11 regional conflicts – in particular in neighbouring Afghanistan and Iraq – have brought about a great deal of introspective debate with many commentaries by bloggers questioning the possibility of more atrocities to come.

1 October 2003

Tonight Channel 2 was showing a documentary about the Iran–Iraq War. They were interviewing maimed or injured war veterans and some who are still to this day in hospitals or mental institutions. The whole programme really upset me. People who through no fault of their own had to go and fight for their country are now – 15, 16 years after it ended – still living abject lives, and wish that they had been martyred too.

Yet even with what we have inherited from the last war, our leaders expect us to go and fight when America attacks. As if we have sincere and noble leaders worth risking our lives for? As we say, 'A yellow dog is the brother of a jackal!'

It makes no difference whether we have our Supreme Leader or 'Uncle Bush', as I am a mere number and don't count ... Our people have no power and are mere observers.

Email: hamedyou@gmail.com
http://weblog.hamedyou.com

22 April 2003

We have a student magazine, with a society section, and sometimes, whenever possible, we run a poll on topical issues among the general public. With the daunting prospect of war between the United States and Saddam, we thought it might be interesting to do a poll on the issues surrounding this subject. Yet when we'd finally compiled our questionnaire, it was so obvious that we weren't going to be able to get away with asking a single one of our questions. Well, everyone including our respondents would have been well and truly 'buggered'. What we could have got away with asking though was:

1. In the hypothetical event of the Islamic Nation of Iraq being

attacked by the tyrannical armies of the Great Satan; would you
agree with such a war?

- No
- Who am I to agree or disagree with anything?
- Whatever our great Supreme Leader says
- All of the above

2. How can the people of Iraq independently topple the Ba'ath
regime?

- Through theological circles
- Through mosques
- With leadership from the clergy
- Through prayer

3. What sort of regime would you like to see in Iraq?

- Islamic government controlled from Najaf
- Islamic government controlled from Karbala
- Islamic government controlled from Qom

http://pouyaa.persianblog.com

With Saddam's regime toppled, Iran was plainly encircled by the forces of the
'Great Satan' (the United States). More than 200,000 US soldiers were stationed
in the neighbouring countries of Afghanistan, Iraq and Azerbaijan.

'Death to America!' chants are nothing new in Tehran, but with US soldiers on
its doorstep, Iran's state media organs such as Kehyan were whipping-up anti-
American feeling more than ever before. Keyhan is no ordinary publication and
to the Islamic Republic it is what Pravda was to the Soviet Union. Its editor
Hussein Shariatmadary was directly appointed by Ayatollah Khamenei the
Supreme Leader of Iran and is part of his inner circle. On 24 June 2003 there was
the heaviest loss of British life in a hostile act since British forces entered Iraq at
the start of the war in late March 2003. On 26 June Hussein Shariatmadary
wrote:

The American and British military are now within easy reach of Islamic
and revolutionary countries. The revenge of the blood of innocent
civilians massacred by these savage militaries is easier than ever before.
Today there is no need for revolutionary Muslims to go to the effort of
carrying bombs and explosive materials to faraway bases, when the
punishment of the American and British military is possible with the use
of grenades, Molotov cocktails or even sticks and stones. This is a
blessing from God: Islamic countries have been given a golden
opportunity for revenge against these aggressors.

Since 9/11 the official line from Iran's Supreme Leader and newspapers like
Keyhan has been that the attacks were co-ordinated by Israel and the United
States as a 'stratagem for world domination' (and as a testament to this 'fact', the
subsequent conflicts in Afghanistan and Iraq). But blogs have allowed Iranians
to discuss world affairs outside the official parameters, as in the following blog
by journalist Roya Sadr, which lampoons such conspiracy theories. The following extract, written in the style of the hard-line press, is a mock book review concerning the relationship between the late Sadeq Hedayat (an Iranian writer of the
1920s and 1930s who translated Jean-Paul Sartre and Franz Kafka into Persian)
and Madeline Albright (the former US Secretary of State).

---

3 October 2003

Sadegh Hedayat, Madeline Albright and 9/11*
... from the secret and underhand traitorous dealings of Sadegh
Hedayat with the leaders of the White House, headed by the
murderous Albright; this world-shattering new publication reveals
that 9/11, the Bay of Pigs, the Gulf Wars and Caspian Sea disputes
are all a result of the fanatical campaign for world domination
headed by Hedayat ... The author of your edifying publication is
indebted to a passer-by called Reza for findings that now merit
further scrutiny by future generations ...

P.S. After reading the book, I realized Albright was born in

Czechoslovakia and Hedayat was heavily influenced by Kafka, so there must be some truth to it …

* Recommended to all devotees of action-murder mystery genres.

Email: admin@bbgoal.com
http://www.bbgoal.com

Toppling Dictators

In a speech on 15 December 2003, Iran's Supreme Leader Ayatollah Khamenei declared that: 'I heard the US President has said the world is better without Saddam. I want to tell him that the world will be even better without Bush and Sharon.'

In contrast, news of the capture of Saddam – the moment when the US administrator Paul Bremer uttered the words, 'Ladies and gentlemen, we got him' – was greeted with joy by countless Iranian bloggers. Even though, in the aftermath of Saddam's demise and the ensuing violence in Iraq, many have voiced their doubts as to the West's intentions.

---

15 December 2003

I will now forever think highly of Paul Bremer, if only for saying: 'Ladies and gentlemen, we got him.'

Email: amirhesabdar@yahoo.com
http://amirhesabdar.blogspot.com

---

14 December 2003

Saddam was arrested … I have just told my mum the news. Her first reaction was: 'When will it be the turn of our lot?'

By Sonnet

---

15 December 2003

It was startling and sudden ... And I'm stunned ... I remember
that day; at 11 years old being told that the war had ended ... I
couldn't understand that wars could end ... I didn't know that
there were places in the world where people didn't fight their
neighbours ... In my childish mind, I believed that life was what I
was experiencing ...

Today Saddam, who robbed me of my childhood, freedom and
peace, and robbed the dignity of humanity from countless others ...
was arrested in the neighbourhoods of his birthplace looking like a
tramp ... And I am still stunned ...

The monster of my childhood days has been snared ... I can now
truly believe that one day I will witness the collapse of things that I
don't believe in ... I feel so close to the people who are celebrating
and dancing in the streets of Iraq ... Be happy ...

But I want him to be tried justly ... without iniquity ... even
though, while attempting to crush the kernel of humanity, he
denied justice to others ... Where I am today he has also caused
devastation, killed people and committed atrocities. I know what
Saddam is ... But don't let that monster yet again distance you from
human dignity. Treat him justly.

Email: sanaz5674@yahoo.com
http://khojaste.persianblog.com

8 April 2003

I was glued to the TV screen ... It was truly gratifying to watch the
toppling of Saddam's statue, with people dancing at the fall of the
dictator ...

All you dictators out there ... build your statues and carry on
displaying your creepy smiling portraits on every available wall
space ... try and scare us with your constant warnings about our

enemies ... And keep repeating it again and again ... to mask the fact that today, you are more terrified than anyone else.

Email: afsoonkhanoom@yahoo.com

http://afsoon.blogspot.com

SADDAM IN THE DUSTBIN OF HISTORY BY MANA NEYESTANI
(3 FEBRUARY 2004)

21 December 2003

What should Saddam's punishment be, now that they have got him?

Every time the rockets roared over our heads without warning ... my little sister used to run around the house hysterically scream-ing ...

I remember the time when an Iraqi rocket hit a Tehran maternity unit ... My friend and I were walking to school with our mums when we were confronted with this huge digger truck, shifting the rubble. Giggling, I turned round and told my mum, 'Don't worry if our

school gets hit today: one of these diggers will dig us out' ... I'll
never forget the ashen look on our mums' faces as they let their
tears flow ...

Email: saba@eparizi.com
http://saba.eparizi.com

15 December 2003

Evidently today ... dictators can die ... they can get arrested or be
overthrown! Just as it happened to Heydar Aliyev, Saddam and
Shevardnadze ...

What will be our method of choice?

By Rosewater for your tresses

DEATH TO AMERICA – NOT

19 July 2002

Death to America! Death to Bush! Death to Colin Powell! Death to
Elizabeth Taylor! But I want to go and live in America.

Email: arareza@Gmail.com
dentist.blogspot.com

Iran is perhaps one of the few countries in the Middle East where people don't
attribute their hardships to their undemocratic US-backed rulers. To Iran's hardline leaders, the United States is ceaselessly the 'Great Satan', with the archive
footage of 'Death to America!' chants during Friday prayers routinely shown on
news items. Yet according to surveys by Iran's own Ministry of Culture and
Guidance, fewer than 1.4 per cent of the population actually bothers to attend
Friday prayers.

After visiting Iran in May 2004, the New York Times columnist Nicholas D.

Kristof declared that: 'Finally, I've found a pro-American country.' He revealed that wherever he went people had 'been exceptionally friendly and fulsome in their praise for the United States, and often for President Bush as well.' Kristof added that for Iranians, 'being pro-American is a way to take a swipe at the Iranian regime' and that left alone, the Islamic Republic is heading for collapse, with a better 'chance of a strongly pro-American democratic government in Tehran in a decade than in Baghdad.'

An American blogger living with her Iranian partner in Iran, writes:

---

21 August 2003

What I like

I could never say anything as bad about Iran or Iranians as Iranians say about each other and their country. I guess that is why I am surprised that many Iranians think I am only critical about Iran. (It's too bad K. has not posted in such a long time, because his posts make mine look more positive.)

Here is what I like:

I like being an American here. Everyone is so nice to me. Everyone seems to think that Americans are wonderful. One restaurant owner had to restrain himself from hugging me when he discovered that I was American. People shake my hand. They talk to me. Sometimes they tell me that they don't like Bush, but they always tell me how much they like Americans. This is so refreshing after a couple of years of living in Europe, where all I heard was how evil Americans were.

I like the fact that I can get a really good challah at a bakery in Tehran. It's almost as good as my grandmother's, but not quite.

I like the fact that everyone has an opinion and that they tell me what they think. I like all the complaining and grousing. I like all of the discussions. I like that people are unafraid to voice their opinions.

I like learning Persian. I enjoy speaking the language.

I like the way that Iranians are dissatisfied with their society and their government. I like that they are working to change it (slowly). One thing I always complained about in the Netherlands is that Dutch people are too satisfied. Everything seems finished there. Everything bad that happens in the Netherlands is the fault of their immigrants. In Iran (like America, I think) there is a sense that society is an ongoing project. Things are most definitely unfinished and moving forward.

I like how K.'s sisters care for his mother who is ill. I like that his older brother taught his daughter to wrestle and that he calls her, 'My lion'.

I like the way his family helps each other ... I like taking the bus between cities ... I like the fact that Iranians have managed to hold on to their cultural identity despite efforts to squelch it ... I love pistachios.

Email: responses@gmail.com
http://www.viewfromiran.blogspot.com

An opinion poll conducted by three separate Iranian institutes – including the National Institute for Research Studies and Opinion Polls (NIRSOP) and published by the Iranian News Agency (IRNA) on 22 September 2002 – revealed that 64.5 per cent favoured resumption of talks between Iran and the United States. This was despite the prevailing atmosphere of tension, with many Iranians believing that a US attack on Iraq was imminent. And regardless of the 'Axis of Evil' membership bestowed on Iran by President Bush, the poll also showed that only 26.1 per cent considered the US policies on Iran to be wrong.

In Iran the crisis of the regime's legitimacy has created a substantial backlash against anything it endorses. The Iranian people's favourable attitude towards a hostile America is possibly just another expression of their general resentment of their current leadership.

The Iranian reformist parliament commissioned the polls as part of a study of ties with the United States, although the researchers involved soon found themselves in prison. Taking into account such opinion polls, it seems that the numerous pro-American blogs written by Iranians are the rule rather than the exception.

'On the evening of 11 September 2001, young people gathered in Madar Square, on the north side of Tehran, in a spontaneous candlelight vigil to express sympathy and support for the United States. A second vigil, the next night, was attacked by the basij, a volunteer force of religious vigilantes, and then dispersed by the police. The vigils may have been the only pro-American demonstrations in the Islamic world after the terrorist attacks on the United States.'[11]

However, despite a genuine sympathy for the plight of Americans on 9/11, it must be pointed out that there are also many on-line commentaries against US foreign policy. After all, as Jahangir Amuzegar, Iran's Finance Minister in the pre-1979 government, has said: 'Iranians' fierce nationalism is characterized by intense suspicion and outright resentment of outside influences.'[12]

---

7 April 2004

[An American blogger living with her Iranian partner in Iran]

A few months ago it was rare to hear a bad word about Bush and our policies in Iraq. That is changing. Iranians have been overwhelmingly supportive of Bush. The Karbala pilgrims were among the most enthusiastic supporters. That is changing. People here are starting to question the US role in Iraq and Bush's warlike tendencies.

Email: responses@gmail.com
http://www.viewfromiran.blogspot.com

---

8 April 2003

Thousands of demonstrators in countries like Pakistan, India and 'Arab countries' are taking part in 'peace' protests; they walk over

other people's sovereign flags, burn George Bush dummies. Some
of them even carry the Iraqi flag and pictures of the tyrant Saddam.
Are these demonstrators truly anti-war?

We have been bombarded with these scenes by an enthusiastic
state-controlled media; yet there is nothing in these images that
conveys peace ...

What is our media so upbeat about? At the sight of a horde of
Bin Laden lookalikes foaming at the mouth, holding a picture of a
tyrant (Saddam) in one hand and a psychopath (Bin Laden) in the
other?

By Our Voice

Death, Mayhem and Destruction

September the 11th and the ensuing terrorist attacks around the world have
brought about global reactions of shock and dismay. Iranian blogs offer a fresh
perspective and a chance to eavesdrop on the intimate conversations of an
Islamic society in relation to such global turmoil. Here are those seldom-heard
voices normally drowned out by the sabre-rattling of fanatics.

---

6 September 2003

After 9/11 ... one of the most shameful pages of human history, we
are witnessing a joint operation of the 'sons of Allah' and America's
neo-conservatives, who march hand in hand killing innocent
humans, taking our world to the edge of an abyss ... But world
opinion can see what the leaders of this new world are up to ...
People are tired of war and those who seek war ...

Never in the history of mankind has there been such an acute
need for peace ... for me personally, 9/11 provided an awareness of
the infinite extent of human cruelty ...

Yet it has also affected our country. People are more aware of our suffering and the Islamic terrorism that had slaughtered countless numbers of our countrymen ... As the world knows more about Islamic dictatorships ...

With the American invasion of Iraq, the lack of stability there, and with the Islamic Republic using its forces to bolster the activities of terrorists ... If the US doesn't bring stability and democracy to Iraq ... the greatest beneficiaries will be the rulers of the Islamic Republic.

Email: siprisk@gmail.com
http://siprisk.blogspot.com

---

15 October 2004

If George Bush, Dick Cheney and the Fox News Network swapped places with Ayatollah Khamenei, Rafsanjani and our own state-controlled television network ... nothing much would change in the world. Just as everything in Iran is the fault of the Americans, in America, Middle Eastern terrorists are to blame for all the woes of the world ...

And these American elections are interesting too. There's a lot of fuss right now about Dick Cheney's daughter being a homosexual!!! Well, perhaps such things are important to the American people. After all, religion will always be an issue. Can you see that there is not much between the US and Iran and religion is always going down the wrong course ...

It's not about Christianity or Islam – all roads end in God. But I don't know why these days all the nasty roads end in God ...

Email: kooche@Gmail.com
http://weblog.kooche.net

---

11 September 2003

Although I have no doubt about the evil nature of our rulers and their ability to perpetrate acts of pure wickedness ... I knew with total certainty on 9/11 that no Iranians could be involved ... And no, I'm not talking about the joke that has been going round: 'You can never find four Iranians in this country who agree on the same thing ... let alone plan ahead and get it done' ... It basically comes down to my difficulty in imagining anyone from Iran or even the rest of the Middle East who could be capable of such acts ...

I can understand that we have psychotics in this world ... or even despotic rulers who systematically terrorize ... but for me the most shocking aspect of 9/11 was that this was not some lone gunman but a group of people who voluntarily colluded in this evil act ... Didn't any of those involved have moments of sanity and say to themselves: 'What we are doing is pure evil'? ... I just don't get it ... I always thought we were more humane than those westerners ... we care about our families and could not hurt others so callously and indiscriminately ...

But it's no longer just 9/11. We are seeing so many acts of pure evil around the world committed by Muslims ...

Until now ... the West was more capable of such evil crimes ... they were the ones who carried out indiscriminate killings ... like the Holocaust, Hiroshima, Bosnia ...

I always felt that we were better than the callous men who rule Western countries ... I just cannot understand how someone who calls himself a Muslim could be capable of such acts ...

Not that I believe in the conspiracy theories that are fed to us by the media, blaming Israel and the United States ... It's just that I still can't get over the fact that we can be so evil too ...

And although, thank God, no Iranians were involved ... I cannot stop feeling an enormous sense of shame, guilt and helplessness.

By Spirit

14 October 2002

Yesterday during the BBC news report on the Bali bombing, the reporter kept repeating that the majority of Bali Muslims are peace-loving and do not in any way support the bombers.

The thief said: 'I don't know why every time something goes missing around here they come after me. But, interestingly, they always find the stolen loot here.'

Now that has become the story of we Muslims, where it's left to the non-Muslim TV, out of common decency, to defend us as peace-lovers. We are useless.

Email: weblog@ksajadi.com
http://www.ksajadi.com/fblog

16 November 2003

I personally remember our war against Iraq, when I served for a year and a half ... before being discharged due to injury ... Even with Saddam as the ruler of Iraq, during this month we respected a mutual ceasefire ... But these bombings this week in Istanbul in the month of Ramadan ... (Not that I agree with war in any other month.)

I curse you ... shame and eternal damnation for those that are bringing such mayhem to the world in the name of a contrived religion ...

Email: eghbal_r@yahoo.com
http://rezaeghbal.blogspot.com

5 December 2002

Yesterday I was wondering why there weren't any Iranians or Afghanis among the Taliban terrorists, but quite a few Pakistanis ... I walked into this shop [in London] owned by a Pakistani; the whole shop was full of various posters of Islamic groups and pictures of

Mecca. And scattered throughout the shop were collection boxes for various Islamic charities (a source linked to some of the terrorist groups). It was sunset and the man was breaking his fast while listening to a woman singing in Urdu.

I thought to myself, if he was an Iranian and had lived in Iran and had actually got a good beating from the Islamic Morality Police for listening to this woman's voice ... There would be no collection boxes, nor even the remotest possibility that his British-born son might go off to fight with the Taliban.

Email: weblog@ksajadi.com
http://www.ksajadi.com/fblog

---

23 November 2003

Death, mayhem and destruction

So many dead ... although the world only became aware of Islamic fascists on 9/11, as a society we have been forced to co-exist with them for nearly a quarter of a century ... to the West it was the dawn of a new world threat; but through a monumental tragic irony many Muslims could also see in the wreckage of the Twin Towers the timely death of Islamic Fascism ...

In the past they have served their purpose ... These mad dogs were well fed and used at the 'last stand' against Communism in Afghanistan ... Another rabid bunch, Hamas, were a valuable tool against a brainless but secular Arafat ... And in 1953 in Iran, the CIA used some of them to topple the democratic government of Dr Mossadegh ...

All societies have their mad dogs, but while theirs are marginalized, scorned and subdued with anti-psychotic medication ... tragically ours have at times been very well fed by outsiders and nurtured by our own ignorance and desperation ...

Now they are saying that those responsible for the bombs in Turkey were the extremist Islamic 'Turkish Hezbollah'. A group that,

according to the Turkish officials' own admittance, were set up by
them to combat the secular Kurdish separatists ...

When is this madness going to stop?! They train, finance and
equip a bunch of dishonourable fanatics to be guard dogs and then
they are shocked when they are attacked themselves ...

I no longer have the heart to describe the details of the carnage
in Turkey last week ... but if you too, like everyone I speak to these
days, are feeling helpless and dejected ... do not lose all hope ...

What we are witnessing is the gruesome self-destruction of all
these Islamic fascists ... the more they go on ... the more they
inspire nothing but mass revulsion and disgust among Muslims ...

And there is hope, because finally we are no longer alone ... the
world is also suddenly aware of the mad rabid dogs that have
brought nothing but mayhem and destruction to our societies for
so long ...

And finally, even if it is not for our sake but for their own safety,
they will stop hiring and financing these rabid mercenaries ...

By Spirit

In the realm of the blogosphere – where anonymous individuals are free to voice
any opinion whatsoever – one is constantly confronted by a chorus of disgust
against the mutant Islamists.

As the western Islamic scholar Olivier Roy pointed out some time ago, the
failure of radical political Islam in the early 1990s is that Islamist movements
were running out of revolutionary steam. Roy argued that in the future they
would either become restrained mainstream political parties – as has happened
in Jordan and Turkey – or they would morph into a sort of individualist neo-fun-
damentalism with an emphasis on lifestyle issues rather than political change.

As has been seen throughout the region – from Egypt and Algeria to Iraq –
since 9/11 the fanatical militants appear to have overestimated their own popularity. Most people in the world are motivated more by economic security and
social justice than by extreme revolution and brutal puritanism. When militant

Islam starts to show a ruthless streak and to threaten the rhythms of daily life and economic stability, the hitherto silent majority will turn against it.

In Iraq in October 2004, fighters loyal to the radical Shia cleric Moqtada Al-Sadr started handing over their heavy weapons when faced with a massive loss of popularity. It had first been demonstrated months before, on a march towards Najaf, when crowds of ordinary Iraqis protested against Sadr's militant methods. On the other side of the Muslim world, in Indonesia, there have been reports that the Jemaah Islamiah movement appears to have turned away from large-scale bombings due to overwhelming public disgust and damaging negative publicity about heavy casualties in the group's attacks before 2003.

But Iran, uniquely, has been controlled and ruled by radical clerics, and people have lived through and suffered the consequences of the 25-year forced march towards the utopia promised by the godfather of Islamic militancy Ayatollah Khomeini. So Iranians have no illusions to shatter. They are all-too aware of the difference between the paradise they were promised and the harsh reality of living under the rule of Islamic fundamentalists.

3 CELEBRATION OF THE CENSORED

11 August 2003

We are all Islamic psychopaths

A while back, French voters made sure that the fascist National Front leader Jean-Marie Le Pen did not get elected. But wasn't it shocking that in a country like France – the cradle of democracy – a fascist has so many supporters that he is successful in the first round of elections?!

It's appalling, but we can explain it away, because the whole world knows the French. We think of France and we are reminded of the birth of democracy. We think of Simone de Beauvoir, Sartre, Matisse, and their gallant resistance against fascism during the Second World War. A 'Le Pen' could never taint the French. Just as Hitler's vile existence did not taint the whole Christian Western world ... but Bin Laden taints us all, every single one of the 1.2 billion Muslims in the world.

What is there to be done with our own Islamic fascists? Our electoral system does not give us an opportunity to vote against them. Have we put up a fight? Yes, for 25 years our prisons have been packed to the rafters, we have seen the best of our kind sent to the gallows and buried in mass graves. Are the fascists in the minority? Yes. In two recent subsequent general elections they gained only 10 per cent of the votes. But they are armed and willing to kill for their beliefs and we are only willing to die for ours …

When outsiders see the actions of a few psychopaths like Bin Laden or Saddam or yet another villain named Muhammed willing to bring mayhem to this world, we are all tainted. The whole of the Islamic world is then made out to be psychopathic. We know about the French and their gallant fight for democracy, but do they know anything about our struggle?

We have been fighting against fascists for at least the last 100 years. Our great-grandfathers during the Constitutional Revolution [1906] tried to bring democracy to this land. But the British with their Anglo-Iranian Oil Company were against it and soon killed it off. Do they know about the democratically elected government of our beloved Dr Mossadegh? Do they know that the CIA toppled him nearly 50 years ago and replaced him with (to paraphrase Roosevelt) a 'son-of-a-bitch, but our son-of-a-bitch'. And the sick joke is now they want to give us democracy!

They only hear the psychopaths among us. Don't they know that many like me believe in the maxims of Hussein [the grandson of the prophet Muhammad], who said, 'If you are a non-believer, at least be a libertarian.' He did not practise our faith like these tyrants.

Do they know that in every Iranian heart beats the poetry of Hafez, Rumi, and Shamlou; or that we habitually whisper to one another as we witness daily acts of oppression:
'Such a strange time it is, my beloved' [Ahmad Shamlou, 1979]

By Godfather

Iranians are proud of a literary heritage that has produced names such as Omar Khayyám, Hafez, Saadi and Rumi (who is currently one of the best-selling poets in the United States). In Iran poets have an iconic status that is uncommon in the West, because throughout history our poets have given us the symbolic language of resistance. Predictably, there is a lot of poetry scattered throughout these on-line journals. Ordinary Iranians pepper their everyday flowery conversations with quotations from Persian poets, despite the fact that the State has erased many of these poets from its official history of Iran.

THE BLACK-CLAD REVOLUTIONARY MILITIAMEN APPROACHING WOMEN THAT HAD DEFIED THE NEWLY INTRODUCED LAWS OF COMPULSORY HEJAB (1979).

During the early days of the Revolution, the Morality Police were sent out on to the streets to enforce the newly introduced laws. As the celebrated Iranian poet Ahmad Shamlou says in his poem 'In This Dead-End' (1979), the Morality Police smell your breath if they suspect you of drinking alcohol and punish anyone caught in possession of banned books, music cassettes or films; or anyone caught kissing in public; and sometimes women's lips are cut with razors ('And surgically they place smiles on lips') for wearing lipstick.

> Your mouth they smell
>> Lest you have said I love you.
>> Your heart they smell

Such a strange time it is, my beloved

And Love
Is whipped
at roadblocks.

Love must be kept hidden in the pantry at home

In the twists and turns of this dead-end cold
Fire
is kept aglow
by burning songs and poems.

Do not peril by thinking.

Such a strange time it is, my beloved

He who beats at the door in the midst of the night
Has come to slay the light.

Light must be kept hidden in the pantry at home

There the butchers
Presiding over the streets
with their bloodstained cleavers and chopping blocks

Such a strange time it is, my beloved

And surgically they place smiles on lips
and songs on mouths.

Joy must be kept hidden in the pantry at home

Roasting Canaries
on a fire made of lilies and Jasmines

Such a strange time it is, my beloved

The devil drunk with conquest

Relishing a spread in the realms of our grief.

God must be kept hidden in the pantry at home.

['In This Dead-End' (1979), Ahmad Shamlou]

Hossein Rahmani © www.iranqpg.com

MOURNERS AT SHAMLOU'S FUNERAL IN
IRAN, 2000

Soon after 'In This Dead-End' was published, Shamlou's work was banned in Iran until his death (aged 75) in July 2000. Yet his poetry can be found through-out the Iranian blogosphere. A lifelong campaigner for freedom of speech, Shamlou was imprisoned several times by the former regime of the Shah and went into exile for a while. Shamlou's death was not mentioned in Iran's state-controlled media, but on 27 July 2000 the BBC reported that 'tens of thousands of mourners packed the streets of Tehran for the funeral procession of Iran's greatest contemporary poet'. During the funeral procession mourners chanted 'I have never feared death', a line from one of Shamlou's most famous poems:

> I have never feared death ... My fear is to die in a land where the
> gravedigger's wage is higher then the price of an individual's freedom ...

Shamlou was a journalist, playwright and broadcaster and also translated a variety of authors – such as Kafka, Lorca and Sholokhov – into Persian. Imprisoned and persecuted by the authorities, he left Iran in 1977 to publish a prominent anti-monarchy newspaper in London. He was active in organizing Iranian writers to fight against the censorship of the Shah's regime and then the Islamic State after the Revolution. He found the new Islamic regime to be just as dangerous as the previous one.

Although he has published more than 70 books and was a serious contender for the Nobel Prize for Literature in 1984, little of Shamlou's work is available in English translation and he remains almost unknown in the West. He was a humanist and a socially engaged intellectual whose work is characterized by a passionate belief in justice.

---

17 October 2003

> Anyone out there who was at university a decade ago (as I was)
> would remember how certain extremist Islamic groups had total
> control of Tahkim Vahdat [the national student union] ... But
> just look at it today ... two years ago when I popped in to the
> union office there had been a great transformation ... Not only

was the obligatory portrait of Ayatollah Khomeini absent [but]
it had been replaced by a poster of Ahmad Shamlou.

Email: vahidharati@yahoo.com
http://vahid.blogspot.com

THE REVOLUTION DEVOURS ITS CHILDREN

The regime's ruthless intolerance of criticism does not only apply to the likes of
Shamlou. Even warhorses of the Revolution like Hashem Aghajari have encountered the wrath of the ruling clerics. A devout Muslim, Aghajari was dismayed by
what he saw as repression in the name of Islam, so he turned against the system
he had helped to create and spoke out in the name of freedom. His death sentence for apostasy generated a lot of frank and controversial debate among
Iranian bloggers. Aghajari was not only a respected university professor but a
veteran who had lost a leg in the war with Iraq (1980–88). He was arrested after
giving an address commemorating the twenty-fifth anniversary of the death of
Dr Ali Shariati.

© Nehzate Azadi

DR ALI SHARIATI

The populist ideas of Shariati – a charismatic sociologist and left-leaning
Islamic intellectual – drew the youth of Iran into the revolutionary movement. 'I
have no religion, but if I were to choose one, it would be that of Shariati's,' said

the philosopher Jean-Paul Sartre. Shariati had studied at the Sorbonne and Sartre's attempt to reconcile existentialism with Marxism and humanism greatly influenced his own attempt to fuse social scientific concepts with Islamic political thought.

Shariati is recognized as one of the founding fathers of political Islam, yet a quarter of a century after the Revolution, his diehard fans still contend that his ideology was hijacked and falsified and later openly discarded by extremists. There is a cruel irony in the fact that the ideology many believe brought about the Islamic Revolution advocated an end to blind obedience to religious authority. Shariati argued that every Muslim had the right to engage in his or her own independent reasoning about the meaning and relevance of the sacred (Sharia) law.

Shariati was aiming for what he called 'Islamic Protestantism'. However, his critics argue that his political philosophy was riddled with the dogmatism of the ideologies of his time. They are convinced that the Islamic Republic of Iran came about as a direct result of the Shariati movement and its leader's warped ideas.

Hasan Yousefi Eshkevari, a cleric and Islamic scholar and the head of the Shariati Foundation in Iran, was imprisoned for his outspoken defence of the separation of State from religion, and for speaking out against the compulsory wearing of the veil for women. He has been accused of several serious offences, including apostasy; charges that normally carry the death penalty.

The following blog was written by Muhammad-Ali Abtahi, a mid-ranking Shia cleric and once the parliamentary ex-vice president to Khatami. In a climate in which Shariati has become a hate figure among the unelected ruling clerics, Abtahi bravely discusses him and his vision of a modern Islam.

---

17 June 2004

I was a young man when I first heard about Shariati ... the enemies of his day, who were predominantly the clerics ... made him known to us ...

Shariati is what we need today [when] the era of revolutions has
long gone ... And a progressive look at religion is needed today
more than ever before ... Shariati was a symbol of modern Islam.
Long live his name and memory.

http://www.webneveshteha.com/

Followers of Shariati's Islamic ideology have enraged the regime by repeating
Shariati's call for an end to blind obedience (taqlid) on the part of the laity. In his
speech, the war veteran Aghajari called for reform within the Islamic clerical
establishment. 'Dr Shariati would have said that this clergy is not descended from
heaven,' he told the crowd, 'they are modern, although their minds are medieval.'
Hardline clerics have publicly demanded the death sentence for Aghajari, com-
paring him to Salman Rushdie, the British author of *The Satanic Verses* and the
subject of a death order or *fatwa* issued by the late Ayatollah Khomeini.

The announcement of Aghajari's death sentence was followed by mass student
demonstrations in many parts of Iran, starting with a month-long student
protest at Tehran University in November 2002. After a fortnight of student
unrest, Ayatollah Khomeini was moved to demand a Supreme Court review of
Aghajari's case. His death sentence was suspended and is currently on appeal.
Nevertheless, the protest continued to grow, attracting tens of thousand of students across the country – until they were brutally crushed. Throughout this
period, Iran's on-line community furiously debated Aghajari's case.

16 November 2002

What is there left for me to say when all our posts these days are
protests at Aghajari's court verdict? ... I am at least slightly
comforted that we as a community of bloggers have been able to
put out a joint protest declaration against it.

Email: comment_ma2ta@consultant.com
http://www.ma-2-ta.com

18 November 2002

I've just read the full text of the speech that has got Aghajari the
death penalty on gooya.com. Go and check it out yourself. These are
just some extracts:

> ... an interpretation by past generations of Islamic scholars is
> not Islam. It was their account of Islam; just as they had the
> right to understand the Koran, from a personal perspective – we
> have the same right. Their understanding of Islam is not an
> absolute diktat of faith for us.

> ... I have personally come across some of our own clerics, after
> their return from short trips to the West – usually two or three
> weeks of medical treatment. These clerics are so awestruck at
> how justly the authorities of those countries act towards their
> own people. Likewise about 150 years ago a Holy [Muslim] man
> went to Europe; on his return to Iran, he wrote: 'I saw no
> Muslims in Europe, but I saw Islam' (i.e., he saw righteousness).
> In our time, we see Muslims, but we do not see Islam.

> ... When Ali [the Prophet Muhammad's successor, according to
> the Shia faith] sent a representative to Egypt, he wrote: 'You are
> a powerful man. Act with decency and impartiality towards the
> people. There are two groups of Egyptians: either they are
> Muslims, and therefore your brethren, or they are your fellow
> human beings. Behave towards them equally according to
> Islam.' Islam does discriminate between Muslims and non-
> Muslims.

Now, I believe myself to be a practising Muslim, but there is
nothing in that speech that I or any member of my huge extended
family could object to. If Aghajari is an apostate, than every decent

man, woman and child in this country is an apostate ...

Our leaders preach death and hatred. Martyrdom is no longer
about defending one's family and home, as Aghajari once did.
He fought for this country and lost a leg in the process. But
today martyrdom has been desecrated by filthy acts like
strapping bombs to yourself and destroying countless innocent
lives.

And just look at the men who encourage and propagate these
acts: corrupt clergy like Rafsanjani [the ex-President of Iran] who is
today one of the richest men in this country ... While men like
Aghajari defended our homes against Saddam, Rafsanjani's sons
were sent to safety in Belgium. If your kind of martyrdom is
esteemed in heaven and earth, then why don't you or your crooked
sons go and blow up your own fat arses? In a world where Aghajari
is an apostate and the Rafsanjani clan are saints, we should all wear
our signs of apostasy with honour.

By Spirit

SECULAR MARTYRS

In 2003 the writer and journalist Akbar Ganji received the European
Parliament's 2003 Sakharov Prize. This is what the award committee had
to say:

> The Sakharov Prize is intended to honour an individual who has through
> personal engagement defended human rights in his country. One of the
> places where this crucial confrontation is taking place today is Iran.
> Confrontation between political freedom and totalitarianism occurs
> there on a daily basis. The question of fundamentalism is paramount.
> Subsequently, and considering his journey through life, Akbar Ganji is an
> ideal candidate for the prize. Being a former follower of Ayatollah
> Khomeini, Ganji has become a symbol for secular Islam. The fate of

democracy in the Islamic world depends on the successful secularization of Islam.

Celebrated by his supporters as the Islamic world's Vaclav Havel, Ganji is six years into a long prison sentence, although in captivity he has managed to produce a 60-page manifesto on 'Republicanism'. Naturally it was banned by the authorities, but it has been posted on the Internet and hotly debated by bloggers. In 'Republicanism' Ganji advocates the separation of religion and the State. He also accuses several senior state figures of being responsible for a number of 'serial killings' (assassinations) of writers and intellectuals in 1998.

Photo © Majid Saeedi

AKBAR GANJI
ON TRIAL

---

17 October 2003

... Is it not so, that those considered apostates during their own time have a far superior place in history than the allegedly devout ...

They think they have destroyed Ganji, ignorant that he is now immortalized.

http://dowran.blogsky.com

Nearing his sixth year in captivity Ganji is not forgotten. In a move that one blogger likened to the famous scene from the film *Spartacus* where the slaves stand up to the Romans by saying 'I am Spartacus'; during April 2005, in coordinated protest (on the anniversary of his imprisonment) a great number of bloggers renamed their blogs Akbar Ganji for a week.

---

25 April 2005

From today for a week I will rename my blog Akbar Ganji. Just to have the name of this champion of the pen on top of my writing is a great personal honour.

fmsokhan@gmail.com
http://www.fmsokhan.com

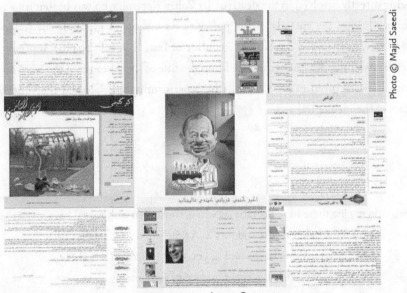

THE FRONT PAGES OF SEVERAL BLOGS RENAMED AKBAR GANJI FOR A WEEK.

As editor of the Sobhe-Emruz newspaper, Akbar Ganji daringly exposed a 'power mafia' network behind the murders of writers and intellectuals. It was organized via key figures in the merchant class, the religious seminaries, the Council of

Guardians, the Revolutionary Guards, the judiciary and the state-run radio and television. The murders also had backing from those in high office. Ganji refers to Iranian ex-president Rafsanjani as the 'Red Eminence' – alluding to Cardinal Richelieu, the power behind Catherine de Medici's rule and chief architect of the slaughter of the Huguenots.

Unlike anything ever seen before in Iran, people formed long lines outside the newspaper kiosks just to read Ganji's latest revelations. He made the previously shadowy Haghani Islamic School in Qom a household name when he pointed out that most members of the 'power mafia' were former pupils.

At his prosecution Ganji was confronted by one of the young rising stars of the Hagahni School, Judge Saeed Mortazavi, who can be credited with the closure of more than 100 pro-democracy publications and the harassment and imprisonment of many writers and political activists in recent years. Mohsen Armin, a reformist MP in the Iranian Parliament, has even accused Mortazavi of being directly involved in the death of Dr Zahra Kazemi, who was beaten into a coma while in the custody of the judiciary. As a show of gratitude for Judge Mortazavi's services to the Islamic Republic of Iran, in April 2004 the Supreme Leader Ayatollah Khamenei awarded him the title of 'Best Leader of the Year', an annual award given to exceptionally high-performing officials and the superstars of the ideological state.

---

2 November 2003

In my life there have been times when, consumed with rage, I have felt infinite helplessness and loss ... A time when you feel that an injustice is crushing your mind ... you want to scream and shout and all you can see is the sneering face of your enemy ... an opponent who seems only to get turned on even more at the spectre of your wet eyes and red cheeks ... times when you feel that God must feel ashamed to have created man ...

Being confronted with the photo of Akbar Ganji facing Saeed Mortazavi [head prosecutor of Tehran's revolutionary court] was one of those times ... It is a foul symbol of a terrorized people forced to look at the smirking faces of the powerful ...

I have lived for 27 years ... 25 years of them under revolution, repression, assassinations, hangings and war ... My youth and childhood passed away during bombings in underground shelters gazing at the trembling hands of my elders ...

I am stunned that we walk past injustices so indifferently ... Sometimes I think this place is the land cursed by God ... Sometimes a photograph of an injustice and that smirk, keeps you awake till dawn.

By The Hungry Philosopher

© Hadi Heidary, www.haditoons.com

CARTOON MARKING AKBAR GANJI'S SIXTH
YEAR OF IMPRISONMENT

ISLAMIC REFORMATION OR BUST

There are many outspoken opponents of the regime. Abdolah Nouri, for instance, was found guilty of publishing sacrilegious articles and imprisoned. Mohsen Kadivar was incarcerated for defaming the country's Islamic system and for 'confusing public opinion'. A formidable critic of Iran's hard-line religious leadership, Kadivar has called for political life to be autonomous from religion, directly challenging many aspects of Sharia law. And as we have seen, Eshkavari has been accused of some serious offences that can normally carry the death penalty under Iran's Sharia laws.

These outspoken critics of the regime are all prominent members of the Shia clergy, as are many political prisoners and dissidents in Iran today. In October 2003 Hussein Khomeini, a mid-ranking cleric and grandson of the Ayatollah, called on the West to do more to support those who wished to end fundamentalist Islamic rule in the country. More recently (27 April 2004), in an interview with the 'Voice of America' Persian service, Khomeini said that had he been in his grandfather's shoes, he 'would never have taken such an action as issuing the fatwa against Salman Rushdie'. He even added that his grandfather was not qualified to issue a fatwa, because 'Islam accords this kind of decision-making authority only to prophets'.

At 82, the Grand Ayatollah Montazeri is one of the most senior-ranking religious figures in Shia Islam. He has been under house arrest since 1997. Many believe that he was freed in 2003, because the ruling clerics feared that his death in captivity might cause social unrest. In July 1988, Montazeri accused Ayatollah Khomeini of the genocide of the jailed opponents of the regime. 'These massacres are incompatible with Islam,' he stated in a letter that was later made public.

Dealing with Montazeri's fierce criticism has proved quite a challenge for the Islamic Republic's rulers. It is a delicate matter placing one of the highest authorities in Shia Islam under house arrest, especially in a supposedly 'Islamic' state. It is tantamount to the regime attacking itself – or at least shooting itself in the foot. Especially as under total house arrest and with only his immediate family members allowed access, the Grand Ayatollah has in effect joined the blogging bandwagon by publishing regular commentaries as well as damning indictments of the regime and his memoirs, online at www.montazeri.ws.

28 January 2003

Yesterday it was announced by IRNA [the Iranian News Agency] that
Ayatollah Montazeri was to be released from his house arrest ...
They must have thought: 'He's 80 and will die soon anyway ... he
barely has the strength to talk ... Let alone criticize us any more ...

The funny thing is ... this new lot of reformists we have in the
Government ... try to claim anyone these days who stands up to the
regime as one of their own ... and give interviews saying that we
support free speech and reform ...

They think we have forgotten that some of these people who are
now 'reformists', called Montazeri a naive fool when he resigned!

Email: hamedyou@gmail.com

http://weblog.hamedyou.com

Despite the general (and erroneous) belief in a unified Shia clergy, the dozen or
so Grand Ayatollahs in the world have their own groups of followers and take
very different positions, even at times issuing religious edicts or *fatwas* that con-
tradict one another. Yet only a tiny section of these Grand Ayatollahs are affili-
ated with the ruling clerics in Iran. And some, like Montazeri, have openly questioned the legitimacy of a Supreme Leader's absolute religious power.

Taking their cue from older theologians, clerics such as Kadivar and Eshkavari
(and groups of young seminarians in the holy city of Qom) are now questioning
whether the mosques should be mixed up with a discredited and unpopular ideological regime. Many now openly speak of the need for an Islamic Reformation.
These clerics are at the heart of a battle over Iran's future, advocating pluralism
over an intolerant dogmatism.

The Islamic scholar Mohsen Kadivar believes that studying divergent interpre-
tations of Islam is not heretical, but rather an essential human prerequisite. Such
views have brought him a large following. Speaking at a seminar entitled 'Towards
Democracy' on 11 May 2004, Kadivar even announced that 'religious tyranny is
more twisted than secular tyranny'. He added that 'democracy ... should not be

loved or denounced merely because it comes from the West ... democracy is currently the best method of governance – as it minimizes the chances of individuals deceiving the people, replacing it with the rule of public wisdom'.

During the May 2000 parliamentary election in Iran, the hardliners managed to hold on to 44 out of almost 290 parliamentary seats. The BBC noted that Jamileh Kadivar was the most popular woman in Iran after she gained the second largest number of votes in the country. The BBC omitted to mention a fact not lost on the Iranian electorate: she is also Mohsen Kadivar's younger sister. The dissident cleric has garnered a great deal of national support since his imprisonment.

© Nehzate Azadi

DISSIDENT CLERIC KADIVAR (LEFT) AT
TEHRAN UNIVERSITY AND (RIGHT) AT A
FUNERAL OF A FELLOW POLITICAL ACTIVIST

2 March 2004

The late Kadivar!
    I doubt that any official media source will dare print what Kadivar said tonight* ... but you can probably see the full text of the speech on his website (www.kadivar.com) ... I dearly hope that these rumours that we hear about more assassinations do not involve him

... But the way he talked tonight you almost felt as if this would be his last speech ...

I don't want anyone to confuse what I'm trying to say here ... It's not as if a twenty-first century doctrine will come out of this man's speeches ... But the simple fact that he is trying to resurrect ideas from 14 centuries ago and apply them to the modern world is an exceptional endeavour ...

* On 2 March 2004 Kadivar gave a lecture in Tehran to about 1,000 people in which he described the symptoms of unjust rule. He outlined in detail the situation in the Islamic Republic, but without actually mentioning the regime or its rulers by name (for instance, talking about 'the repression of all opposition' and 'the inequitable distribution of wealth').

Email: alpr_ir2002@yahoo.com

http://alpr.persianblog.com

23 May 2003

I just love these mullahs who are constantly critical of our ruling clerics ... they are instrumental in exorcizing the fanaticism of the donkeys of this world ...

Twenty-five years of religious rule has had one long-term benefit ... for generations to come no Iranian will ever want to mix matters of state with religion ... And if only those Muslim idiots in our neighbouring countries knew about our failed experiment with an Islamic government they would come to their senses too ... It's a joke they want to do now what we miserably failed at 25 years ago ...

But it is finished ... and when these mullahs are dethroned ... it will be like the Berlin Wall coming down ... then they will all realize ... the mullahs are finished ... You all know what I mean ... We've had our social revolution ... and soon we will be rid of them ... a little patience ... our dawn is near.

By Our Voice

25 November 2002

Every day new intrigues and tyrannies by our repressive turbaned
rulers ... And crazy Muslims around the world that bring nothing
but carnage and shame ...

I swear to God ... if it weren't for clergy Like Eshkavari who keep
telling us that what they do is not Islam ... I would abandon this
little faith I have once and for all.

By Spirit

Radical statements that may eventually change the boundaries and practices of
Islam are coming out of the seminaries of Qom. For instance, Ayatollah Yosef
Sanei has not only declared that women have been 'badly treated' since the
Islamic Revolution, but that there should be nothing to stop a woman becoming
president or even supreme religious leader – which is tantamount to saying there
should be a female pope.

Meanwhile, Ayatollah Taheri, the principal spiritual leader of Isfahan, Iran's
second most populous city, has described the regime as 'an enemy of Islam and
humanity'. In July 2002, resigning from his post after 25 years as the Friday
prayers leader of Isfahan, he condemned the ruling clerics for corruption and
incompetence, adding that the only reason for his public protest was to defend
the faith, which had been marred in the eyes of ordinary people because of its
association with a so-called Islamic government.

Yet while the religious seminaries debate the issue of an Islamic Reformation,
it seems the ordinary people are well ahead of them. People are making a conscious effort to disregard the dictates of the seminaries more than ever before. It
looks like they will transform the boundaries and practices of Islam from the
bottom up, whether the ayatollahs like it or not. It has already been noted that
very few people actually bother to attend Friday prayers.

On 11 March 2001 Muhammad-Hassan Alipour, the managing editor of the
popular weekly magazine *Aban*, was given a six-month suspended jail sentence
and forbidden from practising journalism for five years. He was accused, among

other things, of 'spreading lies, corruption and insulting religious sanctities'. *Aban* was banned for publishing an article entitled 'People Will Move On', which argued that a grassroots Islamic Reformation was already on the move, leaving behind the clerics.

THE FREEDOM TO BE 'BLASPHEMOUS'

While blogging gives some Iranians the freedom to defend their faith, for others it provides an outlet for their resentment and disapproval of a religious system that governs every aspect of their lives.

---

16 September 2003

I don't know what this Allah of ours is, that we call the most beneficent and merciful ... that condemns you to burn in Hell if you don't obey his commands ...

I am neither Allah nor beneficent and merciful, but when I see my fellow men under pressure, displaying their limitations, I feel such a heavy weight of embarrassment on my shoulders that I cannot straighten my back to look them in the eyes ... and if I can, I try to help them ...

I don't try to make them totally lose the plot by terrifying them with hellfire ...

In truth, I don't understand the beneficent and merciful bit and what good it does to us Muslims ...

Email: satgean@yahoo.com
http://www.satgean.persianblog.com

---

26 February 2004

Apologies to all our enlightened and scholarly mullahs out there ...

How to make a Mullah

Email: z8unak@z8un.com

http://z8un.persianblog.com

9 June 2003

I shit on the whole of Hezbollah ... and your distorted Islam and its ideology that you use to diminish a human being through torture.

All your 'bollocks' analyses are obsolete ... this generation has finally, after 23 years, realized what sort of hole it's in ...

The student demonstrations are proof that 23 year of brainwashing from primary school to university cannot even save you today ...

People put an ayatollah and the clergy on the same level as pimps and thugs and they would shove the whole lot of you up a donkey's arse if they could.

Email: fozoolak@hotmail.com

http://fozool.blogspot.com

29 August 2003

Good tidings ... today 'Ayatol-shit' Hakim, the head of Iraqi Shias, was assassinated. Thank you God, as there is one less mullah in the world ...

Yet, I wouldn't have been too unhappy if these senseless Iraqis could have experienced the misery of living under an Islamic

Republic as we have for 25 years ... but I'm jealous in a way ... why
don't our mullahs die off so easily?

Email: DeevMusic@yahoo.com
http://deev.persianblog.com

['The requested weblog has been disabled due to a Terms of Service
violation']

It doesn't take much to be officially accused of 'blasphemy' in Iran – a crime
punishable by death. Iran's ideological state was shaped around Ayatollah
Khomeini and the almost royal powers vested in him as Supreme Leader,
evoking an age when sovereigns were considered God's representatives on
earth. The Western media describes the clerical rulers of the Islamic Republic
as 'fundamentalists', but in reality the revolutionary ayatollahs are a new religious and historic oddity.

In 1979, for the first time in a thousand years, the Supreme Leader of Iran was
made the placeholder for the missing twelfth imam: the messianic figure who
vanished in the tenth century and whose return (accompanied by Jesus), Shias
believe, will bring on an era of absolute justice.

Yet one of the biggest ironies of the Islamic Republic is that the most senior
religious figures in Shia Islam – like the Grand Ayatollahs Sistani and Montazeri
– have pronounced as blasphemous the concept of rule by a Supreme Leader
who claims to be God's representative on earth.

Nevertheless, although tame by Western standards, the off-the-cuff remarks of
bloggers concerning the 'sacred' Supreme Leader are denounced as blasphemous in the Islamic Republic of Iran. Blasphemy carries the death penalty, as do
a variety of offences, from murder, rape and armed robbery to drug trafficking,
adultery and apostasy.

14 January 2004

Dear Leader of the Revolution,
Your Holiness,

Have you ever fallen in love? Have you ever gazed into the crimson
of the wine, when you can still feel the spot where she kissed you on

your eyelids? Have you ever danced? Have you
ever had Maz Maz [Iranian crisps] dipped in
Mast Moseer [a dip]? Have you ever worn jeans?
Do you know what 'Mum' roll-on deodorant is?
Have you ever cried at night? How many years
did you go to school? Have you ever made

Abghosht [an Iranian stew]? Have you ever got a barbeque going?
Tell me, what is Newton's Third Law? Has it ever come about that
you cried when your goldfish jumped out of its bowl and died on
New Year's Eve?* How many times has the scent of springtime in
Shiraz [a southern Iranian city] driven you wild? Have you ever
kissed a dog? Have you ever listened to Persian classical music? Or
what about rap? Do you ever whistle?

Have you ever kissed her neck? What about behind her ears?

Have you ever downloaded an MP3 from the Internet? Do you
ever ask the guy at the kiosk selling cigarettes how he's doing? Ever
walked through town at midnight? Have they ever raided your
home and confiscated your books?

Have you ever been forced into exile? Has it ever happened that
you just can't get the pattern of those tiles in your mother's kitchen
out of your head (for three nights in a row), but you just can't
remember the colour? Have you ever called your mother up from
far away and asked her to describe the colour of those tiles – at the
mention of which you both uncontrollably sob?

Have you ever longed for the windows of your apartment in
Tehran?

* As part of the ancient Persian New Year celebrations, which have been observed in the region for at least 5,000 years, on the eve of the spring equinox Iranians purchase a goldfish as a symbol of good luck.

Email: roozgar@hotmail.com

http://www.hylit.net/nightly

5 November 2003

I'm almost ashamed to admit that up to a couple of years ago I still felt neutral about fasting … I wasn't really conscious of how totally fucked-up a person who wasn't religious would feel … It's Hell itself, this Ramadan … Let's ignore not being able to eat or drink, as even those sons-of-bitches fasting must feel tempted … but what is it to those pimps that I want to have a cigarette? … Are cigarettes food?

It's as if the Almighty gave these pimps a mission to make sure everyone fasts … and God forbid they miss out on even a single good deed in setting us on the path of righteousness … Well I know … thanks to the grace of the Islamic Republic what I've said is repetitive and nothing new to any of you out there.

But I don't know whether to laugh or cry … today I was just putting my asthma inhaler to my mouth when one of these pimps suddenly materialized in front of me and said: 'Sir, it's the month of Ramadan.' I apologize for my language, but I just get really tongue-tied when describing these donkeys …

Email: wastedige@yahoo.co.uk

http://fkngwstd.blogspot.com

4

A NATION OF STEADFAST REVOLUTIONARIES

The Revolution placed great emphasis on 'personal morality' and the performance of religious obligations. Yet state clerics continue to lament the fact that decades of morality policing have not created the steadfast revolutionaries desired by the State. Religious people complain that the mosques were full before the Revolution, but are now often empty. Dissident clerics argue that the Islamic Republic's failings have brought about a loss of Islamic values, because people associate the system with the religion. As the prominent Islamic scholar Hadi Eghbal says in his blog (ghabel.persianblog.com), 25 years of rule by the clerics in Iran 'has not made Islam stronger, but it has brought about a decline in the position of the clergy and religion in society'.

---

19 March 2005

[By middle-ranking cleric and parliamentary ex-Vice President Mohammad-Ali Abtahi]

Religious preachers

... There are lots of discussions around about an aversion to religion, but this aversion is to preachers not to religion. A lot of people cannot accept the disparity between their faith and the preachers of that faith, so they reject it. And for them religion also seems to be in crisis.

In religious regimes when all the actions of the rulers of that regime are attributed to religion, this danger is doubled. And the community of believers end up looking for a faith that cannot be dissociated from the preachers.

webneveshteha.com

Frustrated with a government that rules in the name of Islam, some people have turned away from religion. As *New York Times* columnist Nicholas Kristof put it: 'In much of the world, young Muslims are increasingly religious, but compulsive Islam has soured some Iranians on religion.' (13 May 2004)

23 May 2003

Growing up with the spiritual sound of the call to prayer ... the Allah Akbar [God is great] used to make me feel like a stronger person ... that there was a loving, kind, benevolent God out there ... greater than all my silly problems ... I would run to the mosque and stand there before my God, and leave a stronger person ... All I had to do during difficult times was remind myself 'Allah Akbar' ... When sitting my first exam (aged 7) [or] approaching the girl I had fallen in love with (aged 14) ... or as I was about to be taken to task by my father for driving his car and abandoning it after an accident (aged 17) ... or when my grandmother died (aged 19) ... But now 'Allah Akbar' is the chant of the thugs in the Basij and Hezbollah and fat, corrupt mullahs ...

The call to prayer, the 'Allah Akbar', still makes me feel like a

stronger person ... but I rarely enter a mosque ... all that awaits you
there are the hypocrites, thugs and oppressors ...

We replaced one corrupt monarch with thousands of corrupt
clergy ... yet the only thing they did was destroy our belief in the
religion they said they were safeguarding ... We were already
Muslims and did not have a revolution to become Muslims ... our
dreams were of equality, independence and justice ... but I hope
that when they leave we will still be Muslims ... and my God can be
Great again.

By School Friend

In July 2000 a report by Muhammad Ali Zam, the head of Tehran's cultural and
artistic affairs, was read out to the capital city's council officials. It was the first
time since the Revolution that an officially commissioned government report
had openly admitted the existence of prostitution. It also pointed out that the
average age of prostitutes in Iran had dropped from 27 to 20.

The report also highlighted the fact that many students were neglecting
prayers: 'Seventy-five per cent of the country's 60 million inhabitants and 86
per cent of young students do not say their daily prayers.' The basic irony of
the 'ideological Islamic' state of Iran is that it is becoming less religious by the
day.

In most parts of the world such social absurdities would be discussed at
length by political columnists, but in Iran the sweeping crackdowns on the press
mean that the Internet has become the last refuge for our best journalists.

Here is Ebrahim Nabavi, an uncompromising political satirist renowned for
pointing out the ironies of Iran's regime, writing in February 2004.

All revolutions devour their children, but our revolution ate its fathers
(the Iranian Revolution had many fathers) as well as the children and the
fathers of others too ... Fortunately, after 25 years, we have exported our
revolutionary ideas to the whole world ... Europe, America and Asia ...
but we have exported all of it ... so there is nothing left at home ...

However, the leaders of our country cannot be bothered to announce this
to the world.

In 1999 Nabavi was imprisoned and banned from working for the Iranian press.
Forced out of the conventional media and very recently forced into exile, he
started his own blog, getting an average of 10,000 visitors a day. Yet even this has
proved a challenge, as his site has been attacked by hackers several times and he
has been forced to set up a new site where he could go on writing observations
such as this.

February 2004

Four Portraits by Ebrahim Nabavi

REZA PAHLAVI, IRAN'S OUSTED MONARCH

I

He decreed that they display his portraits throughout town. This was
the best way to intimidate the nation.

II

In one portrait he was holding a young child.
In another he was smiling and benevolently watching the people.

In one portrait he had his hand raised waving to the people.

In another he was holding a rifle pointed at the enemies of the people.

In one portrait he was mounted on a horse.

In another he was standing beside the workers looking at them with compassion.

When he died people joyfully burnt all his portraits …

III

Revolutionaries would secretly hand out his portrait throughout town.

Later people would hide photographs of him at home.

They held his portrait during protests and the streets were filled with his image.

A young man died under a tank while holding his portrait.

They hung huge portraits of him outside all of the offices.

Then men dressed in black would attack and burn down any place that didn't hang up his portrait.

The revolutionary government decreed that his portrait must be hung in all offices.

Artists were commissioned to paint huge portraits of him.

Then someone was imprisoned for tearing down his portrait.

So people removed his portrait from their homes.

Next, revolutionaries secretly destroyed portraits of him.

Photo courtesy of Sara

IV

The more people detested him, the bigger his portraits became and the people were terrified more than ever before.

Email: nabavionline@hotmail.com
http://khabarnameh.gooya.com/nabavi
http://doomdam.com

Photo © Hossein Derakhshan www.vagrantly.com

EBRAHIM NABAVI IN 2002 WRITING HIS DAILY COLUMN FOR THE *HAYAT-E NOU* NEWSPAPER, ONE OF THE LAST PUBLICATIONS HE WORKED FOR IN IRAN BEFORE FLEEING TO EUROPE.

6 February 2004

Most of the leaders of our labour movements and Iran's Communist Party were rich kids, while the people who used to beat them up and stand up against them were from the poor proletariat ...

Email: nabavionline@hotmail.com
http://khabarnameh.gooya.com/nabavi
http://doomdam.com

In another blog, Nabavi comments on the fact that tens of thousands of Iranian women work as prostitutes. Yet illegitimate sexual relationships are punishable by death.

---

3 February 2004

If the Sharia Islamic law and punishments were ever to be applied, 80 per cent of the population would have to be punished and 90 per cent would be considered the enemies of God and the Prophet ...

Is it not strange that after decades of institutionalized religious education, Iran's youth are totally apathetic about such matters and have the keenest social and cultural leanings to 'American ways' in the Islamic world?

Email: nabavionline@hotmail.com
http://khabarnameh.gooya.com/nabavi
http://doomdam.com

THE SHIA PARADOX

Iranians are mostly Shia Muslims. At no time is this more obvious than during the nationwide ceremonies of Ashura at the end of a ten-day period of mourning. Ashura commemorates the slaying of Hossein (the grandson of the Prophet Muhammad) in Karbala, the desert of modern-day Iraq, in AD 680. At the end of Ashura, many Iranians young and old fill the streets throughout Iran and hold silent candlelit vigils in the open air during the hours of darkness in sympathy for Hossein's surviving family, including his sister Zeinab who was taken prisoner after his death. In the aftermath of Ashura, Zeinab became a potent spokesperson for the Shias. The candlelit vigils are a unique Iranian Shia ceremony in remembering the 'burden and loneliness' of Zeinab.

The New York Times correspondent Stephen Kinzer has observed that if there is one crucial theme that runs throughout Iranian history, shaping it to this day, it is the Shia faith and its central tenet that 'God requires leaders to rule justly.' This is why the Iranians 'thirst for just leadership, of which they have enjoyed precious little'.[1]

According to Shia belief and historical accounts, Yazid the Islamic ruler of the time was corrupt and tyrannical, 'oppressing his people in the name of Islam'. In order to strengthen his legitimacy, Yazid ordered Hossein to offer his allegiance or die. Hossein refused, replying: 'The most honourable jihad [struggle] is a just word spoken to an unjust ruler.' In Ashura, on the tenth day of Moharram, Hossein and 72 of his followers, including his brother and children, were surrounded by Yazid's armies in Karbala and massacred. Hossein's last words before he was slain were: 'If you do not care for Islam, do, at least, care for the freedom of your spirit.'

Hossein's last words are often seized upon by secular and religious opponents of the regime. For instance, after his protest resignation from Parliament in February 2004, the cleric Montakhab Nia said that 'the corruption in the name of Islam leads to Ashura ... today the only way forward is to follow Hossein ... the people have to call for the accountability of all those in charge, including prominent figures of the regime, and they must not be fooled by the slogans.'

Shia Islam was made the official religion of Iran at the beginning of the six-

Photo © Hamideh Zolfaghari www.hamidehz.com

SUFI GATHERING

teenth century by Shah Ismaeel, the founder of the Safavi dynasty. Shah Ismaeel was revered as a Sufi master. Sufism or Islamic mysticism provided the foundation of Iranian Shia Islam. Yet since its conception the ideological regime has increased the level of repression against Sufi religious practices. Sufi gatherings are often raided by the Basij paramilitaries who hold their practices in contempt – especially because in many Sufi congregations the men and women pray together and are not segregated.

Perhaps even more ironically, town gatherings to commemorate the passing of a Shia imam are viewed with suspicion by the Shia state clerics who rule Iran because they might provide dangerous rallying points for resistance. Security is routinely stepped up on such occasions and the hard-line Basij vigilantes take control. The authorities' suspicions are justified, for in recent years many congregations have turned into angry rallies against the regime.

In March 2004, Iran's Sharg newspaper and the BBC Persian Service reported that an Ashura candlelit gathering in the affluent neighbourhood of Mirdamad had turned violent. Some 5,000 people clashed at night with members of the paramilitary Basij. The Basij and Hezbollah, the right-wing Islamic irregulars, armed with chains and knives, moved through the crowd on motorcycles attacking people with impunity.

The Basij were sent to keep order, but they ended up brutally assaulting and then arresting people, so enraged were they by crowds of youngsters chanting anti-regime slogans.

'I have never witnessed such an Ashura ... It's as if we are distant from this generation, we don't understand them,' said the distinguished Iranian writer Mahmoud Dowlatabadi.* According to reports, thousands of openly modern, rebellious young men and women had gathered together late into the night, having lit up the area with thousands of candles. They flouted the rules that govern the separation of the sexes and the strict dress codes, many of the girls wearing gothic make-up and black nail varnish.

The scuffles between the Iranian youth and the Basij led to many arrests and

* BBC Persian Service report. In 2000 Dowlatabadi himself was accused of being 'counter-revolutionary and of threatening national security'.

THE CANDLELIT VIGILS OF ASHURA

eventually the riot police were brought in to disperse the crowd. Here again was another paradox: Iran's younger generation denouncing the Shia clerics that rule over them, while holding a night-time vigil for a Shia saint.

Ashura is also commemorated in cyberspace. Even those bloggers who are

fiercely critical of the Islamic regime – such as the outwardly secular anti-regime website www.peiknet.com – close down their blogs for the day during this important period of Shia mourning. And even the founder of Iranian blogs, Hossein Derakhshan – a typical child of the Revolution and a ceaseless detractor of the regime – has expressed his respect for Imam Hossein. Often Iranian bloggers who seem obsessed with Western culture and consumables can surprise us by suddenly remarking on the importance of Ashura. It is just another example of the many contradictions at the heart of modern-day Iran.

---

29 February 2004

My favourite links for today:
- A website by Hossein Ansarian, commemorating the month of Moharram
- Link to Yahoo for the latest pictures of the Oscar ceremony

http://mehdi110.blogspot.com

---

25 February 2004

Moharram is here. The strange thing about the month of Moharram is that even those who don't bother with religion for the rest of the year, during this month suddenly become aware of their religious duties ...

Imam Hossein said: 'I will die to reform my followers.' So why do we only become aware of our failings during this month?

http://hekayat.blogsky.com

---

2 March 2004

An Iranian Symbol Called Hossein
by Hossein Derakhshan

I like the story of Imam Hossein. Because I think the story and its symbols are more Persian than Islamic. It is an account intertwined with ancient Persian culture, which embraces speaking out and making sacrifices for truth and equality, as well as our ancient culture's reverence for women. It is about having the guts to speak bluntly ...

Why do Iranians ignore all the other imams? Why don't we perform festivals filled with passion plays, colour and music to commemorate them? Because they were all conservative; pragmatic but two-faced – all those things that are despised by our culture. Yet the characters surrounding Hossein could have come straight out of the Shah-Nameh [The Epic of Kings, written in pre-Islamic tenth-century Iran by Ferdoosi].

First we have a man with a negligible power base who stands up against unjust rule and instead of collaboration and flattery, refuses to give in ... He has a brother [Abbass], who is handsome and fearless, loyal and kind ... but who is also killed by the armies of deceit ... and then it is the turn of his sister [Zeinab], who is just as potent, courageous and forthright in her fight against the enemy ...

What aspect of this story ties in with Islamic Sharia – or with any other Islamic stories? With the exception of Fatemeh or Zeinab, are there any women in non-Shia Islam that are so openly revered? It is an undeniable and unique fact that these women are players and not bystanders and that their names live on today ...

I believe that the symbolic importance of Imam Hossein to the masses will never disappear from Iranian culture ... He is our icon of struggle against inequality and tyranny ... and this is how we infused our Iranian culture inside this Islamic body, and built this Shia faith of ours.

It was this spirit that led to the rebellion against the monarchy. And it was this spirit that made us stand up against the Arab world [the Iran–Iraq War], which was first backed by Russia, then France and then the United States ... And not an Islamic Sharia ...

No one in Iran is prepared to give up his or her life so that people can pray or have hejab. But they will sacrifice all they have

for freedom and equality ... Perhaps, on balance, Iranians attributed
this phrase to our Shia imam: 'Blasphemous rule will survive, but
not tyranny.'

It was no accident that Imam Hossein had a prominent symbolic
presence in the 1979 revolution.

Email: hoder@hoder.com
http://i.hoder.com

CULTURAL PARADOXES

'Paradoxes seem central to Iran,' writes Richard Plunkett in the Lonely Planet
Guide (2003), 'where grim-faced ayatollahs praise poetry which at face value
describes homosexual infatuation, where alcohol is banned but home-brewing is
a national obsession, where heroin users can be arbitrarily shot while old men
might smoke opium and drift off on a mystical high as they read the Koran. The
people have a Southern European hospitality and a Russian soulfulness and love
of literature, especially for the marvellously ambiguous poetry.'

Perhaps one of the greatest paradoxes is Iran's pre-Islamic history. Its cultural
influences have blended for centuries with non-politicized Islamic practice,
although they are at odds with Khomeini's revolutionary ideological state. As
Stephen Kinzerhas observed, Iranians have been consumed throughout their
history with a 'continuing and often frustrating effort to find a synthesis between
Islam, which was imposed on the country by Arab conquerors, and the rich heritage of pre-Islamic times'. He continues:

> Many countries in the Middle East are artificial creations. European
> colonialists drew their national borders in the nineteenth and twentieth
> century, often with little regard for local history and tradition, and their
> leaders have had to give citizens a sense of nationhood. Just the opposite
> is true in Iran. This is one of the oldest nations, heir to a tradition that
> reaches back thousands of years, to periods when great conquerors
> extended their rule across continents, poets and artists created works of

exquisite beauty and one of the most extraordinary traditions took root and flowered. Even in modern times, which have been marked by long periods of anarchy, repression, and suffering, Iranians are passionately inspired by their heritage.

After 1979 Iran's revolutionary ideas spread throughout the Islamic world. Khomeini hoped to emerge as the leader of a newfound ideological Islam that was modern, political and militant, to counter the traditionalism of Saudi Arabia.

Yet the ruling ayatollahs who want to lead the Muslim world have for a quarter of a century governed the only Islamic country were its main national holiday (when schools are closed for two weeks) is non-Islamic. For the entire Islamic world Eid Al-Fitr, marking the end of Ramadan, is the main national holiday, but not in Iran.

When Iranians talk of Eid they are essentially referring to 21 March, marking the first day of spring and the Iranian New Year, known as Norouz. It is a time of festivities and fireworks and is celebrated by Iranian Muslims, Christians, Jews and Baha'i, etc. In the past, Iranians got married during the New Year celebrations and this continues even today in some rural areas where such traditions are taken very seriously.

---

21 February 2004

It is heart-warming merely observing people busily shopping or spring-cleaning on the eve of Norouz ... We have managed to hold on to our Norouz and Charshanbeh Suri [a fire festival similar to Halloween, held on the last Wednesday night of the year] with our bare claws and teeth ...

By Wild Mint

Norouz is also the spring equinox, a time to celebrate new life, a date that has been celebrated in the region for at least 5,000 years. Even in the eleventh century, the 'golden age' of the Islamic empire in Iran, the Persian poet Omar

Khayyám wrote of Norouz: 'The Norouz breeze caressing a rose is a joy to behold ... A lovely face in the meadow is a joyful sight too ... When yesterday is gone it is no longer enjoyable ... Be merry and forget the past as today is yours to enjoy.'

During the early days of the Revolution, hardliners tried to annul the New Year holidays, but this had failed due to popular outrage. 'For a short while after the Islamic revolution in 1979, the authorities in Tehran attempted to discourage Norouz celebrations and other pre-Islamic customs,' noted the BBC's Tehran correspondent Jim Muir (21 March 2001). 'But they were just too deeply rooted in the Iranian culture and psyche to be eliminated by decree. One of the most important nights in the calendar is Charshanbeh suri – the fire festival – held on the last Wednesday night of the year ... but it is one of many customs going back before Islamic times, which are now being re-embraced with great fervour by the Iranian people.'

On Charshanbeh Suri Iranians throughout the country leap over small bonfires, chanting 'Capture my yellows, grant me your reds!' It means: 'Take my weaknesses and offer me your radiance!'

Iranians continue to mark such ancient days despite the background mutterings of the ideological regime that they are profane. On 14 March 2004, on the eve of the Charshanbeh Suri, Ayatollah Safi-Gholpighani issued a *fatwa* that 'The aim of such heretic occasions is to harm our Islamic identity.'

For many years the revolutionaries have dismissed Iran's pre-Islamic culture as heretical. One of the earliest decrees by the regime was that children given ancient Persian names such as Cyrus, Darius, Ava, Camron or Roxana, would not be issued with birth certificates. People still went ahead and used these names anyway, with the result that many Iranian children have Islamic aliases. After a couple of decades such decrees are no longer obeyed, even by officials. The revolutionaries have found it very difficult to stamp out Iran's pre-Islamic culture and they have tried in vain to diminish its ancient power.

Sometimes this distinguished heritage is so entrenched in Iranian culture that even the state clerics fail to notice it. Iran Air planes, for instance, have 'The Airline of the Islamic Republic of Iran' painted on their sides, but on the tail is the pagan image of Homa, the Persian guardian of travellers.

Photo © Hamed Banaei www.hamedbanaei.com

HOMA, THE PAGAN GUARDIAN OF TRAVELLERS, AT THE 2,500-YEAR-OLD RUINS OF THE ANCIENT CITY OF PERSEPOLIS.

Ayatollah Safi-Gholpighani has condemned the ancient fire festivals, calling those who take part 'barbarians', but in 2004, for the first time in 25 years, the municipal officials of Tehran announced that they would make 40 city squares available for the celebrations.

After 25 years of Islamic rule, Iran's hardline clerics could do little more than reiterate their disapproval, because the people refused to give up their ancient traditions. As the reformist MP, ex-vice-president and middle-ranking cleric

Muhammad-Ali Abtahi points out in his blog traditions such as Charshanbeh Suri are inherent features of Iranian culture.

---

16 March 2004

Two years ago an Arab friend of mine landed in Tehran airport during the evening of Charshanbeh Suri. As he emerged from the airport he was confronted by the relentless noise of explosions. He called me up and was actually surprised that I answered the phone. 'Are you all right?' he asked. 'Are you in hiding? I want to go back straight away! Are there any flights operating out of Tehran?'

I didn't quite understand and said, 'Why? Everything's normal?'

'Then what are all these explosions?' he said. 'The town sounds like a war zone! Has there been a coup d'etat?'

I had to explain to him that this was an ancient Persian tradition … He really couldn't believe it … I said Iranians have a rich history and they are very devoted to their traditions …

When I met him a couple of hours later he seemed reassured. He had seen for himself the really happy, celebrating crowds with their bonfires and fireworks … I told him that no one has ever managed to persuade the Iranians to part with such traditions.

http://www.webneveshteha.com

---

13 March 2004

The (ironic) upshot of 25 years of struggle:

As a stand against tyrannical Mullahs, on Charshanbeh Suri we set off fireworks.

By Hope

---

14 March 2004

Today Commander Ghalibaf [of the Iranian police force] announced that the traditions of the last Wednesday of the year (he couldn't bring himself to actually utter the words 'Charshanbeh Suri') are part of our national customs, and that the security forces have designated safe areas for 'light displays' (not fireworks).

It took those in charge of our civil regime 25 years to realize that they have less power over us than thousands of years of our history. In the first years of the Revolution they called Charshanbeh Suri the heathen tradition of fire worshippers ... but we still privately and with fear jumped over bonfires ... THEY attacked, arrested and took away ...

A few years passed and our people overcame their fears but the pressures never diminished ... again those in charge (who incidentally have no understanding of the people or of society) this time used the excuse of safety precautions and fire hazards and they continued attacking and arresting people ... they didn't think for a second that if all this harassment actually worked it would have done so by now ...

This year to show that they are not so menacing and are actually still a part of this nation, they have distributed safe fireworks among the people ... but they are still afraid to utter the words 'Charshanbeh Suri' ...

I don't know how many years it will take for them to realize that they do not rule over a nation of idiots and that they cannot fool us with such gestures ... and that no one is going to believe that they are part of the people after 25 years.

Email: sanaz5674@yahoo.com
http://khojaste.persianblog.com

18 March 2003

The noise of explosions and smoke have overtaken the whole town ... These are the sounds and smells of the extinction of an ideological religion that is now nothing ... An ideology that for a quarter of a century has controlled our people ...

It doesn't matter what will happen in the future and what price our people are prepared to pay for their freedom; the most important thing is that the majority of Iranians have escaped the influence of ideologies that belong in the Middle Ages. This year Charshanbeh Suri is being celebrated with more commitment than last year ... The flames from the bonfires are higher than ever before ...

From where I sit, I can see most of Tehran and the beautiful fireworks in the sky ... although the sounds of explosions ordinarily would annoy me ... tonight they are exceptionally pleasing.

Email: shabah@shabah.org
http://www.shabah.org

Norouz literally means a 'new day', a tradition that goes back to Zoroastrianism, one of the world's oldest monotheistic faiths (in Shia Iran, Zoroastrianism is recognized as an official faith, although orthodox Sunnism deems it heretical). Preparations for Norouz begin weeks before, while throughout the country people ritually 'spring clean' their homes, followed later by a fire celebration. Norouz ends after the thirteenth day, which also marks the end of the school holidays. Families leave their houses and head outdoors for a picnic, as it is considered unlucky to stay at home on the thirteenth day.

There are many other pre-Islamic customs and celebrations in Iran. Yalda, for instance, during the longest night of the year and the winter solstice, is celebrated in villages and towns throughout Iran. Family and friends get together, read poetry – especially verses from the fourteenth-century poet Hafez – tell jokes and make resolutions for the rest of the year. Traditionally they eat dried and fresh fruits, while it is customary for grandparents to tell their grandchildren ancient tales of the ultimate triumph of good over evil. Iranian Jews are among the earliest inhabitants of Iran and in addition to Yalda they also celebrate the Tree Festival around the same time.

21 December 2004

Congratulations on Yalda night ... let's please be Iranians first and Muslims after ... and don't forget the poetry of Hafez ...

During this night our elders and the wise ... with tales retold in the darkest and longest night ... talk of light and hope ... the stories of pain, struggle and lessons for life ...

The stories of Yalda are the struggles of good against evil ... rekindling the light of hope in our hearts.

Email: niloofar192001@yahoo.com
http://raana1.persianblog.com

22 December 2003

We went to a Yalda gathering last night ... The grandmother there, instead of telling us stories, just sat chewing dried fruit ... But in the end she made up for it by giving us small goody bags to take away ...

By the end of the evening we all had to sing a song and my mum forced me to sing ... I did well to start off with and then messed up as I'd forgotten the words ...

Though I discovered something last night ... Iranian men dance better the older they get ... as the guys my age were no good ... you have to dance Iranian – self-assuredly – not like our host's son who flew across the entire room with each move ...

Email: rere_reera@yahoo.com
http://www.abovethewall.blogspot.com

21 December 2003

Tonight for Yalda we are all guests at my older brother's house until midnight.

• I must remember: When embracing and shaking hands with the other guests ... to do so from the depths of my spirit! Do not forget positive energy ... In view of everyone give Mother two big kisses ...

- To smile all night ... swim on the surface ... don't delve deep into my thoughts ...
- Try and feel things instead of thinking about them.
- Prepare a couple of good jokes so that I am not left out ...
- Be aware of the time, so we start saying our goodbyes around midnight.
- Tell Ali and Leila [his children] about Yalda and the significance of the coming of winter.
- At least for tonight disregard my past and future and live for tonight.
- When we are lying in bed and when my right hand is resting on my ear ... talk to my wife about life and love ... tell her that she was my lost other half and without her life for me is not possible ...

Email: ejavadi2002@yahoo.com

http://nokteha.persianblog.com

THE PARADOX OF EDUCATION FOR THE MASSES

Tahkim Vahdat, Iran's national student union, was formed and heavily financed after a decree by the leader of the Iranian Revolution, Ayatollah Khomeini. It was created to strengthen Khomeini's ideological Islam among the student population. However, it was essentially formed to challenge and drive out the liberal and left-wing student groups from the campuses.

A quarter of a century after the Revolution, Tahkim Vahdat is one of the most outspoken critics of the regime. Active in campuses across Iran, many analysts believe that its official backing (which became front-page news in the reformist press) also helped elect Muhammad Khatami as president in 1997. But with several of its elected leaders behind bars, this nationwide union publicly voted for a withdrawal of support for a parliamentary reform movement in February 2003. It objected that a theocratic democracy was a fallacy and ever since it has been calling for a national referendum to bring real democracy to Iran.

In response to the Islamic Republic's slogan of 'Higher Education for the Masses', universities have been built all over Iran. The Republic's successful education policies have entirely created the well-educated and politicized children of the Revolution – and because they are allowed to vote at the age of 16, they have been the first to express their dissatisfaction with the regime. It is another paradox of life in Iran that the Islamic regime places such value on education for all, while at the same time prohibiting free speech.

Photo © Nafise Motlagh, Iran (2002)
www.nafisegallery.com

A MASKED STUDENT PROTESTOR AT TEHRAN UNIVERSITY. THE HEADBAND READS: 'FREEDOM, EQUALITY'

In 2002 student protests in Tehran soon spread to half a dozen major cities, including Isfahan, Tabriz, Hamadan and Oromiyeh. The students were protesting against a death sentence handed down to Hashem Aghajari, a history professor who openly dared to question the Islamic credentials of the state clerics and their unaccountability to the people.

Many Iran-watchers consider the country's students to be a potent force for change. Many student activists have been arrested and many student magazines, websites and blogs have been closed down, but there are still an estimated 800 student publications in Iran. In 2003 in the Mother Jones's annual round-up of the top ten activist campuses in the world, Iranian campuses gained the top spot 'for unflinching dissent in a nation where speaking out can lead to imprison-ment or worse'.

In October 2001 there was a nationwide crackdown and most of the student union offices were closed by the authorities and many student activists arrested. Undaunted, an official Iranian student publication declared:

> The power of the student movement is not confined to its offices, which
> are now padlocked, but comes from the support it carries from the
> students ... the student movement may appear to some as the carcass of a
> ruined structure. But it is a ruin that will collapse on the heads of all
> those absolute rulers.

Since the major student riots of 1999, disturbances have frequently spilled out of the campuses and on to the streets. Especially in June 2003, which saw ten days of nightly violent clashes between those seeking greater freedoms and the Basij. American officials, including President George W. Bush, voiced their support for the protesters, but this only allowed the regime's hardliners to dismiss the demonstrators as hooligans and the affluent remnants of the monarchy, dancing to the tune of their masters in Washington. To give the lie to such claims, the most persistent nightly protests were reported in the working-class suburbs of Tehran-Pars and Karaj. By the end of the demonstrations, Iranian government officials admitted to having arrested 4,000 people.

It remains to be seen how long a small group of ageing clerics can impose their desire for an Islamic state on a society in which the majority of people are under 30 and have no memory of the Revolution or any appetite for its ideals.

---

22 June 2003

Salaam to all my dear fellow student protestors,

In light of the recent pronouncement by our Grand Supreme Leader that student protesters have taken money from foreign powers to start a revolution, I hereby ask the student or students in charge of funds and in possession of the $500,000,000 received

from the United States that they pay my share into my bank account
(details enclosed) for services rendered:
- Chanting 'The Supreme Leader is a Pimp!': $110
- Chanting 'People are living in poverty but Rafsanjani lives like a
  God!': $267
- Dodging anti-riot police: $77.50
- Saying to a Basij 'Your sister's a whore!': $6
- My fare to and from the demonstrations: $1.10

In the event that my cut is not paid into my account, I hereby state
that I for one am no longer able to give my services to the cause.

Email: soheil_topol@yahoo.com
http://nimpahlavi.persianblog.com

['This weblog has been disabled due to a Terms of Service violation']

---

20 June 2004

Only a few days after the Tehran demonstrations, things have also
started happening in Mashhad ... Every night groups of people
gather in and around Rahnehmaee Street, Tagi'abad Square, and
sections of Ghasem Abad, chanting very bold slogans. They also
write slogans on the walls which are removed the following day ...

Even though it was quite scary, I decided to go along and get a
few photos for my blog ... Unfortunately my ancient camera does
not take good pictures, especially from a distance ...

Though that's not important. Imagine there are a few pictures
here: a large crowd of ordinary people and groups of soldiers with
batons and police cars ... Well that is what the photos would show.

Email: arshinirani@yahoo.com
http://gharibeyeirani.persianblog.com

Protests occur all over the world, but in the Islamic Republic those who take part in anti-government demonstrations can be arrested as *Moharebs* (people making war on God), which carries an automatic death penalty. It's a useful charge to make and has resulted in numerous mass executions since the regime's conception. In July 2003 the former head of the judiciary, Ayatollah Mesbah Yazdi, called on the courts to treat all protesters arrested as *Moharebs*.

Ahmad Batebi, a 'film' student, was convicted of endangering national security purely because of a photo that appeared on the front cover of the Economist magazine. It showed him holding up the bloody shirt of an injured friend during a violent student protest in July 1999. Batebi was initially sentenced to death, but this was later reduced to ten years' imprisonment after international pressure. On a brief leave of absence on medical grounds from Tehran's Evin prison in November 2003, Batebi was reported missing by his family.

Ahmad Batebi wrote an open letter after his imprisonment in 1999:

> 'The soldiers beat my hands and tied them to plumbing pipes. They beat
> my head and stomach with their boots. [They] held me under [a drain full
> of excrement] for so long I was unable to breathe and the excrement was
> inhaled through my nose and seeped into my mouth.'

The photograph of Batebi that so incensed the judiciary is now used by bloggers as a logo demanding the freedom of all political prisoners and is posted on numerous Iranian blogs.

13 November 2003

Ahmad Batebi has disappeared ... for years, when a friend, poet, writer or a thinker ... is late returning home or doesn't turn up for a date, our first thought is that he is in trouble. What black years ... and now that beautiful boy with the blood-stained shirt is missing ...

I am frightened ... there is a heavy silence in the air ... no one says a thing ... where is our Ahmad?

Email: shabah@shabah.org
http://www.shabah.org

13 November 2003

Our mutual honour is missing. Our symbol of resistance is missing. I humbly beg of you in this holy month of Ramadan to pray for Batebi ...

'No animal does to other animals what some humans do to other humans under the guise of humanity.'

By Earth

22 June 2003

I was able to read my blog last night and my heart started shaking ... I had no idea so many of you were following my reports from campus ...

But today I want to write about hope ... I want us to believe that we can all make a difference ...

An old lady turned up yesterday among the demonstrators ... It brings a smile to my face when I remember her ... because she stopped so many students from being beaten to a pulp ... she just kept going up to the Basij and pleading with them, 'My son, for God's sake stop beating those kids!' ... You have no idea how much this meant to us ...

Lets us finally break this chain of hate ... even against those who hit and arrest you ... All the children of Iran ... believe even in our smallest efforts ... I have to tell you that my generation, we don't want to be anyone's heroes or martyrs for freedom. We want to live and the Basij are a part of my generation too ...

http://par.blogsky.com

THE DEFENDERS OF THE FAITH

13 June 2003

A lot of people, a lot of 'beards' [slang for the Basij vigilantes], a lot of bikes ...

Where was I? 17th Street, Amir-Abad, in front of the boys' halls of residence!

It must have been a lot simpler during the last revolution. You could at least stick a flower in a soldier's rifle. How on earth do you attach a flower to an electric baton?

Thirty minutes later ... Kurdistan Street! Visualize a bunch of Neanderthals like a herd of donkeys with chilli up their arses chasing you!

Thirty minutes later, Amir-Abad highway! Thousands having a party! Honking their horns!

2 a.m: Kurdistan Avenue ... Picture 40 or 50 'beards' on bikes. By now the high-ranking special security forces have been brought in. You could tell because their rancid stench filled the air!

Picture this: the Basij beating people to a pulp ... Picture this: the cable in the hand of the Basij beating people ... Picture this: a police officer slapping a Basij in the face and being sworn at ... Picture this: a grandmother looking for her grandson after they got separated ... Picture this: the vans with cages heaving with wild

people ... Picture this: the Basij chanting: 'Our Supreme Leader, we
are ready, we are ready!' ... Picture this: a boy and girl getting to
know each other better ... The stench of tear gas ... The mobiles
being filtered ...

Picture the university gates being torn down by the crowd and
the furious Basij swearing ...

By Lumpy

In a lengthy report for *Forbes Magazine* entitled 'Millionaire Mullahs',[2] the late
Paul Klebnikov (who was allegedly murdered in 2004 by the Russian mafia),
describes the same demonstrations as the last Iranian blogger:

> At dozens of intersections in the capital of Iran thousands of students are
> protesting on a recent Friday around midnight, as they do nearly every
> night, chanting pro-democracy slogans and lighting bonfires on street
> corners. Residents of the surrounding middle-class neighbourhoods
> converge in their cars, honking their horns in raucous support. Suddenly
> there's thunder in the air. A gang of 30 motorcyclists, brandishing iron
> bars and clubs as big as baseball bats, roars through the stalled traffic.
> They glare at the drivers, yell threats, thump cars. Burly and bearded, the
> bikers yank two men from their auto and pummel them. Most protesters
> scatter. Uniformed policemen watch impassively as the thugs beat the last
> stragglers.

Klebnikov describes these gangs of motorcyclists as the 'Hell's Angels' of the
Hezbollah. They are mainly recruited from rural areas and are brought out
whenever the regime needs to threaten the opposition, using 'gangster-like'
methods of intimidation, brutality and assassination. Klebnikov notes that the
regime can no longer rely on the uniformed police or the soldiers (many of
whom share the concerns of the general public), so it has become increasingly
dependent on the Basij and Hezbollah militants. These state vigilantes are
celebrated by the ruling clerics as 'the defenders of the faith' and they pledge
allegiance to the Supreme Leader Ayatollah Ali Khamenei. Whenever there is

a pro-democracy gathering, these shadowy figures arrive at the scene.

---

24 June 2003

Dear Basij,

In answer to your question, the government we Iranians want:

No government official has a job for life.

The people elect the head of our government every four years.

What Parliament votes for is law and cannot be vetoed.

The head of the judiciary is elected.

No power is holy or sacred.

No religious groups or races are discriminated against, even atheists.

No one can investigate your private life.

The Government's ultimate duty should be the welfare of Iranians.

No ideological missions such as conquering Jerusalem or Karbala or leading the Muslims of the world or fighting imperialism.

Those managing our affairs should be experts who know their fields and not the worthless sycophants whose only expertise is their warped theological knowledge.

Without a doubt the worst way to solve the problems of any society is to have a revolution. Just as the nastiest way of solving any international dispute is war. But when a society closes all its doors to change the worst will happen.

Who likes an explosion? Who likes war? But when there are those such as Saddam [Hussein] who have buried alive more than those lost in a war, I for one will opt for fighting against the dictators.

Email: <hayatepayiz@hotmail.com
http://atefe.persianblog.com

['This weblog has been disabled due to a Terms of Service violation']

KHOMEINI'S PROMISED LAND

In July 2000 an official government report by Muhammad Ali Zam, the head of Tehran's cultural and artistic affairs, stated that 20 per cent of the population controlled 80 per cent of the nation's wealth. The daily *Hamshahri* quoted Zam as saying that at least 12 million Iranians were living below the poverty line. It's a damning statistic for a revolution that promised to distribute wealth equally throughout the land. After all, Ayatollah Khomeini was heralded as the 'leader of the world's underprivileged'. In his first address to the Iranian nation in 1979 at the Behesht-e Zahra cemetery, Khomeini said:

> Muhammad Reza Pahlavi, that immoral traitor, fled stealing everything.
> He ruined our nation and filled our cemeteries. He ruined our country's
> economy. Even the projects he carried out in the name of advancement
> pushed the country towards decadence. He suppressed our culture,
> destroyed people and ruined all our manpower resources.

Khomeini then went on to promise free electricity and water supplies and even free transportation and bus services for all Iranians. They would be paid for using oil revenues under a just Islamic system.

This famous speech, in which Khomeini almost promises the Iranian people an Islamic paradise on earth, can be easily downloaded from the Internet. Yet even though every word the late ayatollah uttered in his lifetime has been reproduced in countless books and tapes, this speech at Behesht-e Zahra has mysteriously disappeared from the public archives in Iran.

---

22 November 2004

Khomeini Speaks On Social Justice

Yet again feeling totally mortified, I had to go to my religious studies class today! Anyway, the lecturer said 'I want to give you a test!' Well, what the hell ...

The question: 'Describe four quotes by Imam Khomeini on social justice!'

I read the question up and down ... down and up ... from left to right.

No kidding, that was the set essay question. I was thinking 'God! What sort of a question is this?!' Perhaps it's like one of those totally open global mathematical problems that no one has solved yet ...

kooche@Gmail.com
http://weblog.kooche.net

Ayatollah Khomeini swept to power with the promise of independence, freedom and an Islamic classless society. Today, according to the regime's own figures, 15 per cent of the population lives below the poverty line and the unemployment rate among young people under 30 is about 28.4 per cent.

Writing in Le Figaro in February 2001, the historian Houshang Nahavandi noted that Iran's 'per capita income in 1977 was $2,450, and by all accounts this would be comparable in the year 2000 to $10,000, close to that of Spain. It is, at present, less than $1,500, near to that of ... the Gaza Strip.'

In his study of the 'power mafia' of the clerics, Paul Klebnikov describes the Iranian economy as somewhat akin to the crony capitalism that grew from the ruins of the Soviet Union – but under the direct control of a few state clerics who have amassed enormous wealth since the Revolution. This clerical elite

> has mismanaged the nation into senseless poverty. With 9 per cent of the
> world's oil and 15 per cent of its natural gas, Iran should be a very rich
> country. It has a young, educated population and a long tradition of
> craftsmanship and international commerce. But per capita income today
> is actually 7 per cent below what it was before the Revolution. Iranian
> economists estimate capital flight (to Dubai and other safe havens) at up
> to $3 billion a year.

The Iranian rial now trades at less than 1 per cent of the value it had against the dollar at the time of the Shah's fall. In 2003 the ratings agency Fitch described investing in Iran as 'highly speculative' and burdened with risk. It warned that Iran's fortunes remain closely tied to oil, despite efforts to diversify the economy.

Not everyone in Iran complains of hardship. In some parts of the country shiny, expensive cars roll through streets lined with expensive jewellery shops. Tehran's stock market has risen an average of 50 per cent a year over the past five years, lining the pockets of a tiny minority in a country where many live in dire poverty. A substantial proportion of this stock-market volume is owned by organizations or individuals linked to the unelected ruling clerics.

Critics complain that commerce remains in the hands of the state clergy and their allies who seized businesses at the beginning of the Revolution. Chronic state corruption is undeniable. Even the hardline cleric Ayatollah Ahmad Jannati, who chairs the powerful Guardian Council, has described the financial corruption in Iran as 'unprecedented in the whole world'.

The Iranian people witness corruption, mismanagement and cronyism on a daily basis. In June 2004 Massoud Shariati, governor of the city of Bafq in the Yazd province, announced that the city's zinc mill – the largest in the Middle East – had gone bust after only four years. The closure left more than 4,000 workers without jobs in the small city. Such blatant mismanagement is familiar to ordinary Iranians, who constantly have to deal with the consequences.

While most of the country's industrial sector is owned by the State, major businesses are run by what Iranians call Agah-zadehs. An Agah-zadeh is a son of a clergyman and the word derives from Shah-Zadeh, meaning 'prince'. There is such public resentment against the alleged corruption of the sons of the clergy that the issue has been raised in Parliament and even the conservative press have had to acknowledge their existence.

Typical Agah-zadehs are Mehdi and Yasser Rafsanjani, sons of the ex-president. A journalist (who was later imprisoned) once asked ex-president Rafsanjani: 'How has your son become one of the richest men in Iran?'

Rafsanjani's impassive response was: 'Why don't you go and ask him?'

In September 2003 the Norwegian oil firm Statoil was under police investigation for alleged corruption and bribery in a major deal with Iran. There had allegedly been consultation with Mehdi Rafsanjani. In Norway this was front-page news and in October 2004 Statoil agreed to pay a 20 million-kroner ($3m/£1.7m) penalty imposed for alleged bribery in Iran. In Iran, however, an Agah-zadeh is beyond reproach.

Iran's former president Rafsanjani is the most famous son of the farming town of Rafsanjan and he began life as a pistachio farmer. Today he is one of the most powerful and richest men in Iran.

---

13 December 2003

Last night a few friends were round our house. One of them told a joke that I have to share with you.

When Rafsanjani is asked about his financial standing before and after the Revolution, he replies that 'Before the Revolution I had a piece of land in the centre of the town of Rafsanjan ... Now the town of Rafsanjan is right in the middle of the land I own.'

Email: mahshid_r@hotmail.com
http://zanane.blogspot.com

THE IMPERIALIST PLAGUE: DRUGS, CRIME AND PROSTITUTION

Iran's regime has always denounced crime, drug addiction and prostitution as an 'imperialist plague' imposed by the 'decadent West' on Iran – and very soon they will be banished from the land.

Despite a 100 per cent rise in the average annual oil income since the Revolution, most indicators of economic welfare show a steady deterioration. For 25 years living standards have continued to plunge, leaving ordinary Iranians preoccupied with the economic and social problems of their everyday lives: high unemployment, the boredom and impatience of the young and a disturbing rise in drugs, crime and prostitution.

According to official figures, Iran has two million drug users, with around 200,000 of them injecting themselves intravenously. But experts believe the official statistics are wrong. A government report in June 2002 expressed 'particular concern about a sharp rise in the number of drug addicts among women and young people, and the increased use of heroin and other hard drugs'. Most heroin sold in Europe comes from Afghanistan's poppies. Iran is on the shortest route from the producers in Afghanistan to European consumers, but much of the cargo is sold en route in Iran for negligible sums.

---

4 August 2003

He lay in an alleyway near Taj'rish town hall. People are walking past throwing money.* A couple of policemen are standing by, waiting for the 'death wagon'. I ask what has happened ... And they tell me 'He was an addict' ...

He was alive this morning and now it's only noon ... the shopkeepers and street peddlers carry on with their business ... colourful women and girls pass by, inspecting the cheap make-up that they sell on the streets ... Cheap ... Just slightly dearer than foreign chewing gum ... while the famous beggars and fortune-tellers of Taj'rish carry on with their honest trade ...

I ask another man: 'Had you seen this guy before? Did he always hang around here?' 'He was an addict,' he says and doesn't say any more. Puzzled, he looks at this inquisitive woman and screws up his face: 'A heroin addict.'

I don't want to wake him up and ask where did your journey start ... I don't want to ... it's of no use ... curiosity, pity, the Kaffareh* from the colourful people and the passing of the walking dead around him and ... of no use ... but when the 'death wagon' comes, some mother's little darling, the golden boy that she gave birth to with love and hope ... And now like garbage covered in a sack and all that anyone can say about him is 'He was an addict', 'junky', 'user' ... the 'death wagon' will carry him away, bringing an end to this image ... a mere insignificant image ...

* Kaffareh refers to a practice of penance. It is quite common to see money scattered on the site of fatal road accidents in Iran, and people walking or driving past will leave money. The general belief is that this will banish evil. According to

ancient custom, the money is intended for the burial expenses of the deceased, who may be destitute. It is also common practice to give money (Sadageh) to a charity after being involved in (or even near) a life-threatening incident.

Email: sepaasi@hotmail.com
http://digaran.persianblog.com

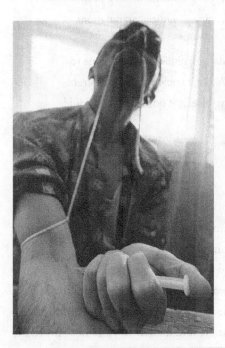

Photo © Khalil Emami, Iran (2002)

25 October 2003

I can't remember exactly when our gatherings filled with music, backgammon and laughter became filled with that unfamiliar smoke ... that woozy, overwhelming brown entity, and when you smoked it ... Its sweet bitter heavy vapours got under your skin ...

I can't remember when the ironed suits, polished shoes and the short colourful skirts were replaced with pyjamas and baggy dresses that were good for lying down ... Heavy ... looking for somewhere to rest your head.

By Wild Mint

12 May 2003

Unemployment ... fear of the future ... the feeling that you are being watched ... the blacklist ... being threatened with death ... poverty ... insecurity ... arrests ... restrictions ... filtering of the Internet ... no freedom ... theft ... rape ... judicial amputations ... prostitution ...

We are getting used to these daily realities and have come to coexist with our nightmares ... We don't know anything different and cannot even imagine anything else. Is it possible that it could ever change?

By The Angry Bull

An estimated 70 per cent of Iran's prison population has been involved in drugs. Recounting his time in prison in the now banned *Payam Emrooz* magazine, the dissident Islamic cleric Mohsen Kadivar noted that 'although the guards were very sensitive to books and newspapers, access to opium and other drugs was very easy and at nights one would often find people smoking opium'. The suspicion is that drugs are made freely available in order to nurture a dependency that renders the addict passive and malleable – and not only in the country's prisons.

Iran has an acute drugs problem, so in April 2004 a nationwide campaign was launched by the Police Directorate of Public Education. However, its major focus was on 'Internet addiction'. Evidently the authorities are more concerned about an epidemic of young people going on-line than it is about them shooting up. The campaign literature pointed out that 'indecent pictures, and becoming familiar with them, causes nothing but depression, religious failing and other forms of psychological and social harm'. It called upon families to be vigilant and to be on the lookout for signs of 'Internet addiction'. It also warned of the 'psychological and religious tensions in families that have irresponsibly used computers and the Internet'.

30 March 2003

This is a symptom of a sick society, where drugs are more accessible
then chewing gum …

    They have taken away from our youth the ability to think, create
or criticize and dispense narcotics to stop them from rising up.

Email: at_857@hotmail.com

http://atash3.blogspot.com

Almost a quarter of Iran's working-age population is unemployed. And as we
have seen, the country's mounting economic woes have also led to a vast increase
in prostitution, which is punishable by fines, flogging, prison and 'stoning' (if the
prostitute is married). Before the 1979 Revolution, 'Shahreno' was Tehran's infamous brothel district. The area was demolished during the first days of the new
regime and some of the women were publicly executed on site.

    Today there are no official figures, but to show that they are cracking down on
prostitution, in a rare public announcement in June 2002, the Basij Islamic
Militia stated that raids on brothels in a six-month period had resulted in 48,900
arrests. The next blogger, a social worker, describes her encounter with an
Iranian prostitute.

21 December 2002

Parisa had been arrested and flogged after a brothel raid. In her
black chador she looked markedly older than her 24 years. Ironically,
I found that her costume of choice was the all-enveloping
conventional black chador, concealing an outfit that would not look
out of place in any red-light district in the world, yet it was practical,
as a prospective client could get a flash of what was on offer.

    'You were married before?' I asked.

    'You could call it that,' she said. 'When I was 14 my father gave
me away to Dariush. Every time we had an argument, Dariush

would tell me to shut it as he had paid 50,000 tomans for me. My father denied taking money for me, but he's a lying dog ... I know 50,000 isn't a lot these days, but ten years ago it was the equivalent of 500,000 [approx. $500], so it's not as if I was worthless.'

'What was Dariush like?'

'He was a pimp. He would bring a friend round, then pop out for cigarettes and return three hours later, by which time his friend would have left. He didn't like to turn up and see them straight after ...'

'When did you get divorced?'

'Our marriage was never registered anyway. One day Dariush just disappeared back to Afghanistan. After he left, his friends kept coming round so much that the landlord threw me out ... It's all good now,' she added with a confident smile. 'Before, the type of men who wanted me were worse off than I was – at best they could share their loaf of "bread and herbs" with me, and at worst they became a burden ... To have a decent man I must be perfumed and powdered, the sort of woman who wears high-heeled boots.' She said this neatly and wisely, as if uttering a proverb.

'I'm doing fine now. I'm seeing a man who wants to take me on as his second wife ... Is there anything wrong with that?' she demanded.

'Congratulations,' I said.

By The Social Worker

---

7 December 2003

Recently a friend was telling me of a prostitute that he had shared a bed with ... He said that she was one of the few people he had come across that appeared to really enjoy her work. I couldn't quite understand his words ... couldn't believe it ... It was all too vague ... I had always imagined that prostitution was a degrading and pitiful experience in exchange for a handful of money ... I remembered

Photo © Payam Borazjani, www.kargah.com

A YOUNG HOMELESS GIRL IN 'SEYD ISMAEL', SOUTH TEHRAN, 2002

my friend's words tonight and thought I'll go to Vali-Asr Street and take a closer look at this community.

But it was raining very hard and there was no sign of the street prostitutes ... A prostitute can stop work on a rainy day, but not an office worker ... It's a truism that to be an office worker is more shameful than prostitution ...

A prostitute sells her body and may even enjoy her work ... But an office worker throws away his time and even worse his soul and mind without any enjoyment.

By The Hungry Philosopher

Today it is an inescapable reality to most Iranians that the regime has miserably failed in its mission to bring women 'Islamic dignity' through its revolutionary ideals.

In December 2002, 22-year-old Mojahed Khazirabi, the star of Iran's national football team, was made a public example of, banned from playing for five years and sentenced to 99 lashes for visiting a brothel.

Yet exactly a year later, in December 2003, the Iranian authorities deported the BBC journalist Sue Lloyd-Roberts because she took photographs of prostitutes. 'We are deporting you tomorrow morning because you have taken pictures of prostitutes,' they told her. 'This is not a true reflection of life in our Islamic Republic. We don't have prostitutes.'

The growing problem of prostitution in Iran has been a subject of mounting concern. So much so that in 2002 an Islamic solution was put forward. Detailed plans were drawn up by the Interior Ministry's Deputy for Social Affairs for the establishment of what, oddly enough, were referred to as 'chastity houses'. Under Iran's Islamic Shia system, it is possible to take out a temporary marriage licence, known as a Sigheh, for even a few hours. A Sigheh is used to cover liaisons between men and women who want to have sex but who, for one reason or another, are not ready for full marriage.

Defenders of a Sigheh or temporary marriage argue that it prevents children born out of wedlock being classified as illegitimate. The main aim of the scheme behind 'chastity houses' was to use Sigheh to arrange and regulate encounters that in many other societies would be regarded as prostitution.

---

28 July 2003

It's not important to me whether the 'chastity houses' are going to be set up in this country or not! They have unofficially been up and running for many years and in reality have always existed ... Yet if they are taken over by the regime, it is unlikely that someone who frequents such places would ever go to one run by the Government ...

In this country nothing is done right ... Because anything that has been taken out of the hands of ordinary peoples and done by the regime has been ruined ...

We should have foreseen what is happening to us today, when

we Iranians started praying on the street instead of our own homes
and took to drinking in isolation at home.

Email: fiftypercentnormal@yahoo.com

http://www.goldoon.com

After the creation of 'chastity houses', prostitutes were to be registered at designated centres under the supervision of health clinics. Couples would then be
directed to special centres where they could consummate their arrangement
without police harassment, but the plan was soon rejected after massive public
opposition.

25 February 2004

[A young Iranian blogger who writes in English]
About a year ago, a few weeks after my arrival in Tehran, I got on a
taxi heading to Takht-e Tavous Street. When I got in the taxi there
was no one in it except the driver and me! After being there for a
few minutes, a young girl who seemed to be in her early twenties
got in. After just two minutes, she started to talk. It went like this.

   Girl: Can you give me 45,000 tomans [approx. $45]?! I desperately
need that sum.

   Driver: I don't have that sort of money, Ma'am.

   Me: No, Ma'am. I don't carry such an amount of money! (This is
the truth because I was thinking I could get things with my bank
and credit card!)

   Girl: I would offer myself or anything you wish to have!!

   Driver: No, Ma'am I am not the type you think!

   Me: (My mouth was open big time and I was looking at her with a
surprised expression on my face – I could not say a word!!) ——!

   Girl: Believe me, I am not who you think I am! I am doing this
because I go to school (grabbing her bag and taking out her university
card) and I live with four roommates. Our rent is due and I owe

them 45,000 tomans. So, that is why I am offering myself.

We all remained silent for a few minutes then the driver said,

'Ma'am, I can't do anything for you. Would you like to stay in the taxi?'

Girl: No, thanks I'll get off here.

I was so frustrated and sad that for the next two days I could not think properly!!

Email: shabahang@netscape.net
http://alireza04.blogspot.com

In recent years even the hardline extremist press has been shattering taboos by routinely admitting to the existence of prostitution and drug addicts. Yet they do so only to protest against falling moral standards, which they blame on the land-slide victories of reformists in the past and the election of Khatami as presidnet in May 1997. In March 2004, Iran's Mehr news agency reported on research carried out by a group of social scientists headed by Fatemah Ghasemzadeh. Out of some 585 street and working children between 16 and 18 years of age, they found that 50 per cent of them had been 'sexually harassed'.

---

22 August 2003

Some facts:

The rate of runaway girls has grown 20 times between the periods of 1986 to 1999, with the average age of girls now at 14.7. (Source: Dr Anvar Sammadi-Rad, Iran Newspaper, Monday 4 June 2001)

68,156 runaways were rounded up in a four-month period during 2001. (Source: Dr Anvar Sammadi-Rad, National conference of social problems, Iran Newspaper, Monday 4 June 2001)

The average age of prostitutes has dropped from 27 to 20 years. (Source: Muhammad Ali Zam, Bahar newspaper, 2 July 2000)

Email: mohammad_ariai@hotmail.com
http://www.deltang25.persianblog.com

---

5 VIRTUALLY UNVEILED WOMEN

'HEY YOU, LISTEN TO MY EYES', SELF-PORTRAIT BY SANAZ

THE FIGHT FOR POLITICAL RIGHTS

Throughout the twentieth century, Iranian women have organized and fought for political rights, from the pro-democratic Constitutional Revolution of 1906 to the egalitarian movement that overthrew the Shah of Iran.

The 1979 Iranian Revolution was far from being just a religious uprising. It was preceded by general strikes raising a broad range of economics and egalitarian demands – including equal rights for women. For instance, striking oil workers in October 1978 included in their demands 'an end to discrimination against female employees'.

In the early twentieth century, Iran made important advances towards the emancipation of women and the creation of a modern culture and modern institutions.

Morgan Shuster lived in Iran at the turn of the century and wrote about his experiences.[1] 'The Persian women since 1907 had become almost at a bound the most progressive, not to say radical, in the world; that this statement upsets the ideas of centuries makes no difference. It is a fact ... In Tehran alone, twelve women's associations were involved in different social and political activities. [Iranian women] overnight become teachers, newspaper writers, founders of women's clubs and speakers on political subjects.'

These women's associations were by no means only in Tehran and there were many prominent groups in towns such as Tabriz, Isfahan and Qazvin. As the historian Janet Afary reminds us,[2] after the Constitutional Revolution (1906), women's associations thrived and the Society for the Freedom of Women and the Underground Union of Women were two of the early groups formed the following year. According to Afary, Iranian women 'took back the segregated streets, claimed a new space for women in the newspapers, created safe educational and political organizations where women's ideas, resources, and creative energies were galvanized and channelled into new projects.' However, she also points out that these women's demands were soon undermined by the dominant regional powers.

Since 1918 there have been demonstrations by women outside the Iranian parliament, demanding equal rights. In January 1953 the democratically elected government of Prime Minister Mossadegh (soon to be overthrown in a joint CIA–British coup) submitted a bill to Parliament granting women the vote – yet a handful of ayatollahs (including Ayatollah Kashani) opposed it. Khomeini – a middle-ranking cleric at the time – gave sermons calling on people to go out and protest against Mossadegh's government and the bill.

Voting rights were eventually granted by the Shah in 1962. Be that as it may,

Photo courtesy of Mr Hashem Hakimi

A TEHRAN WOMEN'S ASSOCIATION, 1933

FIRST ROW (*STANDING, FROM LEFT TO RIGHT*): DR AKHTAR KIYA (KAMBAKASH), MEHR'BANOU DINBALI, ASHRAFF NABAVI, (INSPECTOR, MINISTRY OF EDUCATION), MS ALAVI, MS BAMDAD (HEAD OF A GIRLS TEACHERS' TRAINING COLLEGE) AND NOSRAT TASLIMI MOGHADAM (HAKIMI). SECOND ROW (*SITTING, FROM LEFT TO RIGHT*): FAKHR-AL-ASHRAF, FAKHR AADEL, MS HEKMAT (PASARGADI), (HEADMISTRESS, SHAHNAZ PAHLAVI GIRLS SECONDARY SCHOOL, TEHRAN), HAJAR TARBIYAT (THE FOUNDER OF A NUMBER OF GIRLS SECONDARY SCHOOLS IN TEHRAN), MS ARYANI (HEADMISTRESS OF A GIRLS ELEMENTARY SCHOOL, TEHRAN), MS GHAFARI, AND BATOUL HOMAYOUN. THIRD ROW (*SEATED, FROM LEFT TO RIGHT*): DR SHAMS-AL-MOLOUK MOSSAHEBB, MEHR ANVAR, MS RIYAZI, (HEADMISTRESS, SHAHDOKHT GIRLS SECONDARY SCHOOL, TEHRAN), AND MIR'AFKHAM AFKHAMI.

before the Revolution Iranian women fought for and gained legal rights that are rare in much of the Islamic world even today.

As Azar Nafisi, a professor at Johns Hopkins University, has pointed out, the 'totalitarian Islamic Republic has hidden this history of progressiveness, leading people to erroneously lump Iran together with Saudi Arabia. In Saudi Arabia, people have not yet started to fight for these rights. In Iran, people are fighting to gain back rights they once had.'

14 April 2002

Just as the West has Romeo and Juliet and the Arabs Lailee and
Maj'noon, for Iranians it's the tale of Shirin and Farhad* ... Lailee,
the Arab girl, is a weak, shattered, distraught being and even though
she loves Maj'noon, she cannot bring herself to speak of her love
because of her ethnic background. For solace she cries behind her
veil and is even tormented by her father and brother for expressing
sorrow ...

Oh, but our own Shirin, once she feels that Farhad is her man,
she mounts her horse and leaves for 'Tisfoon' to be with him.
Significantly, there is no father or a brother to torment her or stand
in her way and when those close to her see her passion for him
they encourage her to go after her Farhad ... and the rest ...

Yet in a deliciously cruel historic irony, centuries later,
unlike Shirin, we are denied the expression of the love in our
hearts ...

Email: fiftypercentnormal@yahoo.com

http://www.goldoon.com

* The ancient tale of Shirin and Farhad was written by the Persian Azari poet
Nizami Ganjevi (1141–1209).

4 May 2002

My grandmother had been politically active all of her life ... I
remember whenever there was a political hanging, totally
disheartened she would shut herself in her room ... in her late
eighties she was diagnosed with Alzheimer's ... When I went to see
her last, she was frantically getting ready to leave the house and
kept repeating that she had to go straight away to attend a
meeting ...

'I'm the main speaker. Look after the kids, till I come back!' she
said.

Desperately trying to stop her, I told her she shouldn't: 'You'll get
arrested ... why don't you think about your children?' ... Suddenly
she got really cross with me and said: 'I'm going, whether you look
after the kids or not!' and called out 'Sakineh!' (her maid who had
died 40 years ago) Get my fur coat, it's snowing ...'

Email: shabah@shabah.org
http://www.shabah.org

BATTLING PREJUDICE

Blogs have allowed some Iranian women to express themselves freely for the
first time in modern history and this small freedom may have a big knock-on
effect. It might be objected that the majority of female bloggers do not reflect a
true cross-section of Iranian society, as not everyone has access to computers
and the Internet. However, thanks to the Islamic Republic's policy of free education and its national literacy campaigns, those who enter further education
tend to be from a relatively wide cross-section of society. Iranian students come
from a broad variety of social and regional backgrounds and have access to the
Internet.

In the past, women activists were similarly dismissed by some academics as a
select group of urban middle-class ladies who could not be regarded as speaking
for all women in Iran. They were also demonized as agents of imperialism by the
likes of Ayatollah Khomeini.

Yet early women activists like Mrs Jahangeer, who stood in the way of the car-
riage of the Shah to demand gender equality and the adoption of the
Constitution in 1906 were anything but foreign stooges. They were fighting for
democracy and independence from the control of the imperialist powers of
Russia and Britain, which stood between them and liberation. Mrs Jahangeer
and countless others in 1906 were just as much a symbol of hope for Iranian
women as the suffragette Emily Davison was for British women. Davison
famously ran out in front of the King's horse during the Derby in June 1913 and

was killed. However, unlike the British suffragettes, Iranian women activists were not just struggling against internal prejudices but also against dominant regional powers such as Imperial Russia.

In 1979 Ayatollah Khomeini repealed the existing Family Rights Act (FPA) that had fixed the minimum age of marriage at 18 and had banned polygamy and made divorce and child custody subject to the courts. All of these rights were cast out by a single decree. Furthermore, women were now worth half the value of men in the courts. They needed permission from their fathers or husbands to travel. They lost custody rights to their children. And they could be punished to death by stoning if found guilty of adultery. Ayatollah Khomeini justified this by claiming that the Family Rights Act was unjust and a product of Imperialist rule and exploitation.

Veil or Be Damned

On 7 March 1979 Khomeini decreed that women were required to wear the veil. Ironically, the ruling came a day before the scheduled celebrations throughout Iran to mark International Women's Day. The gatherings soon turned into mass protests against Khomeini's decree and his annulment of the Family Rights Act. This was also the first reported outing of a group calling

Women demonstrating against newly introduced laws of compulsory Hejab

themselves Hezbollah or the 'Party of God', who fiercely attacked many of the demonstrators.

---

18 January 2004

Some of you may remember the beginning of the Revolution, but for those who aren't old enough: until 1979 women did not have to wear the veil ... but soon there were cries of 'Veil or be beaten!' ... And in next to no time an evil institution for the enforcement of rules called the Revolutionary Komiteh raised its head. So in 1979 women put on headscarves, but they were still free to go out with a shirt and skirt or a dress ...

Do you remember the first manteaus? Big shapeless, floor-length coats that women wore on top of their ordinary clothes ... As times passed different versions of the manteau came out ... I remember during those early years suddenly manteaus made in a 'jean' fabric became fashionable, but before long the 'brothers' from the Komiteh would roam the streets and bazaars with carpet cutters, slashing through these manteaus (at the same time tearing through the flesh of the poor unfortunate characters that had taken up this trend). Well, the jean fabric was a representation of the 'great Satan', America ...

Soon fitted manteaus became fashionable. Fitted around the waist, with the shape of the women's breasts visible ... these naturally put into question and demeaned the value of women ... anyway in next to no time they went out of fashion. And then it was the turn of the Maxi manteaus with slits! But oh! these slits were just too much for the 'brothers' of the Komiteh, who were aroused at the spectacle ... So people gave in by sewing buttons on the slits ... Then capes were the latest thing ... except now voices were raised that they were too short and a vision of depravity ... but once women had got them this short they soon evolved into the tight and short manteaus ...

The point is, that as long as you wear a manteau you will not be 'endangering Islam'. Like this woman in the photo, paragliding in Tehran, she is still wearing her manteau with her special gear.

By Shima

Photo © Marc Latzel

SHAHRAN MOUNTAINS, TEHRAN, IRAN (2001)

UNDER THE VEIL

According to historical accounts the veil predates Islam by many centuries. Assyrian kings first introduced it in the Near East, along with the seclusion of women in the royal harem.

It was only in the second Islamic century that the veil became common. It was first used among the powerful and rich as a status symbol – then only 'common' women would be seen in the streets unveiled. Later the Koranic instruction to 'tell the believing women to lower their gaze and protect their private parts and not to show off their adornment except only that which is apparent and to draw their veils all over their bosoms' was taken by some as a ruling to veil one's hair, neck and ears. For a woman to assume a shielding veil and stay within the house was a sign of status: it showed that her family had the means to enable her to do so.

Throughout Islamic history only certain sections of the urban classes were veiled and secluded. Rural and nomadic women – the majority of the population – were not. Even after the 1979 ruling banning women from appearing unveiled, Iran's ancient indigenous tribal women rarely adhered to the revolutionary rules for women and could at times even be observed riding their horses into town,

A TRIBAL WOMAN IN NORTHERN IRAN AND (*RIGHT*) FROM THE GHASGAI TRIBE

A TRIBAL WOMAN IN IRAN (2003)

when urban women could be flogged or imprisoned for riding bicycles.

Many of Iran's tribal women refuse to comply with the Islamic Republic's dress codes – much more so than urban women, who are strictly policed. Take the woman from Iran's ancient Ghasgai tribe in the above photograph: her hair is showing through the decorated gauze fabric that Ghasgai women often wear.

The Basij responsible for keeping the morality laws in place would never dare approach such women, for fear of offending the strict 'Islamic honour codes' of the indigenous tribes and starting widespread tribal rebellions against the regime.

---

8 March 2004

Why is it that women in villages are so much freer in comparison with our urban women (at least when it comes to choosing what to wear)? It's incredible but they are not only freer in how they dress, but also in their activities and movements. Why is it that they don't 'endanger Islam' by not wearing headscarves, as they freely mingle, laughing and chatting with the menfolk? Is it due to their heavy participation in work? Or is it that work will be stopped without women? God Forbid!

Email: bamdadz@yahoo.com
http://bamdad.blogspot.com

---

16 January 2003

Has anyone ever explained why it is that in our Persian language we do not have masculine or feminine verbs or even 'he' or 'she', as they do in English? We say 'Oou', meaning either 'her' or 'him' ... Even though Persian is sophisticated and complex, we do not differentiate men and women in our speech ...

I am taking an English course right now and our professor has said that there are many Farsi words that basically do not have English equivalents ... Especially words related to feelings and emotions (yup! evidence that we are all a bunch of lovesick fools) ...

Why is it then that our ancestors did not feel the necessity to distinguish between the sexes when it came to our language? So where did we inherit this chauvinistic present-day culture from?

By Borderline

With the rise of a uniquely ideological Islam in Iran, western-style clothes were seen as a product of the corrupt influences of the imperialists. Yet this ideology also encouraged people to reject all indigenous Persian traditions, albeit with little success. To the revolutionaries – including many women who identified themselves as 'Muslim feminists' – wearing the veil came to symbolize not the failings of their culture in comparison to western traditions, but its uniqueness and superiority. The veil was a sign of resistance to western values.

The 'Islamic feminists' believed that by veiling they would cease to be sex objects and would be treated on equal terms based on their capabilities and inner strengths. Women such as the chador-clad Ms Fatemeh Haghighatjou, an outspoken ex-parliamentarian who, when told by a journalist that she was referred to as a 'real man', responded irritably: 'I am a feminist and do not view that statement as a compliment.'

Prior to the Revolution, the majority of women covered their heads in public in some way, albeit not to the extent of a strict 'revolutionary hejab'. For many women from orthodox families, wearing the veil helped them define new roles for themselves: it permitted freer movement outside the confines of the home, as well as a route to education and emancipation.

In Iran's revolution, women were viewed as central to the project of changing the public morality. This was reinforced by the belief that the honour of the family is dependent on the actions of its women and of them remaining chaste. The men of the family risk being seen as unmanly if their womenfolk are violated in any way.

---

12 March 2002

Our inheritance from our ancestors is this thing we call 'honour': a reverence for the chastity of women ... Yet this is the thing that separates us from the First World nations ... but we still kill ourselves preserving it ...

In the West, if someone tells someone else that his sister is a whore ... he wouldn't understand the insult ... he would think that her 'thing' belongs to herself ... what is it to you or I? He may even take it as a compliment ... and say to himself: 'I have a resourceful sister' ...

Men ... Gentlemen, leave women's honour to them ... Instead of guarding our 'c***s' ... get on with your work, as this is holding our society back ... Don't deprive yourself from a productive and innovative work life ...

http://neda.blogspot.com

23 April 2003

Men are my guards and they guard their own property and honour ... who am I? I am my brother's, father's, husband's, uncle's honour and even the honour of the honourable boy next door ...

Who should I see, if I don't want all these guard dogs? ...

They don't even honour me dead ... In the obituary columns, instead of my picture they place a picture of a rose ... as an image of a woman can ensnare a man ...

And can bring dishonour to a woman's brother, father, husband, uncle ...

art_rahayabi@yahoo.com
http://rahayabi.persianblog.com

For 'Muslim feminists' donning the 'revolutionary hejab' was the equivalent of the Western feminists of the 1960s and 1970s burning their bras. This 'revolutionary hejab', anti-Western trend has also started to spread recently among young Muslim women in many other parts of the world. Even in Western countries such as France where an estimated four million Muslims live mainly in public housing ghettoes around urban centres. Now some second- and third-generation French Muslim women have found a solution to their exclusion: political Islam. Young women who take up the 'revolutionary hejab' are rejecting the approach of their parents' generation, which tried to assimilate, while at the same time rebelling against a Western society that they feel has rebuffed their parents' efforts.

But Iranian women did the 'revolutionary hejab' thing a quarter of century ago – and what young woman wants to dress like her mother? Judging by most public images of young women in Iran, many of them no longer have any faith in the 'revolutionary hejab' ideals of the 'Muslim feminists'.

Women in Iran have been forced to embody the value systems of society through their dress and social behaviour. Yet today many young Iranian women reject such an imposition and, in turn, have consistently flouted the rules through their dress and behaviour. This tendency is marked in the blogs of young Iranian women and some routinely mock the whole idea of a 'revolutionary hejab'.

---

10 December 2002

From My Personal Street Research

If you wear a short jacket, lots of make-up and a shawl hanging loosely over your head, all men in Tehran will come on to you.

If you wear a tight short jean manteau, lots of make-up, have strands of hair strategically showing, 80 per cent of men in Tehran will come on to you.

If you wear a tight black manteau above the knee, use your dark glasses as an Alice-band, with a thin black scarf, 70 per cent of men in Tehran will come on to you.

If you wear a baggy cream long robe, lots of make-up, and have a few strands of hair showing, 60 per cent of men in Tehran will come on to you.

If you wear long black robes, no make-up, and no hair showing, 30 per cent of men in Tehran will come on to you …

A chador and no make-up … will not get you a man.

Email: khanoomigoli@yahoo.com
http://khanoomgol.blogspot.com

---

29 May 2003

Chat with a friend:

I keep telling her why do you wear black all the time? Black veil, black chador, black shoes! It's dangerous at night! And you always walk with your head down, even when crossing the road! At least wear a coat in a lighter shade! Or perhaps carry a tame beige handbag so that at least you're visible at night!

She never listens. 'A coat in a light shade makes you look bolder and could be enticing ...'

She also tells me: 'When you wear a black chador, it's truly unsightly to have light-coloured shoes sticking out underneath. Too noticeable! And a light-coloured bag? I'm too old for that! Those colours are for school kids! A light-coloured veil? Don't even talk about it! It may make my face look attractive, and again, could be alluring!'

Trying to be as supportive and accepting as possible, I said: 'Perhaps not. You may look just as repellent in a light-coloured veil as you do now, so why not give it a go?!'

By Arched Brows

30 June 2004

Her brother was three years older ... sometimes, after supper on a cool summer's evening, he would go for a ride on his bicycle ... She would normally read a book while her brother was out ... and for the thousandth time on his return ... she would ask: 'Did you have a wonderful time?'

She didn't like girls' clothes.

Mother would glance at her ... in her shirt and trousers and grumble ... 'You look nothing like a girl! What man will ever take a shine to someone who dresses like that?'

Once the boys in the neighbourhood stopped her ... they told her that if they ever caught her dressed like a boy again, they would deal with her ... She was happy that men didn't like the way she dressed ...

She didn't want to marry a man who was just a man.

Not that she didn't want to marry ... she wanted to marry a man who was also human. Because if a man was human he would understand that he had too many rights according to the laws of the land. But the men she knew were all mere men. They inherited, married and divorced according to the laws ...

She wanted to have a daughter of her own someday ... A daughter she could buy a bicycle for ... She would even let her daughter go to China if she wanted to ... Not just for an education though ... but because everyone in China rides a bicycle.

Email: awat_hiva@yahoo.com
http://awathiva.persianblog.com

A YELLOW BANNER OUTSIDE A LOCAL SPORTS CLUB IN IRAN READS: 'ON THE BASIS OF A *FATWA* [RELIGIOUS EDICT] ISSUED BY THE SUPREME RELIGIOUS GUIDE [AYATOLLAH KHAMENEI], WOMEN CYCLING IN PUBLIC IS PROHIBITED.' DISOBEYING SUCH A *FATWA* WITHIN THE ISLAMIC REPUBLIC OF IRAN COULD LEAD TO PENALTIES SUCH AS IMPRISONMENT AND FLOGGING. THESE POSED PHOTOGRAPHS WERE BRIEFLY POSTED ON AN IRANIAN BLOG.

29 May 2002

What would happen if you were no longer legally required to wear the veil? Just imagine if our women were free to wear whatever they wanted; if even mixed bathing on the beach were allowed ... would this be culturally tolerable to Iranians?

You? Would you have any objections to your wife or your girlfriend in public dressed in a mini skirt, T-shirt and no bra with her nipples showing through?

Or you, a woman who lives in Iran, are you prepared to go public in full view of our men, who get so worked up by just glimpsing an inch of ankle underneath your robes that they need to wank?

We're not even talking of white snowy thighs on a mini-skirt-clad woman! Would you honestly feel secure walking past a man who for 20-something years is used to seeing your one eye and his fantasy is just to see the rest of your face?

Reform has to come from the bottom up. People have to change gradually, as our culture cannot change over night.

Email: baakereh@yahoo.com
http://baakereh.blogspot.com

30 May 2002

[Written in direct response to the previous post]

Dear Mr Baakereh,
The day we don't have to wear the veil, Iranian women will shed five kilos of excess gear ...These Korean factories that annually produce millions of metres of black fabric for export to Iran (and that sell nowhere else in the world) will go bankrupt ...

We will live in a more colourful land ... Women will pay more attention to their figures ... If we get hot, we'll wear short sleeves and a coat if we get cold. We'll go out as we dress at home ... If a person cannot trust his wife or girlfriend to go out without the veil, freedom will not be the problem: they have serious trust issues ...

We are no different from the free men and women of the world ... if we were free we would not be so culturally obsessed with the lower parts of our bodies.

We know how to think, how to educate ourselves, how to work hard and improve ourselves. If we had free choice, people who still believed in the veil could wear it and those of us that don't wouldn't. As a society we would learn to respect other viewpoints and not ridicule them for being backward for wearing the veil and we would learn how to avert our eyes.

It comes back to reforming ourselves and not restricting others.

Email: golku81@yahoo.com

http://golku.blogspot.com

GOING FOR THE BURN

The strict moral code imposed under Iran's 1979 Islamic Revolution forbids men and women to mix in social and sporting activities. Segregated sport for women is not forbidden and Islamic women's games have been held since 1993 in Iran. According to official government estimates, in 2004 there were 1,700,930 professional sportswomen. Throughout the year, many Iranians go hiking and mountain climbing. The country's mountain resorts have a less restricted dress code and are especially popular with those who want to escape the gaze of the Morality Police.

Since the Revolution, Iranian women have been banned from attending the men's sporting events, although they have consistently flouted the rules. In December 1997 the state-controlled Iranian news agency and the BBC reported that some 5,000 women had turned out to welcome home Iran's successful football World Cup team at Tehran stadium. There had been frequent requests on Iranian television for women to stay away from the event 'to safeguard Islam's

Marc Latzel ©

SHAHRAN-MOUNTAINS, IRAN (2001)

dignity'. Very few of these 5,000 women were actually football fans. They turned up as a sign of protest, simply because they had been asked to stay away.

Nevertheless, Iranian women are involved in a wide range of sporting activities, from skiing to bodybuilding. Despite the restrictions of Islamic law, many of them are undeniably 'going for the burn'. On any given day, women of all ages

A WOMAN WATCHES HER DAUGHTER SKIING, IRAN (2002)

can be observed in the early hours of the morning in places like Tehran's Mellat Park, jogging or doing aerobics in small groups and there are numerous segregated fitness clubs throughout Iran.

© Copyright Nafise Motlagh www.nafisegallery.com

YOUNG SKIERS IN IRAN (2002)

13 January 2004

Any talk of 'women's sports' in Iran just kills me! I as a woman, when I watch these girls … they make me laugh so much that tears run down my face …

God knows what those foreigners make of our women playing

games wearing 'blankets' and 'duvets' ... Do you know why we only get medals for playing chess? It's because no human being can compete with a ton of gear ... It's total madness ...

At least thank God for the segregated sport clubs that have sprouted up everywhere ... as a lot of housewives go to these clubs ... God knows what would become of us with these stupid mullahs.

By Shima

---

28 February 2003

I've recently joined a step-aerobics class. There are about 20 in our group, from the ages of 15 to 70 ... Naturally, with the New Year approaching we're all hoping to lose some weight so we can put on our best outfits ...

There is this one girl, though, who is more anxious about her weight than the rest of us put together ... she's getting married just before the New Year [spring equinox, 21 March]. Her wedding dress is a size 38 and she needs to get down to 50 kilos ... We're all rooting for her, especially some of the older women who constantly fuss over her with words of encouragement ...

Even I'm starting to feel protective towards her. At the moment we're all concerned about her little plump tummy ... It's a fun group; the women are so supportive and we're doubled-up with laughter most of the time ... all you have to do is tell the women in their forties they look 35 and they're in heaven!

My aerobics class is on the ground floor. I really had to look around to find this class. Our studio looks on to a private garden with huge glass windows and we get a nice peaceful view when it snows or rains ... Our instructor, Narges, is about 35, but they say she has a 20-year-old son!

We were in the middle of our session yesterday when we heard a loud sharp bang accompanied by smoke ... found out later that some idiot had thrown a firecracker over the garden wall! I'm used to sudden noises (due to the silly pranks of my brother), so I didn't even budge and I wasn't scared ... Maybe I was too focused on what I was doing ... I don't know ...

But a few of the women started screaming and Narges actually went deathly pale and shrieked: 'What'll we do if it's a bomb or a fire? Should we run out with what we have on?' Well most of us had skimpy shorts and tops and leotards on ... we leave our robes and stuff in our lockers in the basement.

There are a couple of older women in our group who wear chadors and actually believe in veiling ... they looked seriously distressed. But I said: 'I'd run out as I am! If I stay and die, my dad would be really annoyed with me! He's always told me to put my safety above everything else!!'

Narges replied: 'If I go out like this, my husband would kill me!!' And I said, 'Well, either way you're dead!!'

Anyhow, by then we knew it wasn't anything sinister and we were all laughing ... then one of the young girls said: 'Don't worry. Even if we stay put we'll be rescued, as all the men in the neighbourhood would risk their lives just to get a glimpse of us!' (Hoots of laughter)

Then an older, chubby woman, who is really friendly, bit her lip and said: 'The men would come in and rescue the young and beautiful – I'd have to stay here and die!' And as always, we laughed throughout the entire session.

Email: z8unak@z8un.com
http://z8un.com

Love, Marriage and Legal Identity

Although Iranian women enjoy greater freedoms than in many other Islamic countries, they are still treated as second-class citizens; especially in the courts, where a woman is legally worth half a man. According to Iranian law, a woman can only ask for divorce if she can prove that her husband is either impotent, a drug user, unable to provide financially or has been absent from the home for six months. A mother has the right to custody of a child only up to the age of seven; while girls aged 13 and over and boys over the age of 15 can decide which parent they wish to stay with. *Nooshi and Her Chicks* is a very popular blog. It is written by an Iranian woman who is separated from her husband. She awaits her final divorce decree and the subsequent loss of the custody of her children.

---

17 January 2003

A few months ago, after our constant fighting, my husband left. My son was only a year old and unbeknown to me at the time I was also pregnant with my daughter, Nasha. Now, I cannot do anything but wait for the time when he takes my children away from me.

Email: nooshi.joojehash@gmail.com
http://www.nooshi.ir

Darling Nooshi,

When I first separated from my husband he was exactly the same and kept threatening to take my son. Even though deep down I was frightened and heartbroken, I knew I had to be strong, as all I had to save me was my own inner strength …

I would constantly tell him: 'Come and take your child. Do you think I'm stupid to sit around and bring up your child? I want to get married again and I stand a better chance if you take him.' …
Believe me, I was consumed with panic that it would all backfire on me. But deep down I knew my ex, and most men are the same. It worked. He left us alone for good and didn't even look back – and neither have we … It's now me and my beautiful child and I have also recently remarried … He is a better father than my ex ever was …

Darling, keep strong and don't show any weakness. All we Iranian women have to save us is our own inner strength. Your children will never abandon you for a father who is a father only in name.

Saqi

jagannathah@hotmail.com

8 October 2003

When my father passed away he was 64, yet I never felt he was old. The only time he came across as old or weary was when he was driving, especially when young, impatient drivers would zigzag around him ...

It's the same with Alosha: although he has got taller recently, I hadn't truly felt that he was 'older' ...

He's had a fever the last few days and sleeps in my bed and hasn't had anything to eat for 24 hours – he just can't keep anything down. I feel so guilty. If only I'd taken him to see a doctor on Friday, his throat infection wouldn't have got so bad ... Tonight when he threw up again, I held him, apologized and told him the truth: it was all my fault ... He hugged me and said, 'It's not your fault Mum. It's nobody's fault. Now wipe your tears.'

Getting older or growing old is not always linked with your actual age ... Today I could see the man in my little boy's eyes.

Email: nooshi.joojehash@gmail.com

http://www.nooshi.ir

---

11 February 2003

A lot of you must remember the part women played in the Revolution ... and for what?

All the family protection laws changed to the advantage of men. Before, even if on the surface the child's custody was given to the person most suitable, now it goes to the absolute ruler of our homes: Man ... But there is a lot of difference between a person who breaks the law and the law of the land protecting criminals.

By Lady

8 September 2003

Today, like throughout my life, they have asked my father's name ... Job application form, affidavit, back of a cheque, enrolment at school or university ... They ask my father's name ...

In every legal form that I have ever filled, my identity is referenced as: name, birth certificate number, date, birthplace and my father's name!

The chador-wearing woman at the education office impatiently says: 'Write out your father's name and birth certificate number behind your ID photograph! Father's name, birth certificate number!'

Today is like all those other days that I have mapped out my identity in an official form and they have asked for my father's name ... but what about my mother's lost identity? She has no name, no address.

I wanted to yell out: 'My mum paid for my university education! My mother! My mother brought me into this world!'

I'm not questioning your desire to know my father's name ... But in all these years no one has ever asked who my mother is ... where is her share in my legal identity?

Email: art_rahayabi@yahoo.com
http://rahayabi.persianblog.com

11 January 2004

Who says that we need at least 200 guests at our wedding? I say we can have a fine wedding with 60 people ... Why do we have to hire a place and pay the world for it, when we can have a great celebration right here at home? Why do we have to be lumbered with the expense of a showy professional photographer, when we can record our memories with our own camera? I know my dress isn't the latest 2004 fashion ... but all its beads and pearls have been sewn on with love and laughter and with the help of family and friends ... who says we have to spend all we have on the wedding?

Those who love us will enjoy our special day and those who don't will complain and make a fuss no matter what ... We'll marry standing right here facing Mecca, with the mountains and the skies behind us ...

Darling Pourya, I know I'm stubborn and obstinate ... I know I always do stuff that leaves you speechless ... I love you a lot and I just want us to get our life together ... I miss the peace and tranquillity we had before we started organizing this stuff.

Email: khatoon_77@yahoo.com
http://khatoon77.blogspot.com

Traditionally, as part of the marriage contract, most couples decide on a Mehr (dower). The prenuptial contracts can specify the Mehr as anything from property, a sum of money, gold coins or symbolic items such as a copy of the Koran or a bunch of flowers. If a husband divorces his wife, he is legally obliged to pay the Mehr in full.

The scales are very much tipped against women in divorce law, though there are loopholes within the flexible jurisprudence of Shia Islam. A Shia marriage contract is drawn by the relevant registrars prior to the ceremony, based on the agreement of both parties and there are some who, as part of their contract, agree upon equal rights for divorce and joint child custody rights, and so on.

Although such contracts tend to exist among the middle classes, there are no figures as to what proportion of the population has opted for them. However, they are popular enough for many registry offices to have ready printed copies of them.

The following blogger, 'Lady Sun', decided on these added stipulations in her wedding contract. She became the centre of much attention and chatter in the Iranian blogosphere when it was discovered that she was in fact marrying one of her readers. 'Lady Sun' is one of the first Iranian women to have started a Farsi blog. With her on her big day was her best friend the popular blogger 'Pinkfloydish' (named in honour of her favourite band).

---

13 August 2003

I can't stop thinking about the film My Big Fat Greek Wedding, but in my case both sides are Greek …

In our absurd country, Mehr is this ridiculous device so that a woman who just can't put up with a bad marriage, can turn around and say, 'Keep my Mehr and grant me a divorce.' … As women have no legal rights for divorce … also some women who don't work and have no income can get their Mehr if their husbands throw them out … Our women think it is bad to ask for divorce rights … And those who do ask are told: 'Why do you bring such things up just before a wedding?'

But I'm going to get my divorce rights and I told him right at the outset – and he agreed without any trouble.

22 August 2003

We went to the registry office … It just all felt peculiar … a group of people were there … If it hadn't been for Pinkfloydish, who tried to calm me down by presenting everything in a good light, I would have run off … When the mullah came and started, I still didn't know what was going on … He asked for my consent …
Pinkfloydish said, 'She's picking flowers'* … The second time, her aunt shouted: 'She's writing her blog!' Everyone was laughing …

The third time they were all waiting and I didn't quite realize that I had to say something, but then I said: 'I consent, with the permission of my mother and father' …

They asked for my Mehr and we said … a book of poetry by Hafez, a mirror, candlesticks, and a red rose … I felt triumphant … as I

added my own conditions to the marriage contract ... the rights for
divorce, travel and work, with joint equal property rights ...

*In Iranian weddings the bride is asked three times before she consents. It is
customary for her to be silent during the first two requests, while her friends
say things like 'The bride is busy picking flowers' or 'fetching rose water'. The
groom, however, is asked only once.

Email: khorshid@gmail.com

http://www.khorshidkhanoom.com

'Lady Sun' – a star of the Iranian blogosphere – left Iran in 2004 and now lives in
the United States. The next entry is one of her commentaries from her new
home. The photograph was taken on a picnic with fellow bloggers in Iran in
2002 when she briefly removed her veil for the camera.

Photo © Hossein Derakhshan

3 July 2004

A lot of the older Iranians here [in the United States] are so
discouraging about Iran. They are basically stuck in the exact year
they left Iran. Anything that happens in Iran they view cynically. It
was remarkable that after an hour-long conversation with an Iranian
woman here, I unconsciously started defending [ex-]President

Khatami, the sixth Parliament [the reformist majority Parliament],
the reform movement and Shirin Ebadi. When in reality, in my heart
of hearts, I have a lot of criticisms of what I was defending.

It is really frustrating to be confronted with people far away
from Iran – who view everything bleakly and just curse at every
single thing. Yet I'm also worried that I may turn into one of these
people. I keep telling myself, What if I can't get back to Iran for a
long while and end up giving stupid assessments of the country?
But I keep reassuring myself that if I keep reading the blogs I
will understand Iran better and will not turn into one of these
fossils.

Email: khorshid@gmail.com
http://www.khorshidkhanoom.com

In 2001, when Parliament overwhelmingly passed a law to raise the legal marriage age of girls to 16, the Guardian Council vetoed it, saying it was against
Sharia law. The legal age was lowered to 13 in 1979 after the Revolution, yet this
legislation has largely been ignored by the majority of people. Studies of 'marriage ages' do not show any appreciable change after the Revolution. The
national statistics show that the average marriage age for women is 23. It is just
another example of the difference in attitude between the people of Iran and the
hardline clerics that rule over them. Many Iranians are horrified at the idea of 13-
year-old girls getting married, but the law stands, leaving open the possibility of
what is essentially child abuse.

Unfortunately, even when a woman marries in her early twenties, she surren-
ders many of her freedoms in the service of her husband, as the next blog reveals.

16 March 2002

Salaam. I've just got back from window-shopping for a gift for my
sister who lives in Mashhad ... I like to call her our Jasmine,
because, like that beautiful and fragile flower, she is filled with

warmth and beauty ... but a jasmine flower, like our women, is not safe in our male-dominated society ...

When she was 24, at my parents' insistence, she married. At the time she was a true jasmine and our neighbourhood was drunk with her scent. Our Jasmine was an artist, a painter and a writer. When she sang she spirited you away to a garden filled with flowers ... They gave our flower to a man who had come back from studying abroad ... When I got there he had already presented Jasmine with a small flowerpot ... A pot that when you looked at it completely dissolved in the shadow of her dignity.

He put our flower in that pot and imprisoned her. He denied her beauty ... I don't know why ... perhaps because he was ugly ... Perhaps blind ... He mocked her so much that she no longer believed in her own fragrance ... she stopped painting ... you could no longer hear the sound of her pen, nor her beautiful voice.

Everything she painted was meaningless to that man. Her last painting was of a window facing a garden filled with blossoms. You see, her home has no windows. Our flower has two wonderful little girls now – one I like to call Pistachio and the other Hazelnut ... Our Jasmine has forgotten her songs and her painting and just looks after Pistachio and Hazelnut ...

He's happy, he thinks he has ownership, but I know that our flower will see spring yet again, and will again paint a window for her dark home ... Can any voice out there tell me ... how I can carry her lost fragrance back to her as a gift?

Email: foroogh_payizi@hotmail.com

http://foroogh.malakut.org

---

22 January 2004

Three out of ten Iranian marriages end in divorce.

Divorce as a rule is certainly not a good thing; yet these figures could also imply the growth of personal freedoms; the decline of prejudicial traditions and the improvement in the standing of women in society ... Especially as the new figures show that women make 80 per cent of divorce petitions. (Source: *Khaneh Mah Journal*, No. 4, p. 67.)

Email: art_rahayabi@yahoo.com
http://rahayabi.persianblog.com

1 October 2003

Feminists of the world come to Iran, as this is where women rule!

I was waiting in the pouring rain for a taxi for what seemed like for ever ... a woman appeared and instantly got a ride ... I eventually got to the bank ... busy endless queues ... a woman walks in and speaks to the manager, saying she is in such a hurry ... oblivious to all of us poor men there, a bank-teller, mesmerized by her smile, opened an extra till for her ... Typical! Whether it's in our mad bureaucracies or any social situation that I can think of ... women always come first ...

All of you women out there who keep complaining about your lack of rights in the Islamic Republic of Iran, you know very well that in reality you always get your way and you are far better off than us disadvantaged men.

Email: alifathi_v@hotmail.com
http://ragoniir.persianblog.com

CRIME AND PUNISHMENT

Although some women have managed to find loopholes in the law, such as divorce, there are many other laws where the accused is utterly powerless. One of the most extreme is the stoning to death of an adulteress. Even though the Koran does not sanction punishment by stoning to death, it was introduced in 1979 by Ayatollah Khomeini. Naturally, Iranian bloggers are enraged by this, and

in 2003 there was an outpouring of sympathy for Aminah, a Nigerian woman
who was sentenced to be stoned to death for adultery.

---

25 September 2003

I am so happy I want to explode ... Tonight the BBC Persian radio
announced that Aminah, the Nigerian woman who was to be stoned
to death, has been acquitted ... I am so, so happy ... it felt as if my
own flesh was to be pounded with stones tomorrow ... I was to be
stoned tomorrow ...

And with each stone struck ... remembering my hungry child ...
drops of milk would have fallen from my breasts and shamed this
vile human act into a deep hole of barbarity.

Email: at_857@hotmail.com
http://atash3.blogspot.com

---

25 September 2003

Aminah was freed today ... But we must all remind ourselves that
our own reformist government says that stoning is deplorable – and
she should be killed by a firing squad!

We campaign for Aminah's freedom – and they call for a change
in the method of her execution!

shabah@shabah.org
http://www.shabah.org

Iran's hardline rulers control the major centres of power in Iran, especially the
judiciary. As a result, numerous cases of blatant injustice have been documented
by human rights organizations such as Amnesty International.

The following blogger discusses three recent cases: (1) Afsaneh Nourouzi, a 32-
year-old woman condemned to death for killing a man who had tried to rape
her; (2) Zahra Khazemi, a female journalist who died while in the custody of the

judiciary; and (3) the acquittal of a group of Basij (hardline vigilantes) that had assassinated several intellectuals whom they judged to be apostates.

Nourouzi was acquitted six years ago, but she has spent the last seven years in jail and her death sentence was approved in October 2003. The judge said that her 'immodest attire' had 'prepared the ground for her rape'. Many believe that the real reason she has received a death sentence is that her attacker was the head of police intelligence on Kish Island. The tragic irony is that had Nourouzi not resisted being raped, she might have been charged with adultery, which is punishable by stoning.

---

5 October 2003

I am a dishonoured Iranian man

Today, yet again, there are two cases of injustice in the forefront of our minds. One concerns a group of armed individuals who, in total confidence of doing the right thing, have killed a number of people they condemned as apostates; the other is the case of a woman who killed her would-be rapist, who was a powerful intelligence agent ... in front of her own children, as she was escaping for her life ...

Because of our contemptible laws, the armed group have been acquitted, while this woman has been condemned to hang! Just thinking about these two cases makes me despise who I am. In a country where I live, work, and pay taxes, am I not a party to these injustices? Elections are fast approaching: is not each vote cast in the ballot box a stone cast at a woman being stoned to death? Is it not a knife driven into the hearts of all libertarians who are sacrificed by this ruthless society?

I want to shout out to the world: 'I am a dishonoured Iranian man and am not a party to these crimes! Cross my name off the list! I am a person and I belong to a different time and era! A time when humans don't hunt each other down, and the price of living with honour is not death ...'

For your own sakes and to wash from us this disgraceful

collective stain, sign the petition asking for Afsaneh Nourouzi's freedom. We cannot do anything for Zahra Khazemi, now buried, but think of Afsaneh's freedom ...

For the day when they will ask of us: 'What were you doing during those black days?'

shabah@shabah.org
http://www.shabah.org

Here is Dorna Kozehghar, a recently exiled journalist, writing in *Iran Emrooz*, the on-line political bulletin (10 October 2003):

> The judgement in Afsaneh [Nourouzi]'s case is testament to our repressive backward view of women in Iran. This outlook regards a woman as someone who can ensnare a man and destroy his afterlife. This is precisely why Hezbollah and the Basij are so concerned about our veils above all else – and the way we behave. They even control our laughter in public places ... Women are indeed dangerous creatures. Afsaneh Nourouzi is to die because she is an Iranian woman.

8 November 2003

I am totally against all these petitions that are doing the rounds on our blogs ... I actually feel physically sick at the thought of petitioning the likes of our judiciary and giving them the satisfaction and credit by asking them to free yet another innocent party ...

Things will ultimately be resolved when our people give them a big smack in the mouth ...

All these endless petitions asking, 'Oh, don't beat so-and-so' and 'Free so-and-so' ... for these authorities who don't even know if a petition is something you eat or wear.

http://river.blogsky.com

A FEMALE PROTESTER IN THE CROWD AT TEHRAN AIRPORT
AWAITING THE ARRIVAL OF SHIRIN EBADI (WINNER OF THE
NOBLE PRIZE FOR PEACE), 14 OCTOBER 2003. HER HAND-
WRITTEN BANNER READS: *THIS IS IRAN. I AM A WOMAN. I AM
ZAHRA KAZEMI.* DR KAZEMI WAS BEATEN INTO A COMA WHILE
IN THE CUSTODY OF THE JUDICIARY AND DIED OF A BRAIN
HAEMORRHAGE ON 11 JULY 2003.

Iranian-Canadian photojournalist Zahra Kazemi was arrested for taking pictures outside Evin prison during a student protest in Tehran. With political
activists and lawyers (headed by Ms Shirin Ebadi) determined to expose what
they believed was a cover-up by the judiciary; coupled with pressure from the
Canadian government and the European Union an Information ministry agent
was eventually charged with her death. Yet after a two-day trial in July 2004, her
lawyers refused to sign documents which legitimize the court, stating the whole
trial a farce.

The following is a brief account by an Iranian journalist of one of these court
sessions:

---

18 July 2004

They have finally closed down *Joumhouriat* and *Vaghayeh Etefagieh*
[reformist newspapers]. So there are now no papers left that can put
out uncensored reports of Zahah Kazemi's court session. Well this is

exactly what Mortazavi [Prosecutor General Judge Saeed Mortazavi] wanted.

The situation in court today was sinister beyond words.

Shirin Ebadi was the first member of the defence team who spoke. In one segment she pointed out that there were distinct bruise marks on the thighs of the victim and that it had to be explained how these came about! She also said the victim's trousers were torn and bloody in a 'particular region'. Why was this part of her trousers torn and blood-stained!!!

The accused is an intelligence agent, an interrogator for the Information Ministry. So the courtroom was swamped with the ministry's employees. Their presence in court had given the session an added menacing atmosphere. They really stood out and you knew exactly who they were and where they were from.

The sight of the accused man turned my stomach, even though I knew he was innocent. Albeit an interrogator, so I did not feel sorry for him at all. He was visibly tense and anxious. When it was his turn to speak, he completely lost it and started shouting and sobbing. Then he just stormed out of the court room followed by a few of his Information Ministry colleagues who closed the court doors saying no one was allowed to leave!!! It was as if they ran the whole session and the judge was just there for show! They just calmed him down and brought him back again.

Zahara Kazemi's mother was a total picture of pain and misery. When it was her turn she could not hold back her tears. She told the judge:

Muslim, remember that you will have to answer for everything in the after life.

She kept sobbing:

When they gave me my daughter's body, she was covered in bruises. Her hands and legs were broken. There were burn marks on her chest. The nails on her hands and feet were broken.

When the judge pointed out that there were no mentions of

such abuse in the forensic reports. She got really angry and said:

Are you saying my child had got chicken pox, I saw the burn marks on her breasts myself.

Soltani, another one of the lawyers representing Ms Kazemi's family, said that witnesses had seen her being punched so hard by Bakhshi (the head representative of the judiciary in Evin prison) that she had collapsed on the floor in pain.

I think they had burnt the poor woman with cigarettes. It was vile, vile ...

By Zananeh

STRUGGLING FROM WITHIN

Some people believe the regime is immune to change, but many others, especially women, are experts at finding ways round the constraints of the patriarchal system. These women activists are less interested in whether or not to wear the veil and more concerned with gaining access to education, wider employment opportunities, equality at work and better health care for their families.

Women like Shirin Ebadi, the 2003 Nobel Peace Prize laureate. Dismissed from her position as a judge after the Revolution, she did not follow colleagues overseas into exile, but stayed on fighting against cases of repression, domestic violence and political assassinations. A defender of Islam, she has written authoritatively about women and children's rights under Islamic law.

Since the Revolution, many other women have tried to fight for democracy within the confines of an ideological state. After the death in custody of Zahra Kazemi was made public, Azam Talaghani single-handedly set up a picket outside Iran's notorious Evin Prison. Talaghani had spent many years imprisoned inside Evin under the previous regime. She is the founder and head of the Society of Islamic Revolutionary Women of Iran, but is now, ironically, one of the most outspoken critics of the present regime. She has even stated publicly that the Revolution has brought nothing but 'poverty and polygamy for women'. For more than 20 years she has run literacy campaign programmes for women from very poor backgrounds, so that they can earn a living and win independence from their husbands.

Photo courtesy of Azam Talaghani

AZAM TALAGHANI OUTSIDE EVIN PRISON PROTESTING AT THE DEATH OF DR KAZEMI, 8 DECEMBER 2003

Although she is totally committed to Islam, Talaghani challenges any interpretation of the Koran that supports male supremacy. She advocates instead a much more feminist interpretation. In 1979, when Khomeini decreed that women must wear the veil, (although Talaghani had always worn a veil) she boldly wrote a public letter of protest against the Ayatollah's judgement on the matter. Women should not be 'forced at bayonet point' to wear the chador, she said; they must decide for themselves how they can best dress to please God.

Her father was the late Ayatollah Talaghani and there isn't a town in Iran without a road, a school or a hospital named after him. Constantly arrested and jailed by the Shah for his political opposition, Ayatollah Talaghani was released for the last time in the autumn of 1978 and he immediately became one of the most respected leaders of the Iranian Revolution. When the Shah was overthrown in early 1979, Talaghani began to chart a course somewhat independent of the official policies of Khomeini, who had spent many years in exile.

Khomeini demanded that all political opposition be eliminated, whereas Talaghani protested at the arrests and mass executions (some of the victims were his ex-cellmates). He died during the early days of the Revolution, his last speech warning of oppression in the name of Islam.

Zahra Rabbani Amlashi is also a daughter of an ayatollah, and the daughter-in-law of the dissident Grand Ayatollah Montazeri. In November 2003, when her property (which she had intended to give to a school) was seized by the Revolutionary Guards, she wrote an open letter to the head of the Islamic Revolutionary Guards in which she said:

> I have no criminal record and have been a school teacher for many years
> in the city of Qom. You ceaselessly protest at Israel's illegal occupation.
> You are occupying a house that is my personal property; yet what you say
> is immoral for Israel is good for the Islamic Republic of Iran. The
> dustbin of history is full of tyrants who, due to fleeting earthly power,
> impinge on the rights of others. You, my Revolutionary Guard brothers,
> who fought so bravely against outside aggression during a war, what has
> happened to you that you are now the pawns of oppressors and are
> answerable to no one?

Other women who have shown extraordinary courage in opposing the regime are still associated with it in the minds of many. For instance, Fatemeh Haghighatjou has a reputation as a fearlessly outspoken MP after several scathing attacks on some of the most powerful institutions and individuals in Iran. She has been in and out of the courts and in August 2001 she was given a 22-month prison sentence for, among other things, 'criticizing the Islamic regime'. According to the Iranian constitution, all parliamentary sessions must be broadcast live on state radio, but Haghighatjou's provocative speeches in Parliament have been banned from appearing in the print media.

On 14 November 2003 she yet again stunned Parliament in a speech that was transmitted live on national radio throughout Iran. She gave extensive details of blatant human rights abuses that had been sanctioned and carried out by some of Iran's most powerful institutions. She even said that the Islamic Republic's so-called enemies could not have brought as much 'shame' on Iran as these 'gentlemen' (meaning the ruling unelected clergy) have brought on themselves through their actions. Finally, she called on her fellow MPs to stop playing at democracy and to disregard all other undemocratic institutions that try to over-rule them. It was their constitutional right, she said, to hold a national referen-dum on the future of the Islamic Republic and let the people decide.

FATEMEH HAGHIGHATJOU

In January 2004 Haghighatjou was banned from standing in the upcoming elections, as were 3,600 other candidates, including 87 elected MPs. It spelled the beginning of the end for parliamentary reform in Iran. And because of Haghighatjou's outspoken attacks on the unelected ruling clerics, she was facing banishment from the Government and a prison sentence. Instead she resigned from the Government in protest at the barring of thousands of candidates in the 2004 elections. She said in her resignation speech:

> I resign ... because a staged, dishonest and uncompetitive election was
> held with the aim of producing a docile Parliament. They do not want a
> republic, but a Taliban-style Islam.

It is indicative of the sort of anger she arouses in her opponents that during her last parliamentary session, as she spoke, an enraged hardline cleric and MP ran to the podium and tried physically to prevent her from speaking. Haghighatjou was only able to carry on with her resignation speech because four other women MPs created a wall around her with their bodies.

14 November 2003

I had come across her during the last student demonstrations ... everyone was buzzing around her, trying to tell her their grievances ... someone told me that she had been a student union leader a few years back and is pretty much a legend among some of the older students ... petite, demure, yet weirdly a bit tom-boyish and wrapped in her black chador. To be honest with you, I just couldn't see past her black garb and didn't think much of her ...

We all know that without that uniform she could never have stood for Parliament ... but some women need that uniform just as most of us start growing our beards when we go for any sort of official interview ...

However, when I told this Jennifer Lopez look-alike in the Maths department what I thought of Haghighatjou, I had my head bitten off ... and was told that in this perverse society of ours, her veil stops men like me treating her like an object ... and even if she had the choice, she would carry on wearing the veil because of men like me ...

Well, I for one will never figure out our women. (I mean, do you think Miss Lopez fancies me?)

But I can see that even the most bigoted mullah doesn't know how to handle a woman who looks more devout than their own daughters, and dresses like their long-lost beloved grandmothers used to ...

Today four of my friends and I were squeezed into a taxi and as usual making a lot of noise, when the driver told us to keep it quiet as he was trying to listen to something ... It was Haghighatjou speaking live in Parliament ...

He didn't have to tell us to be quiet a second time ... we were all stunned into silence even long after she had stopped speaking ... When she had finished the driver turned to us and said: 'The only one with balls in the whole Parliament is Fatemeh ...' Well, no one can argue with that ...

But what I heard today, although undoubtedly heroic, felt like
listening to a live national broadcast of a suicide note.

By School Friend

Haghighatjou was born in a working-class family in the south of Tehran and
went on to become a prominent and outspoken student leader. In particular she
called for the highest members of the regime to be made accountable. Later, with
the student vote behind her, she became the youngest ever female MP, struggling
to change the system from within. Not only was she one of the most outspoken
reformist MPs, but she was also a leading representative of a grass-roots reform
movement that was voted for by the vast majority of Iranians in the 1997 and
2001 presidential elections. That movement even had the backing of secular liberals, although, above all, it was backed by the same classes that supported
Khomeini a quarter of a century ago at the start of the Revolution.

In an interview with *Le Figaro* (15 June 2004) Fatemeh Haghighatjou said that
'the best lesson I learnt from my years as an MP is that an Islamic State is inca-
pable of responding to Iranian expectations ... If our nation is to advance,' she
added, 'we must separate religion from politics.'

Pronouncements by committed revolutionary figures like Haghighatjou that
the system is 'corrupt' or 'immune to reform' are a potent indictment of the legitimacy of the regime. A quarter of a century after the Revolution, grass-roots
reformers are protesting that the fight for an Islamic democracy has actually led
to an Islamic dictatorship – and one that imprisons or even kills its opponents,
violates human rights, and distorts the tenets of Islam.

Emrooz, a prominent reformist on-line news portal, often publishes the
writings of Iranian journalists who have been banned from the print media. On
23 February 2004 Emrooz paid tribute to Ms Haghighatjou.

A letter to Fatemeh Haghighatjou's daughter, baby Sara:

Dear little Sara Salaam
I just want to congratulate you for having the most beautiful mother in

the world, a mother who is embraced with the beauty of honesty, faith
and bravery ...

Do you know that in this land of ours every time a daughter is born a
mother's heart is touched with pain? ... as the mothers of this land know
that their daughter's life is worth only half that of a boy's ... But dear Sara,
you need no longer believe that ... the lioness that is your mother ended
all that today ... and proved to the women of this land that there is pride
in giving life to a girl ... a daughter like your mother ... Sara, if only you
were a bit older and could realize the enormity of what your mother has
done ...

Today the fear we have for your mother shakes with terror the hearts of
the bravest among us ... yet your mother stood by the pledge she made to
the people and her God ... She shattered fear with her courage and her
name will live on in the history of this land.

Fatemeh Haghighatjou's defiance of the hardline clerics brought her many
death threats from groups within Iran. When asked about these in an interview
with Germany's *Deutsche Welle* newspaper in February 2004, she replied that
'these threats are dependent on the extent of international pressure. The conservatives always cave in to a lot of foreign criticism, and when there is no foreign
criticism, they do what they want. I predict that in the future, if there is no international pressure, there will be even more crackdowns, arrests and imprisonments, but if there is international concern these things will be reduced.'

THE FAILURE OF PARLIAMENTARY REFORM

In the parliamentary elections of February 2004, a conservative victory was guaranteed after thousands of candidates (including Haghighatjou) were barred
from standing. All pretensions to democracy were abandoned once and for all. A
political climate of absolutist hardline rule and rapprochement with the West
prevailed and everyone could see that Iran was entering into an era of political
repression. Numerous political and social activists were put on trial and there
were more crackdowns, arrests and imprisonments.

As we have already mentioned, International Women's Day in Tehran on 8

March 2004 was hijacked by the Basij vigilantes. In recent years the event had just about been tolerated and celebrated throughout Iran, thanks in large part to the efforts of non-governmental women's groups. Before the big day, seven Iranian women's groups – including the Women's Cultural Centre and the Independent Women's Association – posted news of the event on Internet sites and blogs. The main theme of the day was to have been 'violence against women', but those taking part were instead violently attacked by armed members of the Basij. Here is 'Lady Sun' on the subject.

---

8 March 2004

You get there … They are beating a boy at your feet … they strike with batons … The old men at the park are struggling to free the boy from their hands … 'With what right are you beating this kid? This boy was on his way home!' 'Why are you beating him up? You have no right to hit him! What has he done?'

They turn to us: 'Go away before we give you a thrashing too!'

I can't believe ———— has been assaulted. She is the most discreet journalist you are ever likely to come across …Last year we were all laughing … we talked of peace … Shirin Ebadi [the Noble Peace Prize laureate 2003] spoke with hope and excitement … even a girl in a chador went up and spoke about their organization … The police were stationed around us quietly listening to what we were saying … no one was bothered … No – perhaps we had bothered people, so this year … This year the amphitheatre was empty … no one was laughing.

They chanted slogans. They were beaten up. They were sworn at … and they celebrated International Women's Day.

Email: khorshidkhanoomi77@yahoo.com
http://www.khorshidkhanoom.com

Laleh Park, 8 March 2004. On 8 March, the authorities withdrew permission for a gathering in Tehran's Laleh Park just hours before it was due to begin. Despite the heavy presence of security, several hundred women defied the ban by staying and chanting slogans.

Photo © Leila

THIS PHOTOGRAPH WAS TAKEN MOMENTS BEFORE THE SECURITY FORCES ATTACKED.

9 March 2004

We are the loneliest women in the world and have many hard days ahead of us ... I was so angry and tired yesterday I just couldn't write anything ... As the baton brushed against my ankle, I could hear the voice of the officer in charge of security: 'Give them a good thrashing! Show no mercy!' I witnessed three girls being viciously assaulted, the arrest of two other girls, and a woman who was sobbing with pain ...

But even so we won, as we got our trembling voices heard ...

They called us whores, bitches ... Yes I am a prostitute, if by that they mean 'virtuous' and 'pure' ... I am a whore to their 'virtue' ... We are the loneliest women in the world, with a new era of repression ahead.

Email: golie_1982@yahoo.com
http://golnaz1982.blogspot.com

Iranian women were officially allowed to celebrate International Women's Day in 1979, the first year of the Revolution. After that it was marked by underground women's groups gathering at home. However, the earliest recorded Women's Day celebration in Iran was in 1921, when 50 women gathered in the Caspian Sea town of Anzali.

In 1999, thanks to the efforts of a grass-roots reform movement, women once again openly celebrated on 8 March. Despite the outbreak of violence at Laleh Park in Tehran, numerous peaceful celebrations took place throughout Iran, organized by women's NGOs and university students. The special day was even acknowledged by the reformist ex-vice president and mid-ranking cleric Muhammad-Ali Abtahi in his blog.

---

8 March 2004

Lebanon is an Arab country, but was for many years under French cultural influence. And the Lebanese like to see themselves, as a society not so entangled with Arab culture. But I remember when my third daughter was born and I was taking my wife home from the hospital. The doorman at the hospital quietly asked the driver, 'What sex is the child?'

'Its a girl,' he said.

Without offering any sort of congratulations he came up to me and, as if to comfort me, said: 'Don't be too upset. God is great.'

I was outraged, but what could I do? ...

The high percentage of women gaining entrance to universities in Iran in recent years, and their widespread presence in cultural, political and social arenas, are all due to their own ceaseless efforts.

I remember once someone was trying to defend women from a religious standpoint, saying that even though Mary was 'only a woman', God has mentioned her in the Koran. It is because of such stupid 'defences' in the name of religion that so many insults are made against Islam itself.

http://www.webneveshteha.com

In May 2004, Shadi Sadr – an Iranian newspaper columnist and editor of the 'Women in Iran' website (www.womeniniran.org) – was awarded the 2004 Ida B. Wells Award for Bravery in Journalism. In her acceptance speech she outlined the fundamental changes that have come about in Iranian society and in the indigenous women's movement.

> In recent years a massive growth in the number of young people in Iran has brought about changes that have shaken the nation. In all of these changes, women have played the leading role and as a result have sustained the most casualties, but they refuse to go back to their traditional roles ...
>
> For example, we can now observe a rapid growth in the number of feminist groups at universities and colleges throughout Iran. Second, women's organizations have put aside their ideological differences in order to form national consulting networks based on common goals and objectives. Third, thanks to the Internet, websites and weblogs, new bridges have been built between Iranian women outside and inside Iran, while old ties are strengthened on a regular basis.
>
> And finally, today Iranian women continue to struggle against the compulsory hejab, to gain independence from men and to participate at the highest levels of society. As such, they have imposed themselves on a male-dominated society which still believes women should stay at home.

Photo © Hossein Derakhshan

SHADI SADR, THE PUBLISHER, LAWYER AND JOURNALIST, WITH HER HUSBAND, HOSSEIN NILCHIAN

Perhaps nobody sees us, but we exist and we make our mark on the world around us. I assure you that if you look around carefully, everywhere you will see our footsteps.

WOMANLY PARADOXES

The westernized life-styles that were available to some Iranian women were lost with the Islamic Revolution of 1979. But even the most radical clerics realized that Iran's culture would not stand the strictures imposed in such countries as Saudi Arabia. As one commentator has observed: 'More than many women in the Islamic world, Iranian women occupy public spaces. Even as wives and mothers, they work, vote, drive, shop and hold professional positions as doctors, lawyers, corporate executives, and deputies in Parliament ... They can vote at 16 and that makes them a threat to the power of the clerics who had promoted the anti-contraception policy in the first place.'[3]

Women have transformed Iran since the Revolution. A third of all doctors, 60 per cent of civil servants and 80 per cent of all teachers in Iran are women. Some are even the sole breadwinner in their family; many are war widows or divorced, like the following blogger: a teacher, who also drives a taxi cab.

In the last few years taxi firms using women drivers have sprouted up all over Iran – even in religious towns like Qom, where there is a client-base of women who prefer to have female drivers. Taxis in Iran are an inexpensive form of travel as the majority are communal, with passengers paying set fares for designated routes.

---

26 March 2004

The other day I heard from one of my colleagues that a foreign journalist was in town and wanted to interview some women drivers ...

Well I went along and saw a few other familiar faces there ... including Mrs Elahi who is 60, yet full of energy and wisdom ... She's someone I admire a great deal, as she has had to struggle all her life and has always supported her family without help ... She also has a tendency to be pretty up-front ...

Anyway, the journalist wanted to find out about our motivations for doing what we do, but it was as if she had already written up her article and wanted our answers to fit in with her preconceptions ... 'Ladies,' she said, 'what would you say is your main motivation for choosing this career? ...'

Mrs Elahi immediately answered, 'Money, obviously.'

The reporter looked at her ... as if she had not given the appropriate answer and said, 'I really need more elaborate answers for my report. I have to ...'

Mrs Elahi said, 'What do you want us to say? To lie?'

The reporter got closer to Mrs Elahi. The camera was now focused on her face and she said: 'You live in a country where you are denied many of the basic rights awarded to women. Yet you have taken up a profession that is generally considered a masculine occupation.'

'Well you really fail to appreciate who we are,' said Mrs Elahi, 'and clearly you don't think much of us ... You come from a country where women are astronauts and pilots and you still think it's amazing that we merely drive cars for a living!!' And then she added: 'Listen lady. You can ask as much as you like but my motivation is still money. Anyway, you know best.'

The reporter looked very serious, impatiently waiting for Mrs Elahi's words to be translated.

We all knew that Mrs Elahi was toying with the reporter.

When the reporter left, Mrs Elahi scornfully said, 'May she rest in peace! My grandmother could shoot an apple in half while galloping on horseback. Yet after all these years they think it's amazing that we drive cars!'

16 December 2003

'Will you pay for two fares or shall I pick up more passengers?'

'No, charge for two.'

He asked to be dropped off near the roundabout ... he got out,
put his hand in his pocket and took out a 50-toman note and held it
in front of me ...

'Two fares make 100 tomans,' I said ...

'Oh go away, since when are your sort real drivers?!'

'Listen. Did we not agree a fare at the outset?'

He nastily took out another note from his pocket and gave it to
me. Well, I tore the notes to pieces and threw them in his face and
drove off.

It was money from someone who did not understand the fact
that there is no difference between the efforts of a man or a woman
making a living ... It was worthless to me.

14 January 2004

I take my shopping list out of my bag. My fare is a lady ... She's
pointing out a china tea set in the window to the sales assistant ... I
look at my list ... Gloves, turnip, fruit (oranges and apples), onions and
tomatoes, washing powder, soap, a kilo of mincemeat ...

Half an hour passes and she's still in the shop. I took her to the
butcher's first and then she bought her fruit from the shop next
door ... She was holding on tight to the edges of her chador ... I
know her ... her husband used to have an important post in the
town hall ... She now says he is in business ... The construction
business ... I look at my watch ... My son has been poorly for three
days ... I took him to a doctor in between work this morning ... The
lady upstairs is looking after him ...

She is still pointing out things in the shop window. I have to get
my own shopping done ... But in my own neighbourhood the

prices are less ... I look through my bag ... I had to pay the
mechanic for some work this morning ... I count the money in my
bag: I have 3,000 tomans ... I cross out the mincemeat and the
gloves. I have to give my daughter another excuse for not getting
her the gloves ...

Someone knocks on the window ... it's her. She laughs and
waves her hand ... I open the front door for her, she puts her
shopping in the back and sits down ... I release the clutch and start
the car ... the shop assistant is running out of the shop. Something
in his hand ... She opens the window ... the sales assistant has
lowered his head to the level of the window:

'Sorry, but how much was your cheque?'

'50,000 tomans. Why?'

'You've given me a cheque for 500,000 instead!'

She says thank you and gives him a grey cheque for 50,000, after
examining it carefully. She laughs, tilting back her head ... What a
mix-up!

Email: bahar-goler@yahoo.com
http://manotaxim.persianblog.com

This last blogger describes her passenger – the gormless wife of an ex-local government official – as 'holding on tight to the edges of her chador': the chador has become synonymous with Islamic rule and the ruling class. There are many scathing commentaries by bloggers against compulsory veiling, yet in December 2003, when France announced its plans to forbid headscarves in state schools, many of the same voices were critical of the French.

In 2003 Shirin Ebadi caused uproar among Iran's ruling clerics when she attended the Nobel ceremony to accept the Peace Prize unveiled. She even received public death threats from extremist Islamic groups. Yet Ebadi has spoken out against the French ban on Islamic headscarves in state schools. 'If there is a law [against headscarves], only extremists will profit from it, as it would be an excuse to prevent their daughter's education,' she said. 'The better the girls are educated and the more they go to school, the more emancipated they will become.'

---

5 January 2003

I've just heard the funniest thing on the radio ... really funny ... some of our mullahs have sent a joint statement of protest to Jacques Chirac through the Foreign Office against a ban on headscarves in France ... these mullahs really have a lot of nerve ...

Yes, the same mullahs who are obsessed by nothing more than keeping these vile headscarves on our heads ... Ayatollah Khamenei would rather give birth to Ariel Sharon's baby (not that they don't make a lovely couple) than see us go unveiled ... Yes, these exact same mullahs who blatantly ignore all civil liberties are complaining that the French are acting undemocratically ...

Well the French are acting undemocratically ... but the difference is that I, as a woman, have every right to complain against such narrow-minded xenophobic rulings ... But our mullahs sure don't.

By Arched Brows

---

21 December 2003

On the one hand the French say women should discard their veils and on the other, in Iran, they believe in forcing the veil on women throughout the world. They both batter us on the head with the

TEHRAN METRO, 2003

© Noushin Najafi www.noushin-photo.com

stick of Islam. Do we women ever tell you men what you can and
cannot wear?

Email: saba@eparizi.com
http://saba.eparizi.com

---

30 November 2003

A man who hits his wife or daughter on the head, saying 'Tighten
your headscarf and cover yourself up!' and that man who passes a
law to ban the headscarf are both pursuing their own ulterior
motives ... Freedom is the ability to choose ... in our case, a group
of men is forcing us to wear it and yet elsewhere they force you to
take it off!

Email: mmir82@hotmail.com
http://omgh.persianblog.com

Many commentators over the years have tried to explain Middle Eastern
society in purely black and white terms. However, most countries are full of cultural paradoxes and Iran is no exception. The Revolution's impact on women has
been entirely paradoxical, as it has both opened up new possibilities for them
and at the same time instituted the most repressive controls on their lives.

Prior to the Revolution many traditional families refused to send their daughters to university. They believed it would violate their Islamic way of life. In those
days, educated working women did not wear Islamic covering, but the majority
of women did, especially in the provinces. In 1936, when the Shah tried to make
it law that all women should cease to wear their veils he failed due to popular
outrage.

Paradoxically, the requirement that women wear Islamic covering may have
helped some of them to gain an education and emancipation, especially in
traditional families, as they did not need to go through a drastic cultural
makeover to enter the work force. Yet today Iran's young women have very
different aspirations to those of their mothers, especially if their mothers are

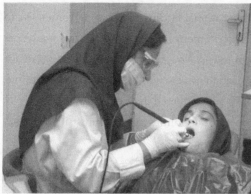

© Nafise Motlagh, www.nafisegallery.com

uneducated. Prior to the Islamic Revolution, the majority of women chose to cover their heads in public in some way. It is impossible to predict whether this will still be the case in 50 years time.

Yet as Elaine Sciolino has observed: 'Iran's women, being subtle and adaptable, came to think of the veil as something more complicated than just an imprisoning garment. For many women, the Islamic dress became a tool to be used to their advantage, a way into public spaces. It gave them the right to be present in public spaces – to work in offices, to attend college, to drive, to walk on the streets.'[4]

Women have been resilient and have worked within the system. As was reported in The Economist (16 October 2003): in Iran 'after a baby boom in the

1980s, family planning reduced the national fertility rate to two. Women live to 72, two years longer than men. In 1975, women's illiteracy in rural areas was 90 per cent and more than 45 per cent in towns. Now, the nationwide literacy rate for girls aged between 15 and 24 has risen to 97 per cent. Last year, for the first time, female students in state universities outnumbered male ones.'

Here is what Haleh Afshar, a professor of politics at York University, has to say on the subject:

> The rule of Islam in Iran has not been easy on women. They lost much of
> the ground that they had won over the previous century and the way to
> recapturing some of those rights has been slow and barred by prejudice
> and patriarchal power. Undaunted, Iranian women have struggled on. For
> the moment they have had to concede the veil and its imposition in the
> name of Islam, though they've done so reluctantly and have continued
> the discussions about its validity, relevance and the extent to which it
> should be imposed. But the bargain that they have struck has enabled
> them to negotiate better terms.
>
> They have managed to revert the discriminatory policies on education;
> they are vociferously attacking the inequalities in the labour market and
> demanding better care and welfare provisions for working mothers.
> Although the road to liberty is one that is strewn with difficulties, Iranian
> women, as ever, have come out fighting and have proved indomitable.[5]

Although they are discriminated against, Iranian women continue to play a considerable role in everyday life. However, this cannot be explained through recourse to the much-used western media paradigm of brave, heroic women subjugated by a post-9/11 caricature of a brutal Muslim male. Such blatant stereotypes merely encourage urbane readers to indulge in raw bigotry while at the same time shoring up a sense of personal decency.

Reading the intimate, on-line commentaries of Iranians, we are sometimes granted a rare glimpse of life beyond the crude stereotypes. The first of the posts below is written by a young man; the other is by a husband on his wedding anniversary.

22 February 2003

We want to say ... to say ... to finally say that we basically don't like you ... You want to make families fatherless and demand that our men die for you ...

You tell us that if we do something 'bad' we will burn in Hell ... you promise us maidens in heaven with everlasting happiness there. Well, we clearly don't understand any of this, and anyway we don't want to sleep next to the virtuous maidens in heaven that we don't personally know. It just doesn't seem right to lie down with an angel you're not properly acquainted with ... You want to incarcerate us inside these gardens with rivers of flowing honey. But we don't care much for honey – we prefer pizza ...

You say Father can get a second wife; but we don't ever want the familiar scent of our mums' beds to change ... You say Father is allowed to give Mum a beating once in a while; well, when we grow up we'll show you who needs a beating ...

When you say I am valued twice as much as my sister, you're essentially asking all of us men to be unchivalrous and we don't like it ... You say that my cousin – who I grew up with and who used to lay beside me while we listened to bedtime stories together – should suddenly hide her hair from me ...

You ask us to bow down to you and you want to rule us ... I ... I ... have a lot to say to you ... and will tell you sooner or later ... you will have no choice but to listen when the time is right.

By Antidepressant

1 January 2003

To my wife on our sixteenth wedding anniversary
We have struggled and yet we have survived ... we have been humiliated, but we have not lost our dignity ...

Do you remember when we were first married? We rented this

room in south Tehran and had to share a toilet with the landlord ...
There was no bathroom and we had to use a public baths ...

Do you remember that time, when we took all the money we had
and went to a posh restaurant uptown? We had a wonderful meal
and gave the rest of the money as a tip to the waiter ... we had no
money left for a taxi ... so we walked all the way home across the
whole town ... we had a lot of energy then ...

Do you remember the time our son was born ... through all
that bombing and war ... in that climate of death we built a new
life ... and the evening our daughter was born ... With two kids
and work, you still went to university and you were top of your
class ...

Do you remember getting war rations for dried milk – to prove
that you had no milk, you had to show your breasts to the 'sister' at
the Komiteh every week ... but we would not have that ... 'We'll
work overtime and buy dried milk on the open market ... But we're
not showing your breasts to anyone!'

I said all this stuff so you know that I haven't forgotten ... our
mutual troubles, growth and love can never be destroyed. We are
just starting ... with more energy than ever before ...

We will go forward to change a world that was unjust for our
children and make it a fairer place for our grandchildren.

shabah@shabah.org
http://www.shabah.org

---

14 November 2003

Dear Father, I miss you so very very much ...

I even miss your compulsive tidiness:

'Someone has been through my drawers. I can always tell even if
a single piece of paper has been moved by a tiny fraction ...'

I miss your stern side:

© Maziar Zand www.mzand.com

IRANIAN FATHER, HUSBAND AND SONS

'What is fear? Stop being so absurd! I have never taught my children fear.'

I miss your advice:

'Don't be too swayed by these boys at university, they fall in and out of love within a 24-hour period at that age.'

The way you spoiled us:

'Don't ever think that you have to put up with an impossible marriage. If it ever gets desperate, you come back to me.'

For always reciting the poetry of Hafez:*

'They closed the tavern door; O God, do not permit that they open the door of dishonour and deceit ...'

I miss you lending me your precious books:

'Why can't you read a book properly, have respect for the written word? I have never destroyed a book by reading it.'

I miss our political discussions:

'Darling, you have to vote ...'

'I will never vote under this regime.'

'Don't vote for their endorsed candidates, just vote so that they know you exist, but that you don't approve of them.'

'Fine, but I will cast a blank vote and I'm not voting for Khatami.'

Your love of Iran:

'It is impossible for me not to cry when I am reminded of Mossadegh** or ...'

Your love of sports:

'Get up you lazy kids! All the other kids are already out and about playing games and you lot are still asleep!'

I am grateful to you for teaching me to drive:

'Remember the way you drive represents your civility and character.'

For teaching me to speak English:

'You learn English at the same time as Farsi, otherwise you are illiterate ... From tomorrow we only speak English at home.'

I am eternally grateful for the times when you sat outside my exam hall and fell asleep in the car waiting for me to come out ... For rushing me to a doctor at my smallest discomfort ... For the books you used to give me, signed To my daughter ... For your good taste in clothes and actually going shopping with me ... For being such a gracious host ... For the face that always used to laugh, even if you had a world full of sorrow in your heart ... For all the sunny days when your laughter used to fill the house ...

I am sorry for the suffering that you never complained of ...

And for the dreams you had that became impossible overnight ...

* The Persian poet Hafez (1326–89). It has been said that most Iranian households keep at least two books: a copy of the Koran and the poetry of Hafez.
** The democratically elected Prime Minister of Iran, who was ousted in a US-British coup in 1953.

Email: afsoonkhanoom@yahoo.com

http://afsoon.blogspot.com

6 VIRTUAL MEDIA

DEFYING MEDIA CONTROL

Two decisive election victories (1997 and 2001) put Muhammed Khatami in office as president under the auspices of a reformist agenda – a staggering 85 per cent of the population voted for change. Unfortunately the reformers have been blocked every step of the way by Iran's hardliners who hold the real power through the judiciary and the Guardian Council. They demonstrated this power by vetoing Parliament through the Guardian Council, arresting many liberal and student activists and closing down reformist newspapers. Many of Iran's best journalists have spent time behind bars, from the respected investigative journalist Akbar Ganji to the ailing 74-year-old Siamak Pourzand.

Some 100 publications – including 41 daily newspapers – have been closed down since the 1995 Press Law came into being. This established a supervisory board and court with authority to impose various penalties, including closure and suspension of operating privileges. On 28 November 2000 an Iranian court banned the country's highest-circulation youth magazine, *Iran Javan*. In a feature on the cinema, the magazine had published a handful of bland photographs from a Hollywood blockbuster, which the court regarded as obscene.

In April 2000 alone, the judiciary banned 16 newspapers. But thanks to the

Photo © Hossein Derakhshan www.vagrantly.com

THE CARTOONIST ARVIN (DAVOUD AHMADI MOUNES)
WAS ARRESTED AT THE AGE OF 17 FOR DRAWING A
CARTOON WITH SLIGHT FEMINIST UNDERTONES. IT WAS
PUBLISHED IN ZAN (WOMAN) MAGAZINE AND AS A
RESULT ZAN WAS BANNED ON 8 MARCH 1999. MANY
OTHER PUBLICATIONS THAT HAVE PUBLISHED ARVIN'S
WORK – INCLUDING AKHBAR EGHTESAD, AZAD, EMROOZ
AND BAYAN – HAVE GONE THE SAME WAY.

Internet, many of the journalists cast out of Iran's mainstream media have started their own popular blogs, covering a range of areas from the cinema to the arts, as well as sport and, of course, politics.

In 1999 the conservative parliamentary speaker Ali Akbar Nateq-Nuri described the press in Iran as 'a gateway for cultural invasion'. Today there are tens of thousands of Iranian blogs, an alternative media that – for the moment at least – defies control and supervision by the authorities.

On his brief visit to Iran in 2004, the New York Times columnist Nicholas Kristof experienced first hand (albeit to a minor degree) the difficulties of being a journalist in Iran. After some clumsy harassment by the security forces, he was eventually detained and after one 90-minute detention it was even implied he was a spy. However, he noted that the regime's attempts to create a credible, effective police state were constantly undermined by its incompetence and lack of control over the flow of information. 'If it were an efficient police state, it might survive,' he concluded, 'but it's not.' He added that:

Photo © Hossein Derakhshan www.vagrantly.com

THE EDITORS OF THE MONTHLY *CAPPUCCINO* MAGAZINE, ONE OF
THE EARLIEST AND MOST PROFESSIONAL E-ZINES TO DEVELOP
OUT OF IRAN'S BLOGGING COMMUNITY. IN A COUNTRY WHERE
MOST PUBLICATIONS ARE SHUT DOWN THE MOMENT THEY
ARRIVE ON THE SCENE, *CAPPUCCINO* HAS NOW ENTERED ITS
THIRD YEAR OF PRODUCTION, PROVIDING IRANIANS WITH
CUTTING-EDGE COVERAGE OF THE ARTS, SCIENCES, POLITICS AND
TECHNOLOGY.

'The Iranian press is not as free as it was a few years ago, but it is now bolstered
by blogs (Web logs) and satellite TV, which offer real scrutiny of government
officials."

DIGITAL DEPICTIONS OF YOUTH CULTURE

The subject matter of many Iranian blogs might appear rather tame to Western
eyes, but most of them go well beyond the limits imposed by state censorship.
For instance, one Iranian blog is kept by 'Psychooo', a Marilyn Manson fan.
Another (www.whiteflag.persianblog.com) contains rock star biographies and
pop music trivia, while a blogger called 'One-heart' maintains Iran's only Celine
Dion fan club. 'Harrypotterfriends' contains news, trivia and reviews of the
Harry Potter novels and Persianwizards.com has everything Iranians might want
to know about the bespectacled wizard.

1 September 2003

Salaam to all witches and wizards!

**Write your own unique plotline for the eagerly awaited sixth Harry
Potter chronicle. Submissions should include:**

- Name or pseudonym, age and sex
- A title for your story
- A summary of your plotline – approximately 2,000 words – should
  be sent to iranhpbook6@yahoo.com

All entries will be posted on this blog soon.

http://iranhpbook6.persianblog.com

These blogs might appear somewhat superficial, but self-expression is a very rare
privilege in Iran. It seems that the regime's attempt to shield Iranians from the
West's 'cultural invasion' for a quarter of a century has backfired magnificently.
The country's youth is now almost obsessed with the Western culture they have
been deprived of for so long and its very illegality gives it an added cachet. For
some of them, Marilyn Manson, Celine Dion, Harry Potter, David Beckham, lipstick and Saint Valentine's Day are cherished symbols of freedom.

In September 2003, billboards in Tehran showed an advertisement for engine
oil featuring the head and shoulders of David Beckham, the English footballer.
They were hurriedly draped in black cloth, in what appeared to be a backlash
against 'Western cultural invasion'. So blogs such as 'David Beckham Love'
(www.davidbeckhamlove.persianblog.com) would undoubtedly be frowned upon
by the authorities. At present, however, Iran's David Beckham fans can freely
admire him and discuss him at length.

31 July 2003

Salaam, I am one unlucky guy … David has moved to Real Madrid
and I have to come to terms with it … I've been in complete denial,

but it's finalized … his family are happily settling down in Spain …
it's the End.

12 August 2003

The first ever game without Beckham and of course Manchester
United lost (I was seriously miserable) and look at the effect his
mere presence has had in Real Madrid … continuous successes …
    All I can say is that I hope 'our Ferguson' now realizes what we
have all known for a while that he has completely lost his mind!

Email: david_r_j_beckhamlove@yahoo.com
http://davidbeckhamlove.persianblog.com

MESSAGES IN BOTTLES

It may seem bizarre to an outsider that Iranian bloggers tirelessly post long and
detailed descriptions of films and laboriously type out by hand numerous
banned books. Those Westerners who read Lady Chatterley's Lover or smuggled,
hand-written texts of Tropic of Cancer when both books were still banned in the
West might be able to identify with Iran's bloggers. However, the ban in Iran does
not apply to just a handful of books. In a society with such strict guidelines and
censorship laws, the only place where Iranians can openly discuss such com-
monplace things as the latest Matrix movie or a new Brittney Spears album is an
anonymous blog.

    'Farsibookson-line' (www.farsibookson-line.blogspot.com), for instance, con-
tains hundreds of hand-typed and uncensored books ready to be downloaded. It
is as if there is an invisible conveyor belt taking anything that has been rejected
by the Ministry of Culture and releasing it in cyberspace. Banned material always
ends up on the Internet – and in Farsi. In the Iranian blogosphere you can even
download a copy of The Satanic Verses by Salman Rushdie, who was the subject of
a fatwa issued by the late Ayatollah Khomeini. You only need to go to
www.kaafar.com (kaafar means 'atheist').

Elsewhere, Iranian bloggers conduct on-line writing competitions judged by some of Iran's leading authors. Unfortunately there are no prizes and the winners are unlikely to get their work published in a country where prominent writers such as Abass Maroufi cannot always publish their own work in Iran due to strict censorship laws.

Maroufi is a member of Germany's PEN and in 2003 he was one of the judges of an on-line short-story competition. In 1996 he was sentenced to imprisonment and flogged because his literary magazine *Gardoon* had published articles critical of Iran's Islamic regime. He has written several books and plays and in 2003, when the censors at the Ministry of Culture asked him to make more than 200 changes to his latest, eagerly awaited novel, Maroufi refused. Instead he posted the entire manuscript of *Fereydoon Had Three Sons* on the Internet (www.fereydoon.malakut.org) for his fans to download. Maroufi has written about judging a writing competition in his blog.

---

23 November 2003

We are now down to 44 stories competing for the prize ...

We are writing on the pages of the Internet and casting to the waves ... messages in bottles ... a testament to the secrets of our hearts ... When human conduct, law and honour has crumbled ... other wheels are put in motion ...

They are writing stories; they are bearing witness to human life and hardships ... This is not the end ... the competition is just an excuse ... for them to write ... for us and you to write ... when we turn around and look back from a distance, we will eventually see how many trees were planted.

Email: abbasmaroufi@gmx.de

http://maroufi.malakut.org

July 2003

[By literary critic Seyed-Reza Shokrolahi]

Photo © Maziar Zand, www.mzand.com

It's true that our story writing skills – like many of our other endeavours – have not yet reached a level comparable with the literary output of many nations, and it's true that you can't swap the joy of reading the likes of Greene or Salinger with anything else ... and it's true that we may have to wait for many years for an Iranian novel worth reading ... But still there is no reason that we should look down on Iranian writers and that we should boast about actively ignoring them ... Iranian stories good or bad – reveal the misshapen and indistinct thoughts of modern Iranians. I'm not saying read everything published ... read them if only to improve your cursing ability at our own writers ...

- Iranian bestseller this month: Abass Maroufi, *Symphony of the Dead*
- Foreign translation bestseller: J. D. Salinger, *Raise High the Roof Beam, Carpenters and Seymour: An Introduction*.

Email: design@khabgard.com
http://www.khabgard.com

SALAAM CINEMA

After 25 years of strict, state-controlled censorship, a vast and resilient black market has evolved. Banned foreign CDs, videos and computer games are pirated and sold on the streets for a fraction of their price in the West. DVDs of the latest blockbusters from America are sold clandestinely all over the place and are often available in Iran long before they have their European premieres. And Iranian bloggers review these forbidden fruits of Western culture with a unique passion.

---

11 July 2003

On occasion something happens in life that makes you want to believe in miracles. Like today! Coming across a copy of Kieslowski's Three Colours Blue / White / Red among the videos at home – without anyone remembering having borrowed it from a friend ...

This was one of those majestic miracles that only a higher being can bestow on a special someone like me. Thank you God!

Email: pedram_kiano@yahoo.com
http://natoor.persianblog.com

---

18 November 2003

A group of generous people today have sent me 128 films ... Yes 128 ... I was initially sent the list of the 128 films that they have managed to download and I cannot believe that I'm still alive?! Films by:

Akira Kurosawa, François Truffaut, Ingmar Bergman, Kislovski, Bonnell, Martin Scorsese, Roman Polanski, Woody Allen, Stanley Kubrick ...

Shall I tell you more??? Are you still standing or have you fainted too?

I didn't tell you all this to induce mass fainting out there ... but to say that these good friends not only see the films themselves but also pass them on to whoever else is interested.

Email: arezou_mn@yahoo.com
http://goosband.persianblog.com

---

5 February 2004

I've just seen The House of Sand and Fog ... Congratulations to all Iranians for Shohreh Aghdashloo's nomination in the 2004 Academy Awards for Actress in the Best Supporting Role.

But as we are gathered in this unassuming virtual setting ... there are no foreigners around here and anyway if there were they couldn't understand us ... as a result we can be honest ... so let me be blunt ... The film was not that great ...

But I'm happy about her nomination, as it's especially good for Iran to be mentioned not in the usual context.

sepehr_blog@yahoo.ca
http://www.sepehrm.blogspot.com

---

1 November 2003

Tonight I saw Scanners and once again I applauded the great soul of David Cronenberg ... The first time I ever watched the film was with my dad on his Beta Max Sony 15 years ago.

In total fear and dread we had picked the film up from a friend of my dad's ... Worried that the Komiteh or the Hezbollah 'human peddlers' might catch us ...

Even when it came to watching it, we had the sound down really low, just in case our landlord might hear and report us to the Komiteh. Tonight I downloaded it from my computer and saw it without fear or worry!

blueman_blog@yahoo.co.uk
http://raincoat.blogspot.com

20 November 2003

I watched Mel Brooks's History of the World yesterday. Great film!
What a jester this Mel Brooks is ... As it began with Dom DeLuise's
parody of a Kubrick setting, you knew you were in for a treat ...
Thank you, Mr Brooks ...

In reply to some of you who asked where I get my films ... I
usually buy them for 4,000–5,000 tomans [$4–5] from Bazaar Reza ...

But I'm looking for someone reliable who can deliver films to
order ... know anyone good? Let me know ...

I know, I know ... I watch too many films and for a couple of
weeks now I keep meaning to start reading [the Persian translation]
of Virginia Woolf's To the Lighthouse ... but haven't had a chance ...
the end of term is fast approaching and I also have to keep
reminding myself I'm also a student.

22 November 2003

The Matrix Revolutions is truly a shambles ... a total freefall ... what
were the Wachowski Brothers thinking?! I could never have
imagined such a ridiculous and puerile ending to the trilogy ...
Halfway through I thought maybe I've bought Star Wars by
mistake and was falling asleep ... it was so incredibly
overdone ...

I also wanted to buy Finding Nemo ... but I've bought so many
films recently that I couldn't afford it ... I think I'll have to end up
selling my DVD player to pay for my spending habit!

Email: hamid@hamidreza.com
http://hamidreza.com

1 September 2003

It was the night before an important exam ... but my need to see a
good film won out. No one around to tell me I was sublimating. I

put my books away and dived towards the film cabinet and with a cartwheel picked up Paris, Texas.

The stunning cinematography and images created by Robby Muller always get me energized. But damn the existential saga and what it does to a fugitive from revision ... yet as I'm such a pathetic know-it-all, I tried to readdress the balance of that night's viewing ... I also watched Bergman's The Silence ... Good ending? No?

On the day of my exam, I spent the first 45 minutes just reading the questions ... was just getting my bearings ... as I hadn't slept the night before; I must have dozed off ... Travis was there staring at me from behind the glass, so I stared right back, and then Ester walked towards me and said: 'Poor Anna, hurry up and help him solve this equation.' Just as I had come to the answer, I raised my head and both my lecturer and the adjudicator were staring straight at me.

Email: marmoozim@yahoo.com

http://citizenkaveh.blogspot.com

---

14 August 2003

Tom Hanks does not play an Iranian

Nasseri is an Iranian exile who has actually been stranded at Paris Airport for 15 years. Inspired by his tale, Steven Spielberg has bought the rights to his life story as the basis for the new Tom Hanks vehicle, The Terminal. Catherine Zeta-Jones plays Hanks's love interest, a flight attendant (although the wretched Nasseri has had no such luck). But due to the way things are between Iran and the USA, the Nasseri character has been changed to an East European called Victor ...

I look forward to seeing the film, but I just find it so hard to swallow ... Are we so culturally repellent that even a director as skilled as Spielberg cannot portray an Iranian in a lead role? ...

He made the world face their nastiest fears of aliens and had us all fall in love with the grotesque ET ... but seemingly there is a limit to Mr Spielberg's talents; not even a Spielberg can show someone from the Middle East in a good light ... Still, it would have been great to see Tom Hanks playing an Iranian.

By The Friend

ELVIS, SCHUBERT AND CELINE DION

17 August 2002

Today is the 25th anniversary of Elvis's passing ... I have always liked him. Today, tens of thousands of his fans gather at Graceland to pay homage ... I hope that one day I will be able to visit Graceland.

Email: fiftypercentnormal@yahoo.com
http://www.goldoon.com

1 December 2003

A piece of sad news
Iran's Celine Dion fan club offers its condolences to the Dion family at their time of sorrow at the passing of Adhemar Dion.

Adhemar, the father and the elder of the Dion family, passed away after a period of illness, on Sunday morning, 30 November, at home. His wife and children were at his bedside.

Email: m.barvarz@gmail.com
http://one-heart.persianblog.com

6 September 2003

Music sometimes makes tolerable the endurance of our burdensome and hectic lives and invites us to remember the lost beauties of this world. For me it's works such as Beethoven's Symphonies 5, 6 & 9; Schubert's Symphonies 8 & 9, Trout Quintet;

Mozart's Symphony 40 and Requiem; Gustav Mahler's Symphony 3 & A Summer Morning's Dream; Franz Liszt's Rhapsodies ...

I don't want to write about myself; I don't. All I'll say is that I'm a coward and frightened. For this reason, I don't write about politics. I'm 32 and past getting melancholy and emotional about things. But I'm restless.

I don't want to whine ... but I'm tortured by the stupid stuff systematically offered to us by our media and publications.

By Salvation

---

7 January 2004

Marilyn Manson says: 'I was created to show the wickedness of people, as through my appearance I reveal the true face of humanity.' ... What about us? What do we reveal with our appearances?

Email: marylin_1985@yahoo.com
http://psychooo.persianblog.com

FORBIDDEN ICONS IN THE BLOGOSPHERE

In the Iranian blogosphere you can read a book, watch a film or even download a medley of international chart-topping hits or a bit of hip-hop or heavy metal. When Khomeini's regime came to power in Iran, it censored music. War songs or bland instrumentals were the only legal music. One of the most devastating edicts was the ban on women making music or performing. Only in 2002 were women granted permission to perform in concert halls – provided it was an all-female audience.

The ban on female performers cut short the careers of many Iranian singers, among them Googoosh, Iran's first lady of pop. She had grown up in the public eye, assisting her father in his act as a little girl and then becoming an Iranian pop diva. But all that ended when she was forbidden from performing in public.

Paradoxically, Googoosh's professional silence has added to her fame and she is a much-loved icon across the region. In 2004, for instance, Emomali Rakhmonov, the President of Iran's neighbouring country Tajikistan, announced that Googoosh's birthday would be an official national day of celebration.

GOOGOOSH IN THE 1960S (*LEFT*) AND THE 1970S AT THE HEIGHT OF HER FAME

Her music defined an era for Iranians in the same way as the Beatles did in the West. In 2002 in a BBC World Service poll of global musical tastes, 55 songs by the Beatles were selected, while Googoosh, who has been silenced for decades, had 40 songs in the list – one of them voted the most popular song in the Middle East.

She might have been silenced by the regime, but Googoosh is alive and well in the Iranian blogosphere, illegal downloads of her songs mingling with MTV chart-busters on Iranian computers. She has been silent for more than two decades. No stage appearances, no new recordings. Yet she has many new fans among the younger generation. They once listened to her songs on bootleg tape cassettes and can now hear them on-line.

In 2000 Googoosh finally left Iran. She has since given a series of sell-out concerts at more than 100,000 venues packed with Iranians living abroad. In one of her many interviews since leaving Iran, she recalled how, at a time when she was divorced and depressed in the early 1990s, she met one of Iran's leading filmmakers Massoud Kimiaei. Today he is her husband. On their first date he took her to a private recording studio in Tehran. After years of silence, she put on her headphones and did what the regime had categorically forbidden her to do. Behind the closed doors of a private recording studio, she sang.

---

2 August 2001

Hossein Derakshan

When we were in Iran, Googoosh was there too, but she couldn't sing. And then we came abroad, and she left soon after and now we are both away from home – but she can sing and we can hear her ... The 12,000-capacity venue was three-quarters full ... Everyone was so excited when Googoosh came on, they screamed and whistled. She was really emotional and her hands were shaking. Anyway, she began to sing ... people sang along, danced and also cried once in a while ...

She finished her show in Toronto with the song 'If my work is done' ... tearful, with a trembling voice and eyes blackened with her mascara running down her face. When it finished she left the stage before her musicians ... Perhaps she left so that she could cry behind the scenes. As if she really thinks her work is done.

Personally, without any hesitation, I would say to her: That's just wishful thinking ... We've only just found you again after 20 years.

Email: hoder@hoder.com
http://i.hoder.com

---

5 May 2004

A few weeks ago I was watching a Googoosh interview on one of the overseas satellite channels ... She was talking about her latest album due for release on 15 April ... The 15th was some way off then ... The next day I'm doing a bit of shopping on Naderi Street in Ahvaz [Southern Iran] ... when – totally dumbfounded – I suddenly see the latest Googoosh album on sale ...

Then again, just before the Oscar ceremonies, I got hold of a copy of The House of Sand and Fog ... it was visibly marked and subtitled as a tape for 'Academy Award voters' ...

Now the fact that Iran doesn't adhere to any international copyright laws coupled with the fact that under the current state censorship we can't legitimately have access to such material anyway ... Iran has become a pirate's paradise.

Getting back to Googoosh, though, they say that a few years back a Tajik official in a diplomatic session had asked his Iranian counterpart if it was possible to meet the lady in question. The Tajiks just like us, are crazy about her. But when this 50-something woman sings, she sings of our essence.

Email: masoome@gmail.com
http://naseria.blogspot.com

Googoosh was only recently able to leave Iran, but many other musicians and artists condemned as 'corrupt degenerates' by Khomeini left straight after the Revolution. The production of Iranian pop music moved from Tehran to Los Angeles, where it thrives today. Despite the ban on such music in Iran, bootlegged tapes and CDs are widely heard in the country and a recent newspaper report claimed that every album produced in Los Angeles sells three or four million underground copies in Iran.

REVOLUTIONARY POP

Unable to control this black market in pop music and in an attempt to pacify the restless younger generation, Iran's hardline clerics have given their blessing to a particular kind of homegrown music. Despite brutal clampdowns on writers, intellectuals, journalists and pro-democracy activists, they have permitted a kind of tame 'revolutionary pop'.

After railing against the dilution of Islamic principles and warning of a foreign cultural invasion, the unelected ruling clergy have actually allowed Iran's state-run radio and television to broadcast 'revolutionary pop'. However, this newfound largess and concern for fostering new talent does not apply to all artists.

IRANIAN POP SENSATION *OHUM* IN CONCERT, TEHRAN 2004

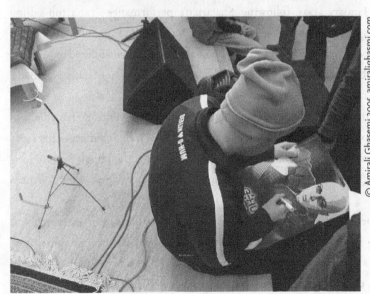

SHAHRAM, VOCALIST AND LEAD GUITARIST WITH *OHUM* SIGNING A CONCERT POSTER FOR A FAN

The Songbird of Dawn

Muhammad-Reza Shajarian is Iran's most renowned classical vocalist and received UNESCO's Picasso Award (1999) in recognition of his outstanding contribution to the arts. More recently his album *Without You* was nominated for the Grammy Award in 2004. Shajarian lives in Iran and teaches at Tehran University's Department of Fine Arts, yet his songs are not allowed to be broadcast on the state-run radio or television. Although little known outside Iran, to Iranians Shajarian is an icon, keeping alive a style of music that was headed for extinction after the Revolution. Now in his sixties, he performs regularly throughout the world, but rarely gives concerts in Iran.

In January 2004 he made a rare public announcement that he would give a fundraising performance in Iran for the people of Bam, who had suffered a devastating earthquake. He was offered a 3,000-capacity venue by the State. There was a mad rush for tickets, people queuing overnight for the chance to see one of the three scheduled shows. Although the average price of concert tickets was about 90,000 rials (about $10), the BBC Persian Service reported that tickets were being touted on the black market for a record 1,500,000 rials (about $172).

On 21 January 2004, following Shajarian's performance, Iran's top-selling *Sharg* newspaper reported that his equipment and the instruments of his musicians had been impounded. The state-owned venue had been offered to him free of charge, but a subsequent request for an immediate payment had been made. The price tag was about $40,000!

Shajarian might have been excluded from the state-controlled media, but Iranian bloggers can still listen to his music on the Web and discuss his every move. After *Sharg* broke the story of the $40,000 sting, the popular group blog *Sobhaneh* (Breakfast) wearily commented that 'Once again they torment Shajarian.'

Many believe the singer chooses symbolic lyrics that can be interpreted as criticizing the current regime. In addition to classical Persian songs, he often sings lyrics written by dissident poets. The authorities had been outraged that at his charity concert he had performed 'Morgeh Sahar' ('The Bird of Dawn'), written in 1906 by the pro-democracy constitutionalist Malek-o-Sho'ara Bahar. This

© Mehrdad Oskouei,
Iranian Art Quarterly www.tavoosmag.com

MUHAMMAD-REZA SHAJARIAN

famous anthem of the pro-democracy constitutionalists is frequently sung at student demonstrations and sums up Iran's 100-year history of struggle for democracy.

> Bird of dawn, cry out,
> Refresh my pains,
> Break this cage,
> Bring forth a transformation!
> My tangled-wing nightingale,
> Break out of this cage!
> Chant the anthem for the freedom of humanity
> With every breath for the soil of this land and its inhabitants ...
> The tyranny of the tyrants ...
> Who have relinquished our home to the winds.
> O God! O Universe! O Nature!
> Make our darkest night dawn.

---

17 January 2004

I wanted to write a few words about the Shajarian concert last night

... But I'll just tell you about the euphoria and exhilaration of the audience during the performance of 'The Bird of Dawn' ... That's all!

Email: black_mak82@yahoo.com
http://blackmak.blogspot.com

17 January 2004

The voice that embodies this land's pride

For many years Master Shajarian has not performed in Iran. Yet he has broken his silence for the memory of the people of Bam ... Notable was his performance of 'The Bird of Dawn', to which a thrilled crowd sang along ... People raised their hands above their heads and within seconds, in one voice, the whole auditorium accompanied the Master. Yet among all those voices his could still be heard.

Is it not extraordinary that this nation still expresses its pains with the songs of the Constitutional Revolution?

As Ms Parsi has said: 'If one day researchers had to write about our social history during the last 25 years, one indicator of the condition of people who lived during this time, would be Shajarian's body of work. As he has always sung about and for the people.'

Email: mohammad_ariai@hotmail.com
http://deltang25.blogspot.com

30 January 2004

Muhammad-Reza Shajarian after so many years sang for and because of the people. And what singing! Again Shajarian sang 'The Bird of Dawn' at the end of his concert ... How that song embodies our life!

http://darvishkhaan.persianblog.com

Putting On a Show

Just as blogs allow people to discuss the corrupt music, cinema and literature of the West, there are many others that deal with the arts. Blogs such as 'newday' (www.newday.persianblog.com), which is dedicated to art and architecture, or 'honaremoaser' (www.honaremoaser.persianblog.com), which is devoted to contemporary art and features analyses and biographies of Western artists like

© Nima Kiann
www.balletspersans.org

Roudaki (Vahdat) Concert Hall, 1970s Iran

Picasso, Gustav Klimt, Andy Warhol and Damien Hirst. Another blog (www.pardeh-namayesh.persianblog.com) is kept by a theatre critic and includes reviews and recommendations of recent plays.

---

9 February 2004

I remember during a film festival queuing with a friend from nine in the morning until eleven at night to see a rare showing of Bizaei's Dog Killings.

In the end everyone pushed in, and even though we were the first to arrive, we were forced to sit right in the front ... but it was all worth it, just to see the great master at work.

Email: sepehr_blog@yahoo.ca
http://www.sepehrm.blogspot.com

Bizaei is considered by some in Iran as a member of the vanguard of Iranian cinema and theatre – yet his work ordinarily does not see the light of day and many have been banned. Unlike many of his junior contemporaries within

Iranian cinema that are recognised outside Iran, he adamantly refuses to compromise his work by giving in to the censors. Even so restrictions come in different forms and practices as this veteran director was recently only permitted the use of 'hall 4' in one of Tehran's largest theatres; a small room usually allocated to new up and coming talents. Alluding to the snub, Bizaei told the Iranian Students News Agency (ISNA), to evade the censors 'for many years … I have been trying to write a play that can be performed in a small private room, at home'.

---

19 October 2003

It's going to be a quiet week, yet this week's theatre
recommendations are:
- The End of the Line – Shadow Theatre
- Molière's, The Misanthrope starring Abolfazl Pour'arab –
  Vahdat Hall
- Bahram Bizaei's The One Thousand and First Night – Shahr Theatre,
  Hall 4

Email: donya_ye_theater@yahoo.com
http://pardeh-namayesh.persianblog.com

© Mehrdad Oskouei Tavoos, Iranian Art Quarterly www.tavoosmag.com

BAHRAM BIZAEI

Staging Molière in the Islamic Republic of Iran may conjure up bizarre images for some, but it is not unheard of. In 1851 plays by Molière and many other Western writers were performed in the theatres of the Dar ul Fonoun in Tabriz, Iran.

In *Translation Movements in Iran* (2000), Massoume Price describes a tradition dating back to the second millennium BC.

> In Seleucid, Parthian and Sassanian time Greek plays were translated and performed and Greek philosophy and science were well known by the Iranian scholars. Iranian artists participated and performed at the major art festivals in Rome, India, Alexandria in Egypt and Byzantium in cultural centres such as Constantinople. Such cultural exchanges created an international class of artists, intellectuals and performers well versed in a number of languages and traditions.

© Mas'oud Pakdel, Tavoos, Iranian Art Quarterly
www.tavoosmag.com

MOJDEH SHAMSAI STARRING IN *THE ONE THOUSAND AND FIRST NIGHT* (2003), A PRODUCTION BY THE VETERAN THEATRE DIRECTOR BIZAEI

The Fajr Theatre Festival met with a chorus of outrage from the state-controlled media because the actors were dressed in Iranian tribal costumes. As we have seen, Iran's tribal women tend not to comply with the regime's strict dress codes and freely expose their hair in plaits. In an attempt to comply with the regime's guideline for theatrical performances, the actresses wore false plaits, but the state media still worked itself up into an hysterical frenzy over this 'depraved performance'.

THE FAJR THEATRE FESTIVAL IN IRAN (2003)

For centuries Iranian artists have combined modern features with elements taken from Iran's 5,000-year-old cultural heritage. It's a rich and complex artistic legacy that includes painting, textiles, metalwork, ceramics, poetry, calligraphy, architecture and more recently cinema.

Although the regime tries to exclude from Iranian society anything that runs counter to its own political agenda there are many paradoxical legacies from the past, such as Tehran's Museum of Contemporary Art, which was founded by the former Queen Farah Diba. It holds a vast collection of art, including works by Pissarro, Whistler, Rodin, Monet, Van Gogh, Toulouse-Lautrec, Kandinsky, Matisse, Picasso, Giacometti, Dali, Francis Bacon and Warhol, among many others. Some of these artists were banned as 'degenerate' by the Nazis and their work was also consigned to storage after the Revolution in 1979, because they were deemed 'offensive'.

The same can also be said for Iranian filmmakers, although they must get permission from the Government to make films. And despite the international success of Iranian cinema in recent years, many prize-winning films – such as

© Nima Kiann www.balletspersans.org

IRANIAN BALLET STARS OF THE 1970S IN A PERFORMANCE OF THE
ANCIENT PERSIAN LOVE STORY *BIJAN AND MANIJEH*

Jafar Panahi's *The Circle*, which won the Golden Lion at the Venice Film Festival and the Freedom of Expression Prize at the Sundance Film Festival – are never publicly shown in Iran.

Iranian artists have both very ancient and entirely modern cultural legacies to draw from and despite the obvious state restrictions there are still many contemporary artists active in Iran.

In May 2004 the award-winning director Mohsen Makhmalbaf complained that in recent years 'the productions of Mohsen Makhmalbaf and the Makhmalbaf Film House have faced the problem of inadequate screening, a kind of hidden censorship ... Many of these films are either prevented from being shown or are shown in a couple of cinemas for a short time and disappear before anyone finds out about them'. He was also angry that Iran's Ministry of Culture and Islamic Guidance had refused to allow him to shoot his latest script, *Amnesia*. It took him years to write, he said, and 'reflects two decades of the pain and suffering of the Iranian people'. It is not surprising the authorities rejected it.

And yet, despite the massive restrictions placed upon them by the regime, a small band of tireless individuals still manage to get their films made, create

Photo of Farah Diba courtesy of Darius Kadivar

Photo © Maziar Zand www.mzand.com

FARAH DIBA, THE FORMER QUEEN OF IRAN, AS AN ART
STUDENT IN PARIS IN THE 1950S. ONE OF HER FORMER
HOMES IS TODAY THE NIAVARAN MUSEUM.

works of art, give concerts and organize art exhibitions – like the Conceptual Art
Exhibition at the Niavaran Museum in September 2003 or an exhibition of
British art at the Tehran Museum of Contemporary Art in February 2004, which
included Damien Hirst's never-before-seen *Resurrection* and works by Gilbert
and George and Henry Moore. The organizers even managed to sneak in the Brit
Art of the Iranian-born sculptor Shirazeh Houshiary, which incorporates
ancient Jewish, Christian and Buddhist chants.

He/She/Ou at the Niavaran Museum (2003)
'Ou' is a Persian word meaning 'he' or 'she'. The exhibit consisted of Guita Aslani's paintings and her live choreographed theatrical models. The film and photography for the show were by Hamid Jafari and the music by Ali Shahrashoub.

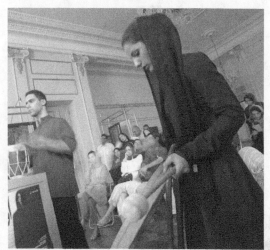

LEFT, ARTIST GUITA ASLANI

7 SPREADING THE NEWS

'Weblogs – personal or collective websites where people comment on current events – are a new and promising development which is having a big impact on society,' said the international organization Reporters Sans Frontières. 'Weblogs are much used at times of crisis, such as during the June 2003 student demonstrations, when they were the main source of news about the protests and helped the students to rally and organize."

Iran's urban university students have tried on and off to demonstrate for political change in Iran since 1999. During recent student demonstrations many blogs functioned as notice boards telling people where and when to join the demonstrations and including follow-up news and photographs, with some student activists writing daily reports.

---

12 December 2002

A remarkable thing about the Saturday demonstrations was the behaviour of the female students and some of the older women who joined us ... The girls were less cautious than the boys ... for instance, after we lined up in front of the university gates, the girls always started the chants ... Also the few who actually stood up to

the Basij were women in their forties. They had this air of authority
about them and carried considerable clout among the other
demonstrators ...

But if I'm honest it was a bit awkward. There I was anxious that I
may end up in a prison cell or breathing in tear gas ... yet every time
I lit a cigarette a couple of the older women protesters gave me
dirty looks ... (It was like having your mum or your aunts around ...
I was polluting the air and my body, you see!).

By Metal

Masoud Behnoud has been a leading author, journalist and social commentator
in Iran for four decades. He has maintained his integrity under two autocratic
regimes, which has led to prison sentences and more recently to his exile. Today
he works for the BBC and is one of the most prominent Iranian bloggers at
www.behnoudonline.com.

He likens the growing use of the Internet in Iran to the 'cassette-tape campaign' mounted by Khomeini to overthrow the monarchy. The Shah had controlled the country's media and assumed that the exiled Khomeini would not be
able to reach the Iranian people. Yet in exile Khomeini received many Iranian
visitors and sent home taped cassettes of his sermons to be peddled around
town. In these tapes he promised an end to the corrupt tyrannical monarchy and
a utopian Islamic state where the country's oil revenues would pay for 'free electricity, water, buses' and 'free land for all that needed it'. All political parties
would be free, too, so 'no political prisoners would exist in an Islamic state'.
Moreover, 'prisons would be turned into museums'. In fact, Khomeini made all
kinds of promises: free elections, freedom of the press, a new status for women,
etc., etc. He managed to turn the common tape cassette into a vast communication network and the stuff of revolution.

Behnoud believes that most of Iran's opposition has been driven underground to plot what he calls an 'Internet Revolution'. Through the Internet
'Iranian intellectuals who have been subjugated by the state secret service since
the start of the Islamic Republic ... are experiencing unparalleled unity.' While

Photo © Hossein Derakhshan   www.vagrantly.com

Masoud Behnoud (*in light-coloured jumper*) with Shamsolvaezin as guest speakers at the University of Toronto in 2004. Shamsolvaezin was the editor of a number of outspoken daily newspapers that were closed down by the judiciary.

the state-controlled media churns out the same old propaganda, with most of Iran's leading journalists silenced or behind bars, 'Internet sites and weblogs by dissident Iranian youths are independently shouldering the entire mission of a public media network and resistance against the conservative clergy.'

Covering a Natural Disaster

According to official estimates, on 26 December 2003 more than 30,000 people died during an earthquake measuring 6.7 on the Richter scale in Iran's ancient city of Bam. In the aftermath of the disaster Iranian bloggers tried to come to terms with this national disaster, their on-line commentaries offering a more intimate and honest assessment than the state-run media.

Some bloggers were immediately affected by the quake. Dr Marajn Haj-Ahmadi, for instance, was based in the provincial capital town of Kerman, which borders Bam. In the aftermath of the disaster her blog was one of the most read, along with 'Baba' (www.baba.eparizi) an anonymous blogger who only tells us that he is a 30-something ex-newspaper journalist who was made redundant when his newspaper was closed down. His personal motto is 'The people have a right to know.' This mystery journalist dispatched himself to the disaster region, posting his inimitable reports exclusively for Iran's virtual community.

26 December 2003

It's four days since the disaster, but still many streets and old neighbourhoods have been shut off by the quake and have seen nothing of any rescue workers ...

Without a doubt the most loved creatures of Bam in this period are the rescue dogs ... their muzzles are covered in blood and dust due to their ceaseless efforts, but their barks bring hope and the possibility of recovering someone alive ... If I hadn't heard with my own ears the incessant prayers being said for these dogs, I wouldn't have believed it ... I heard someone say: 'May they one day be rewarded by God.' ... But in one of the most developed areas of Bam – the graveyard – I found an angry man sobbing and saying: 'If only "They" had trained more rescue dogs instead of training all these **** we wouldn't have to suffer so much.'*

* After a similar earthquake in 1990, the Iranian regime turned down many offers of outside help and denounced sniffer dogs as 'unclean'.

Email: baba@eparizi.com
http://baba.eparizi.com

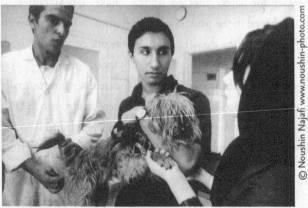

A VISIT TO THE VETS, TEHRAN (2003)

28 December 2003

[by Marjan Haj-Ahmadi, Kerman]

Condition Red

The hospital is swarming with personnel ... they bring groups of 50 injured at a time from the airport ... All the hospital beds are full ... We have even put patients on mattresses on the floor ... in every cubic metre there is a patient ... To examine them you first have to clean off the dust ... Internal bleeding, broken hips, backs and ribs ... yet eerily no one complains of pain ... It's as if they want to suffer in silence ...

'I saw myself going under the rubble' – 'I had twins' – 'She died in my arms' – 'I had six children' – 'Let me go back to Bam. My children are under the rubble. Perhaps they are still alive. I have to go and tell them where to look. If I don't go, who will get my children?' – 'I saw my sister go under the wall, there's no way she's alive.'

In Radiology patients are waiting on stretchers in queues ... medical students, even the dentists at the hospital are carrying stretchers. Not a single patient has any relatives with them ... So many members of their families have died that instead of reminding them of the dead we ask if anyone they know has lived ...

We send the injured to the wards quickly to make room for new patients ... so many are on the floor in the hall and even the prayer rooms are full of patients ... The operating theatres have been in use non-stop ... We keep going back and examining patients but among all these people it's easy to miss a few ... Casualty smells like dust ... the dust of Bam ... A town that no longer exists ...

The first day I was really strong, but now I can't control myself and my eyes well up as I examine each patient and hear their stories ... some of the staff are in even worse shape ... We're all losing it ... Some of my colleagues had family in Bam; others have worked in Bam ... right now we can only account for one doctor in Bam who

has survived and so many have died ... Our youngest patient is a
newborn, probably 20 days old. They dug out mother and chlld
together, thankfully both alive, with the baby still suckling on his
mother's breast ...

Last night they brought in an eight-month-old baby and he just
laughs all the time ... and you look at the baby and you're reminded
that life must go on ...

---

27 December 2003

Someone was rocking my bed ... I put my head under the covers
and realized that now the room was shaking ... The windows were
shaking ... A roaring sound, as if a gigantic truck was going past ...
My mother was shouting from downstairs: 'Marjan! Get up, it's an
earthquake!'

I got up and another tremor came on ... I wanted to get to the
door but I was thrown to the wall ... My father comes in and says:
'These are aftershocks.' Mother frantically says, 'What if they're
"before shocks"?'

By the time Muhammad opened the locks the ground was still
shaking ... When we got outside it had all stopped, but it was so
cold we eventually went back in again ... Mother said we should all
sleep in the same room, but we ignored her and all went back to our
own beds.

But Mother sat up all night ... In Kerman we have got used to
earthquakes, we get a few mild tremors every year ... all I can say is
that we were lucky this time, but Bam ...

Email: hajahmadimarjan@yahoo.com
http://saltdesert.persianblog.com

A RESCUED EARTHQUAKE SURVIVOR, IRAN

4 January 2004

I have not been able to sleep for the last ten days. Not since the
night when Bam shook and took 30,000 dreams under the rubble. I
make sure my son sleeps next to me ... I want to be his shield when
this ruin crashes on his head in this backward world of ours ...

I am worried that sleep will engulf me ... and the dust will
swallow up my son.

Here in this forgotten corner of the world ... lost in this third
millennium, I am worried about the crumbling ruins collapsing on
my only child's head ...

Not far away in the civilized world, people would laugh at my
deepest fears ... No rubble will disturb their dreams ... I can hear
them snoring.

Email: mitrajournal@yahoo.com
http://zane-azad.blogspot.com

27 December 2003

I look at my wife ... We have been married 17 years ... she has a generous heart not unlike water and eyes that are directly connected to her heart ...

Today Ali and Leila took their end-of-term exams ... they are both huddled in front of the TV. Perhaps they are wondering how the kids in Bam did in their exams ...

I ask her to look around for what we can donate. With all the bills to pay we will have 25,000 tomans [about $28] left this month ... In the evening I go to one of the collection points with some goods and 20,000 tomans [$22] ... While there I whisper, 'God, I have no expectations of you ... but when an earthquake strikes ... let me die before my wife and children.'

Email: ejavadi2002@yahoo.com
http://nokteha.persianblog.com

A Test of 'Divine Grace'

In the aftermath of the earthquake in Bam, the state-controlled media constantly repeated the message that such disasters were 'inevitable' and there was little to be done from preventing them. They even went so far as to say that an earthquake is a test of 'divine grace'. Meanwhile, numerous bloggers took to cyberspace to vent their fury, angry at the backwardness of Bam and an overall lack of development in their oil-rich country. Why had their rulers failed to adopt the sort of safety measures that are common in other earthquake-prone countries? A similar earthquake in California a month before had resulted in just three casualties, while in Iran a whole town had disappeared.

22 January 2004

The whole of our blog community is screaming in one voice that
the regime is directly responsible because it has done nothing all
these years except get involved in racketeering.

Email: viraneh2002@yahoo.com
http://viran.blogspot.com

© Copyright Nafise Motlagh
www.nafisegallery.com

TRAGIC AFTERMATH

28 December 2003

Even though Iran is an earthquake-prone country what have those
in charge done?

Our country doesn't even have a few sniffer dogs to locate
people under the rubble! All they can do is conduct the prayers
during funerals.

The earthquake was not a tragedy; our useless rulers are the
tragedy.

By Ordinary

TRAGIC AFTERMATH

---

11 January 2004

The earthquake of oppression and dictatorship
California and Iran are both earthquake-prone areas ... In California
three people died and in Bam nearly 50,000 died.

Doesn't this point the finger at this regime of thieves and
racketeers? Life will continue in Bam.

But for how long are the people of Iran to endure the political
quakes of oppression?

Email: gashtal@hotmail.com
http://siprisk.blogspot.com

---

30 December 2003

I wanted to put my hand into the TV and force the man talking
about the Grace of God to tell people instead how to make stronger
buildings – and what precautions to take before during and after a
natural diaster.

The guy next to him I wanted to strangle, as he rambled on in a
soothing voice and a smug smile! As if it had rained gold on Bam.

At least 'may God bless the ancestors' of the BBC for their
coverage.

Email: rere_reera@yahoo.com
http://abovethewall.blogspot.com

---

10 January 2004

These days all roads lead to the historical city of Bam. Wherever I
look there is such unity and generosity among ordinary people.
Some of them don't have much to spare themselves ... But no news
of donations from the offspring of the clergy who suck the blood of
our nation ...

The earthquake was a tragic thing, but more tragic has been its aftermath. When you see that two student halls of residences, a nursery, hospitals, and even most government offices built in recent years have been destroyed ... What other explanation is there ... that they did not even take into account ordinary building regulations when it came to these buildings ... They spent as little as possible so that they could carry on filling their own pockets.

By Star

Discontent at the regime's inadequate preparation for a national disaster and its inability to cope afterwards was not confined to the blogosphere. On 4 March 2004 Iran's daily *Shargh* reported that the surviving residents of Bam had rioted in protest at their awful living conditions more than two months after the quake. Iran's Fars news agency quoted Bam's Friday prayer leader, Asghar Asghari, as saying that two people had been wounded by bullets fired into the crowd. These incidences were followed by the resignation of Ali Shafie, the governor-general of Bam, after the quake survivors and their families accused him of holding up the distribution of foreign aid in the region.

Two months after the disaster, either through bureaucratic chaos or state corruption – or perhaps a combination of the two – officials at the Iranian Red Crescent announced that they had only received about $2 million out of the $12 million donated to them for relief assistance. Almost $10 million held by organs of the regimes could not be accounted for or even located.

The head of the Iranian Red Crescent, Ahmad-Ali Nourbala, said there was evidence that international groups had sent more than $11.8 million in aid, but his organization had seen only $1.9 million of it. Meanwhile the Iranian government had not given the Red Crescent the amount they were promised. In the reformist newspaper *Hambastegi* Nourbala predicted that 'their failure to give a clear answer would lead to national distrust and international disgrace'.

Wary of watchful eyes, in May 2004 the Iranian government expelled Dan De Luce, the *Guardian*'s correspondent in Tehran, for making an unauthorized visit to Bam. Luce had written an article (published in the *Guardian* on 2 April 2004) in which he reported that the earthquake survivors were critical of the Government's reconstruction effort.

Iranians are painfully aware that living under an oppressive ideological state affects every aspect of their lives – from shelter to food and education and medical treatment. Because the leaders of the regime are not accountable to the people, there is much scope for corruption. On 20 January 2004 Abbass Maroufi, one of Iran's leading writers, sent an open letter to the heads of the Iranian government:

> In the aftermath of the Bam earthquake, the Russian rescuers were there
> before you. One earthquake has shown us that you men in high office are
> adept at oppressing thousands of people, but you can't even send four
> rescuers.

Bahram Akasheh, a professor of geophysics at Tehran University, told Reuters (29 December 2003) that a quake as strong as the one that destroyed Bam could damage or destroy 80 per cent of the buildings in Tehran – the capital with 10 million inhabitants. 'The building codes are almost universally ignored in Iran,' he said, 'and Tehran is especially vulnerable to quakes because there is a major fault line running across it.'

In Bam buildings that had existed for centuries have vanished. Iranian houses are known for their walled gardens planted with almond trees, pomegranates, damask roses and featuring turquoise tiled pools – referred to by Iranians as *pairi diz* (literally, 'around wall'). The *pairi diz* that made its way into English as 'paradise'. Today, however, these too are disappearing. They are replaced by high-rise tower blocks, thanks to property developers doing deals with unscrupulous construction companies and corrupt government officials. The result is that they put up substandard death-traps.

Organizing Action

In the absence of a democratic political system, many Iranians have turned to non-governmental organizations (NGOs) as the only way to fight for social

Tehran, Iran (2002) Photo © Hamed Banaei
www.hamedbanaei.com

THE DERELICT GATES OF PARADISE
A COMMON SIGHT IN IRANIAN TOWNS: BEAUTIFUL OLD HOMES
WAITING TO BE DEMOLISHED AND REPLACED BY DANGEROUS
SOVIET-STYLE TOWER BLOCKS

change. Today there are more than 8,000 NGOs operating in Iran. According to experts they are being formed with or without official permission to deal with on-going problems such as environmental and child-welfare issues, drug addiction and homelessness. Many workers and students are turning to NGOs as the only way to fight for social change. It is a massive phenomenon in Iran that may conceivably prove a serious challenge to the regime.

As Hooshang Amirahmadi, professor and director of the Centre for Middle East Studies at Rutgers University has pointed out: 'The Bam tragedy marked a turning point when there was an obvious break between the State and the NGOs. The legitimacy of the State has sharply declined due to its inefficiency and lack of accountability.'[2]

Nevertheless, ordinary Iranians responded to the disaster by piling up food and clothes at collection points across the country. Bloggers like 'Shineh' (www.shineh.com/zelzele) got involved in a variety of NGOs organizing their own collection points and the transportation of aid in many parts of Iran. They were sometimes able to notify their fellow bloggers of the whereabouts of survivors relocated to hospitals in urban centres. They organized hospital visits, charity sales and recruited volunteers ready to help in Bam.

4 January 2004

On Friday bloggers in Mashad went to visit survivors of the Bam earthquake who have recently been brought here ...

FRIDAY, 2 P.M., OUTSIDE IMAM REZA HOSPITAL

Photo © Arman Anzanpour

Email: viraf@ardaviraf.com
http://ardaviraf.com

30 December 2003

At the hospital we kept asking the patients if they needed anything we could get them ... Most of them just politely refused, saying 'No thank you' ... but there was a young girl who looked jaundiced with long waist-length tangled hair ... the only thing she wanted was a hairbrush for her dusty hair.

Email: Email: arezou_mn@yahoo.com
http://www.goosband.persianblog.com

15 January 2004

Bloggers' Charity Sale
Friday, 16 January 2004
9 a.m. til 8 p.m.
Parvaresh Fekri Art centre
Bolvar kehavarz, Hejab Street

Performance of live music by young artists
Joining us during the day will be a number of celebrities and sport personalities. Charity Sale in addition to blog-keeping multimedia lessons

Email: reza_ag61@yahoo.com
http://ttarane.blogspot.com

INTERNATIONAL RESCUE

In the aftermath of the quake, aid and rescue missions were dispatched from nearly 30 countries – including the United States, the Islamic Republic's Great Satan. (In a similar earthquake in 1990, the Iranian regime turned down many offers of outside help and the clergy denounced sniffer dogs as 'unclean'.) Yet despite all the international help, during his trip to the area the Supreme Leader of Iran made no reference to the mainly Western countries that had rushed to Iran's aid. Speaking at Friday prayers, Ayatollah Ahmad Jannati, the head of the powerful Council of Guardians, accused the Americans of trying to use the earthquake to seek relations with Iran:

Our answer is to slap you in the face and to say that for the worthless aid you sent we cannot forget our problems with you and extend the hand of friendship and open relations ... If you're so full of compassion, why don't you go and help the Palestinians, whose earthquake you created?

In sharp contrast to this official rebuff, the blogging community – prompted by Hossein Derakhshan – organized a Thank You note for the aid workers. It was signed by hundreds of bloggers within hours.

---

7 January 2004

[by Pedram Moallemian]

Inspired by Hossein Derakhshan, this is a note to thank all those teams currently leaving Iran after participating in the rescue and relief efforts in Bam. If you wish, please use the comments section to add your own short message of thanks.

To all rescuers, volunteers and others who travelled from around the globe to take part in the rescue and relief effort in Bam, Iran.

Thank You!

At a time when our people were in dire need, your presence was a beacon of hope that proved to them they are not alone.

You proved the words of the Persian poet Saadi, who said:

The sons of Adam are limbs of one another,
Having been created from one essence ...
When the calamity of time affects one limb,
The other limbs cannot remain at rest.

We thank you for your efforts and will never forget your sacrifices.
Thank you!

Email: pedram@eyeranian.net
http://www.eyeranian.net

---

30 December 2003

They have all come! Americans, Serbs(!), Turks, the Swiss and
Iranians – shoulder to shoulder with the people of Bam (even
though our TV networks do not show us this).

Why is it that some people willingly abandon their Christmas
and come to help others they have never met and are never likely to
meet again? ... Because we are all one ... Why do we only
remember this at times of misery?

The days of men of honour have come to an end, but let's
remember that it was not always so. We all know well that proverb
from the great Ali [successor of the prophet Mohammed according
to the Shia faith] who used to say:

'Don't be surprised if a strong man of honour should die of
shame, if he witnessed a thorn heaved with undue force from the
feet of an old Jewish lady'

...

Email: silence1355@yahoo.com
http://shortcut.persianblog.com

9 January 2004

Foreigners are still helping the earthquake survivors ...

The help of foreign aid workers during their Christmas holidays
when they left their homes and families and came to Bam is worthy
of deep gratitude ... Even though the Government did not thank
them, we the people will never forget ...

By Bear

30 December 2003

They have sent trained dogs to detect humans buried under the
rubble. But in our country dogs are unclean creatures and if the

dog-trainers are unveiled women they should not help the
earthquake survivors ...

You see, it's better to die than to be rescued from the rubble by
such people ...

And of course we should totally disregard the fact that these
women have totally abandoned their sacred Christmas
celebrations and time with their families to come to our
aid ...

Email: saba@eparizi.com
http://saba.eparizi.com

30 December 2003

I want to know how many thousands of people dead under the
rubble would have lived if all this money that our rulers have spent
in the last few decades on Palestine, Lebanon and Bosnia, had been
spent on the sort of safety measures that are the norm in other
earthquake zones.

Anyway, how many of Lebanon's Hezbollah or the Palestinian
Islamic organizations sent help to Iran? How many came from
Bosnia to help us? How much aid came from the Iraqi Shia? What
about our brothers in Libya or Syria? Let's compare them with the
aid sent by those countries they call 'Western criminals' and 'world
oppressors'. It seems there is more honour among this world's
criminals and oppressors. Even Israel has offered help and the gods
have been offended. If this had happened in Israel, would we have
offered our help?

This sentence, which I heard on Larijani's [the ex-Director
General of Broadcasting] network, is always ringing in my ears: 'This
afternoon a young Palestinian on a martyrdom mission joined God,
and sent four Israelis to Hell.'

Now the ones who were sent to Hell put aside all grudges and
ideology and decide to help in a time like this, but those whose

death is equal to being reunited with God don't even bother with a
message of sympathy.

Email: kamyar@eehum.com
http://eehum.com

ENEMY SOLDIERS

Iran's judiciary chief Ayatollah Shahroudi recently described the Internet as a
'Trojan horse carrying enemy soldiers in its belly'. He's right. The Iranian blogosphere is full of what Ayatollah Shahroudi would call 'enemy soldiers'.

Many bloggers use the word *Hezbollahi* as an expletive, understood by everyone in the on-line community to mean 'extremist', 'lunatic', 'nerd' or 'bully'.
Never does it mean the 'party of God'. The heroes of the Islamic regime are not
the heroes of Iranian cyberspace. In fact, Ayatollah Shahroudi really wouldn't like
cyberspace at all. There are Iranian bloggers who attack the veil and blogs dedicated to home brewing in a country where drinking alcohol could get you publicly flogged. There are even electronic shrines dedicated to the 'good old days'
under the Shah.

No government in the world is more outspoken in its hostility towards Israel
than the Islamic Republic of Iran, but many bloggers question the regime's
support for radical Palestinian groups – some even say 'Why meddle in the
affairs of others to no avail?' However, there is great sympathy for the Palestinian
cause in Iran, as in much of the Islamic world. But many Iranians are frustrated
at their rulers' impotence and uselessness in dealing with the situation. They
appear wholly preoccupied with holding on to power and at best merely pay lip-
service to the Palestinians' cause.

DISCARDED MILITANCY

In Iran a crisis in the legitimacy of the regime has created a substantial backlash
against anything it endorses. As the *Guardian*'s Dan De Luce explains: 'The ideological extremism that accompanied the Revolution in 1979 has virtually

expired, except among a dwindling minority.' He adds that while other Arab governments have struggled to repress militant Islamists, there was sustained militancy in Iran. As a consequence it has now 'run its course'.[3]

However, it is hard to say whether the chorus of disapproval from bloggers condemning militant groups also applies to the rest of Iranian society. But in a country where the majority of people have overwhelmingly rejected the ruling clerics through the ballot box, a widespread dissatisfaction with the regime is apparent. To many Iranians, groups like Hamas or Islamic Jihad are unappealing because they share the same methods and ideology as Iran's own corrupt and discredited rulers.

Perhaps militant groups are largely unloved by the majority because they are endorsed by Iran's ruling clerics. Or perhaps it is because Iranians have for long endured the real consequences of radical Islam and have decided it is not the way forward. Iranian bloggers often complain about the senseless slaughter. They also routinely complain about Iran's struggling economy – from the decline of the health service to a hike in the price of petrol – while their leaders continue to fund radical Islamic groups around the world.

Mohsen Kadivar, a prominent cleric, recently criticized Iranians for not paying enough attention to the fate of the Palestinian people. 'It is most unfortunate,' he said, 'that when the leaders of Hamas were assassinated by Israel, Iranians showed no reaction at all.'[4]

In the summer of 1999, among the calls for democracy and freedom of student protestors was a familiar slogan: 'Forget Palestine ... let's deal with our own problems!' Such is the fear of Middle Eastern radical groups that a widespread (and totally unsubstantiated) rumour often goes around during demonstrations that Palestinian and Lebanese Hezbollah shock troops have been brought in by the authorities to deal with demonstrators.

Yet even long-established Palestinian groups feel they could do without the interference of the Iranian regime. For instance, on 30 October 1998 Iran's Supreme Leader Ayatollah Khamenei lashed out at the Palestinian leader Yasser Arafat, calling him a 'traitor and a lackey of the Zionists'. Two days later, Sheikh Hassan Nasrallah, the leader of Lebanon's Hezbollah (which was set up by Iran), called on Palestinians to kill Arafat. The Palestinian Authority Secretary General at the time, Tayeb Abdelrahim, responded by saying that 'an extremist faction in Iran, led by Khamenei, wants to aggravate the situation in the Palestinian territories to spark a civil war'. He added that: 'The Palestinian Authority is utterly convinced that the hard-liners in Iran have succeeded in infiltrating certain Palestinian factions which worked with Iran and received its aid in the past.' Meanwhile the unfortunate Palestinian people are harangued by the very ayatollahs who profess to support them.

For a quarter of a century Iran's official solution to the Palestinian problem has been simple. In the words of Ayatollah Khamenei: the 'cancerous tumour of Israel has to be removed from the landscape'. However, it is a sentiment that has little support from the majority of Iranians.

---

2 May 2004

Death to Everybody!
Death to America! Israel! Britain! Imperialism! ... Death to your mother, aunt and sister too! ... Death! Death! Death! They have been chanting 'Death to America and Israel!' for 25 years ... and what have these useless leaders achieved? ... Israel is still the bully of the neighbourhood and the Palestinians are swamped in misery ...

But I can't get over how we Iranians today are considered the most fanatical people in the world – all because of a bunch of nit-ridden illiterate mullahs ... When I was growing up, Hajji Yousef, the mullah who used to teach us the Koran ... would say that 'Moses taught us wisdom, Jesus love and Mohamed life' ... so where did all these death chants come from?

Although we do have our fair share of bigots and racists, I don't think we as a society are more intolerant than any others in the world.

If Iranians were so intolerant ... then why have so many people throughout our ancient history sought refuge in our land?

By the twentieth century, Iran was a major centre of Armenian life in the Middle East. There was a mass exodus of Armenian refugees to Iran after the Turks massacred them in the 1800s, and many more came here to escape from the Russians ... They stayed and today they are our dear brothers and sisters.

Jews around the world regard Cyrus the founder of the Persian Empire as anointed by God, after he offered them sanctuary within his kingdom 2,500 years ago ... Iranian Jews are the oldest inhabitants of this land and our honourable forefathers ...

In recent years – according to UN statistics* – we have had 1.4 million refugees from war-torn Afghanistan and 600,000 Iraqi refugees fleeing Saddam ... I know ... I don't usually write about this sort of thing ... but what got to me today was an e-mailed article sent to me by a friend – posted on this website: wiesenthal.com [20 April 2004].

The Wiesenthal Centre in remembrance of the Holocaust has recently honoured Hussein Sardari who, as a young Iranian diplomat in Paris, succeeded in having hundreds of Iranian Jews classified as 'non-racially' connected to the rest of the Jewish people, thereby saving them from the Nazi death camps. Additionally, in 1942, he turned over 500 blank Iranian passports to Jewish acquaintances in Paris to help save other non-Iranian Jews fleeing from Nazi persecution ... They are calling Hussein Sardari the 'Iranian Schindler' ... After World War II he was charged with illegal conduct for having issued unauthorized passports ... but was ultimately pardoned.

Ok ... I read it and felt proud ... but it was nothing exceptional as far as I was concerned ... it is something that most Iranians that I know would have done ... But it really got to me ... We need to claim back our tainted honour from these nit-ridden hateful mullahs before it's too late.

*According to UNHCR's global refugee figures (June 2004), Iran ranks second in the world in providing asylum to refugees.

By Friend

Ex-President Khatami and his ex-parliamentary deputy – the prominent blogger Abtahi (*FAR LEFT*) – attending the Ilanot Jewish celebrations in Iran, alongside Iranian Jewish community leaders and rabbis

Ordinary Iranians appear to be tired of the 'death chants' of the regime. They want to project a positive image of their country to counterbalance its reputation in the West as a nation of terrorists.

---

3 December 2002

[In 1941 an estimated 300, 000 Polish refugees are believed to have made it to Iran after their release from Stalin's prison camps]

One of my grandmother's most memorable stories was about a frosty winter's day during World War II when a ship brought a group of Polish women and children to the port of Anzali:

'On that day your grandfather had come home in a frenzy. He asked me to quickly pack some food and some plates and cutlery. He wanted me to go along too, as they might have problems they could not discuss with the men. He also said that I should bring some of my clothes and some of the girls' clothes too.

'Gholam, your grandfather's apprentice, had arrived. And I had made some jam sandwiches and even packed what was left of dinner and we were on our way. Your grandfather had rushed off to fetch Seyed Hashem, the town mullah, and to ask him what we should do ...

'When we got there, it was so heartbreaking ... beautiful women and young girls like flowers with green and blue eyes ... but they looked like they had just come out of a coal pit ... They were hungry, thirsty and flea-ridden ... The only doctor in town had been called and some tents were brought over from the town hall ... The doctor had asked us women to help and wash them with Soblimeh soap ... you cannot imagine the commotion ... the whole town running around getting things from the shops.

'When our Mullah Seyed Hashem arrived he told us it was our religious duty to look after these people who had come to us for sanctuary ... "Treat them with total respect," he said. "It doesn't matter if they don't practise what you practise ... Treat them like guests in your home ... divide them among yourselves, but don't separate the children from their mothers. Now get hot water ..."

'The clamour of people bringing hot water from their homes to the beach ... All the town barbers on the beach cutting the Poles' flea-ridden hair. And we took them in the tents and washed and dried and clothed them ... You have no idea how beautiful they were when they were washed!

'The next day Seyed Hashem in the mosque said "These are women of honour ... they have also asked me to let it be known that they sew, embroider and knit and would like to be paid for this. Send your girl to be taught by them and pay them so that they can run their own lives."'

My grandmother sent my mum to be taught by Marous, who taught her lacework, embroidery, knitting and beadwork. The girls in Anzali had all their wedding trousseaus embroidered. And the

brides of many families were these blonde and blue-eyed beauties.
When I was in primary school, Houma and another girl, Maryam,
had inherited their beautiful blue eyes from their Polish
grandmothers. And every time I looked into their eyes I
remembered my grandmother's stories about that day …

But there is a big question that tortures me today … are not the
two million Afghans in Iran also looking for sanctuary? Are we not
the same people? Didn't Seyed Hashem, the old town mullah,
believe in the same things as our present rulers? What happened to
us? What did they do to us?

Email: bamdadz@yahoo.com
http://bamdad.blogspot.com

On 21 June 2004 three British naval vessels and their crews were seized by Iran's
Revolutionary Guards, who claimed they had strayed across the maritime
Iranian borders. However, the British servicemen objected that they had been
'forcibly escorted' into Iran's territorial waters before being taken captive. The
servicemen were then paraded on Iranian TV wearing blindfolds. Here is
Hossein Derakhshan on the subject.

23 June 2004

It's as if the Revolutionary Guards want to officially set fire to the
whole of Iran by broadcasting those humiliating images of
blindfolded British soldiers … It's not clear what these
Revolutionary Guards want, but they are trying to take control of all
the centres of power … and as always our unfortunate people have
to pay for the actions of 20 or 30 thugs and hooligans …

Not only are they not Iranian … they are not even human.

Email: hoder@hoder.com
http://editormyself.com

Interviewed on CNN (7 January 1998), ex-President Khatami pointed out that 'anti-Semitism is indeed a Western phenomenon. It has no precedents in Islam or in the East. Jews and Muslims have lived harmoniously together for centuries.' And here's another paradox: although the Iranian authorities hate the state of Israel, anti-Semitism remains a social taboo in Iran – even among the most radical members of the regime. Iranian Jews are the oldest inhabitants of Iran and even under the present constitution have a right to choose a Jewish representative in Parliament. Although the Iranian people have deep sympathies with the Palestinians, they also cannot accept the view of the unelected ruling clerics that every man, woman and child in Israel is a legitimate target.

The Iranian Jewish exile Roya Hakakian has recently published a memoir about her life in Tehran before and after the Revolution.[5] Growing up in Tehran, she never experienced anti-Semitism: 'The people who persecuted Jews in Iran were the same people who persecuted anyone who didn't fall in line with the Government ... Our neighbours never turned on us and we always maintained close ties with our Iranian friends.'

On the other hand, the Iranian-born Moshe Katsav – who was sworn in as eighth President of the State of Israel in 2000 – told the *Jerusalem Post* (5 May 2004) that he 'found it incomprehensible' that Iranian Jews chose to live anywhere other than Israel. Nevertheless, the article went on to say that 'most of the Jews still resident in Iran are quite happy to be there and despite the anti-Israel hatred that often translates itself into anti-Jewish feeling, generally speaking, they are not persecuted. Katsav has met them when they have travelled abroad, and they are usually in a hurry to return to Tehran.'

---

16 August 2004

[by Hossein Derakhshan]

The rulers of Iran ... should realize that ordinary Iranians are not so devoted to Palestinians or angry at the Israeli people. Anyway, there are more Iranians in Israel than there are in Palestine. I for one don't know any other nation that can claim an Iranian-born president and defence chief except Israel.

23 December 2003

Why are we the only country in the region that does not accept the existence of the State of Israel?

We must not forget that during the Iran–Iraq war, Yasser Arafat was Saddam's best friend and along with all other Arab-speaking nations supported Iraq against Iran in the war.

Email: Hoder@hoder.com
http://i.hoder.com

Most of the bloggers in this book are the ones with the highest number of visitors or 'hits' per day, so in a way they represent the views of a great many regular readers. Common themes, topics and areas of concern recur throughout these on-line journals and most of them object to the irrational, hate-filled rhetoric of the hardline clerics.

Such objections are not limited to the Internet, however. In 2001, for instance, in response to the regime's refusal to accept the existence of the State of Israel and any so-called 'peace process', the middle-ranking Shia cleric Nouri asked: 'If they [the Palestinians] have agreed to a "peace process", why do we have to be more Palestinian than the Palestinians?' Nouri – who was ex-President Khatami's former vice-president and Interior Minister – was later sentenced to five years in prison for political and religious dissent and his brother, a young reformist MP, died in suspicious circumstances.

After the Revolution, Ayatollah Khomeini's big idea of a revolutionary, political Islam spread throughout the Islamic world. In every Islamic country, especially those with the poorest populations, Tehran moved to set up networks of militant activists as a means of seizing power for radical Islam. However, back home in Iran the foot soldiers of the ideological state – the Revolutionary Guards actively spreading the message from Lebanon to Sudan – are hate figures that arrest and torture anyone who speaks out against the regime.

But one man's terrorist is another man's freedom fighter and Iran's rulers proudly and openly support such groups around the world. They even hold annual conferences that are like a who's who of international terrorism. A meeting in Tehran in 2004 to celebrate the twenty-fifth anniversary of Ayatollah Khomeini's seizure of power proudly announced the arrival of members of Hamas, Hezbollah, Islamic Jihad, Ansar Al Islam and the leader of Iraq's insurgent Mahdi Army, Mogtada Sadr.

A popular Iranian joke about Iran's standing in the international community goes like this: 'Before the Revolution Iran had one enemy in the world: Syria. After the Revolution, it has only one ally in the world: Syria.' Perhaps you need to be Iranian to find it funny. Today, unsurprisingly, many Iranians regard the regime's support for international Islamic radicalism (or 'terrorism') as a major cause of their falling living standards, not least because it has scared away international business.

After 25 years of being told it is their religious duty to liberate Jerusalem one day, most Iranians are more concerned with their own liberation. Many others who sympathize with the Palestinian cause, see similarities between their own rulers and the 'occupiers'.

16 November 2003

The Iranian rulers reject any peace process between Israel and Palestine because they are in actual fact against an independent state of Palestine ...

If there were peace, then the hatreds between the two tribes would gradually disappear and that would leave no role for our leaders, who love to meddle in other people's business.

Email: eghbal_r@yahoo.com
http://rezaeghbal.blogspot.com

17 August 2003

In Memory of Rachel

You've probably read about it on the Internet: Rachel Corrie, the 23-year-old American who gave her life as she stood in the way of Israeli bulldozers to stop the destruction of homes in Palestine.

As I look at you, Rachel, all I feel is shame and inferiority, especially as I live under a mob that say they worship God. If only they would officially admit to being non-believers, then that would give me some peace! A clan that talk day and night about Imam Hussein, who used to say, 'If you are non-believers at least be libertarians' and they … what can I tell you? It is as if freedom, honesty, sincerity are historical terms.

The innocence in your eyes, takes me to the depth of history and back … When throughout the world today … a world filled with mirages … false prophets and pseudo-intellectuals … Consumers of mud from East and West, Left and Right … thousands of groups, parties, unions, signing useless protocols.

We are force-fed so much mud that I don't even know whether the feelings I have are real or were fed to me. Is my love real, is my breathing real, and is my God a real God?

Rachel you are a rare being! I don't want to know whether losing your life was 'right'. What is important is that you were what you were; you did what you had to do. You were a voice against the false smiles and poses, the ironed suits, the summits and the humanitarian slogans and the endless political point-scoring and photo opportunities. I hate politics!

Email: silence1355@yahoo.com
http://shortcut.persianblog.com

11 November 2003

In the news today ... more dead in Iraq ... Iran has no atom bomb
... Nicole Kidman has decided that she no longer wishes to discuss
her private life ...

In the Gaza Strip a number of people (it is of no significance
whether they were Israeli or Palestinian) will never ever fight each
other again, because they're all dead ...

Interestingly, Andre Agassi (son of Muhammad Agassi, the
Iranian Olympic Boxer) is still a great tennis player.

Email: deltangestan@yahoo.com

http://deltangestan.blogspot.com

24 March 2004

Most of the people I know are either totally indifferent or happy
about the assassination of Sheikh Ahmed Yassin* (which ultimately
is an illegal act) ...

What does this illustrate? When a group of people (supposedly
among the educated or enlightened members of this society) are so
pleased at the deaths or murders of religious leaders?

* Sheikh Ahmed Yassin, the spiritual head of the Palestinian militant group Hamas,
was assassinated in an Israeli air strike on 22 March 2004.

Email: dr_salardr@yahoo.com

http://www.doctoractor.persianblog.com

REVEALING THE UNSPOKEN NEWS

As the Iranian journalist Behnoud has observed, the endless articles and commentaries and up-to-the-minute information posted on the Internet 'connect

young dissident civilians through an invisible thread, revealing the unspoken news of corruption among the clergy and their infamous offspring; mafia-like networks of power and murder; interrogators who kill dissidents on the orders of the highest authorities and so on ... This information is spread the next day by word of mouth in [communal] taxis and at universities', tempting even more Iranians to invest in a computer that will give them the chance to join in the clandestine conversation.

---

14 May 2003

All of a sudden our blogs are so political ... is there nothing else that we can talk about? Discussing forbidden subjects in small groups used to take place in barbers or our communal taxis.

Our taxis have always been centres for the most exciting political news (I think not even the most reputable of news agencies could pass on such a huge volume of news at such speed) and now we have transferred our national obsession with politics to our blogs.

By Foam

Behnoud also notes that with the despotic ruler Saddam Hussein overthrown on Iran's doorstep, 'blogs that before the war in Iraq dealt mainly with Madonna's latest offerings, Western music and films and photographs of Victoria and David Beckham, are now quite politicized, with bloggers becoming ever more blunt, daring and reckless.'

In fact, blogs have become an unconventional alternative news source. 'Goftaniha' is a blog written by Amir-Farshad Ebrahimi. In September 2000 two lawyers – Shirin Ebadi (Nobel Peace Prize 2003) and Mohsen Rahami – were given suspended prison sentences of 15 months each and banned from practising for five years. They were accused of videotaping the confession of a penitent plain-clothed secret agent (Amir-Farshad Ebrahimi), alleging that prominent conservative figures supported the activities of violent, right-wing vigilante groups that had brutally attacked political gatherings and student protests. Today, this ex-secret agent (who recently fled Iran) keeps a popular blog offering a distinctive take on current affairs.

---

25 January 2004

[by Amir-Farshad Ebrahimi]
When Faezeh* was standing for Parliament ... we were asked to go along and interrupt her election campaign ... beat up a few people and chant slogans against her ... So she could pose as one of the people and get some votes ... but people could see through all that and soon she didn't even dare to stand in the next elections ...

* Faezeh Rafsanjani is the daughter of ex-president Hashem Rafsanjani, head of the Expediency Council and believed to be one of the most powerful unelected clerics in Iran today. During Faezeh's election campaign there were local news reports of her speeches being disrupted by hardline Islamic vigilantes.

11 January 2004

Soheil Karimi* – a recognized executive member of Hezbollah Central Office ... implicated in the attempted assassination of Abdolah Nouri [a dissident cleric], and who was recently arrested by the American forces in Iraq charged with spying – has now been freed. He has probably been exchanged for al-Qaida members in Iran ...

* Soheil Karimi, purportedly an employee of Iran's state-run TV, was held for four months on suspicion of spying by American forces in Iraq.

Email: a_farshadebrahimi@hotmail.com
http://www.goftaniha.com

Amir-Farshad Ebrahimi's blog is not entirely exceptional. The Iranian blogo-sphere is filled with the sort of discussions that many would only dare whisper behind closed doors – such as the recent on-line debate about Ardeshir Afshin-Rad, a young film director found dead in his flat after being attacked by security forces.

---

6 March 2004

The news of Ardeshir Afshin-Rad's death had been going round the cinema circles before it was posted in many Internet sites ... The only thing about his death that can be corroborated is the entrance of security forces to a gathering were Ardeshir was present before he met his end ... One version of the story is that he fell from the fourth-floor balcony to his death while trying to escape from security agents ... Another version is that he was assaulted by the security forces and then thrown from the balcony to conceal the cause of death ...

But in the prevailing atmosphere ... I doubt that even his own family will pursue the reasons for his death.

By Ghost-Writer

---

8 March 2004

Ardeshir Afshin-Rad was killed as he tried to escape from members of the security services ... other reports say he died as a result of torture and assault at the hands of the security agents of Ansar [Hezbollah].

What can I say? I am truly sorry ... My agony is more than I can express in words.

Email; rere_reera@yahoo.com
http://abovethewall.blogspot.com

A COVERT MASS CELEBRATION

While some blogs are used to spill the beans, others are used to spread the word – like the news that the Iranian dissident and human rights lawyer Shirin Ebadi had won the Nobel Peace Prize.

Iran's first female judge, Ebadi was forced to resign after the 1979 Islamic Revolution. She turned her law practice into a base for rights campaigning, particularly for Iranian women and children. She often took on the cases of dissident writers, intellectuals and pro-democracy activists which other lawyers deemed far too inflammatory. She even assisted the students who were prosecuted after six days of clashes at Tehran University in 1999.

In a country that routinely imprisons many lawyers for taking on such cases, she has had to pay for her beliefs, yet even in solitary confinement at the notorious Evin Prison she found sympathizers. In July 2001 she told the *Payam Emrooz* monthly review (a pro-democracy publication that was later closed down) that after one interrogation session with the security agents, a female guard said to her:

> 'Damn that Law College you studied in! Why on earth couldn't you
> defend yourself? ... Why is he accusing you so deceitfully?' Irrationally, I
> looked at her and said, 'There is a new conspiracy coming up.' Like a
> sister she touched my shoulder and said, 'Trust in God.'

Many young people view Ebadi as a daring heroine standing up to the ideological state. Naturally, she is disdained by the clerics and Iran's state-controlled media ignored the story of her winning the Nobel Prize for many hours. Eventually, there was a brief 15-second announcement at the end of the late evening news, though it omitted any mention of her human rights work, stating merely that she had been awarded the peace prize for her work with 'a children's charity'.

In stark contrast, within minutes of the announcement by the Nobel committee, bloggers were posting messages of congratulation. An Iranian statistical analysis website, www.damasanj.com (which is similar to Bogdex), works out which news stories are most read and disseminated throughout

the Iranian blogosphere. Items about Ebadi's Nobel Prize dominated the Top
Ten rankings.

---

10 October 2003

Shirin Ebadi is the winner of the Nobel Peace Prize!
My hands are shaking as I type this ...
This news is too big ...

Congratulations to all Iranians – especially our women ... now I
have to go and have a real good sob ... I will update you with all the
news links to this story as soon as I stop shaking.

Email: zahra_rose61@yahoo.com
http://www.zahra-hb.com

SHIRIN EBADI ADDRESSING TEHRAN UNIVERSITY STUDENTS ON
INTERNATIONAL WOMEN'S DAY 2003

And this is how the BBC covered the news on 14 October 2003:

Thousands of people have greeted Iranian Nobel Peace Prize winner
Shirin Ebadi in extraordinary scenes at Tehran's city airport on her return
to the Iranian capital. Human rights groups and non-governmental

organizations, swelled by crowds of local people, gathered at the city airport to give her a hero's welcome.

The BBC described the area surrounding Tehran's Mehrabad Airport as brought to a 'standstill by traffic jams'. Crowds of people abandoned their cars and walked the rest of the way to the airport, chanting slogans calling for the release of all political prisoners and singing pre-revolutionary Iranian nationalist songs.

SHIRIN EBADI BY MANA NEYESTANI, ONE OF IRAN'S BEST YOUNG CARTOONISTS WWW.HADI2NS.COM

12 October 2003

Our voices will be heard

Today I really felt that all our pains and struggles are not for nothing ... Shirin has struggled relentlessly ... despite all the dangers to her own life ... without ever expecting anything in return ...

Today we exist, our voices exist, and our voices will be heard.

Email: omid@khushe.org
http://omid.khushe.org/weblog

Surrogate Media

Under normal circumstances, when a country wins the Nobel Prize for the first time it should receive significant media coverage. But Iran is not normal. The state-controlled media were reluctant even to mention Shirin Ebadi, so it was left to bloggers to provide detailed commentaries about her life and work, as well as their reaction to the win. They also used the Web to organize a reception for Ebadi at the airport on her arrival, then posted the latest photos of her arrival in Iran.

---

13 October 2003

We will go to the welcoming rally of Shirin Ebadi, who for many years has struggled for freedom in this land ... tonight the airport will be a scene of a national celebration ...
   Tuesday 9 p.m. Mehrabad Airport – International Arrivals.

Email: mana_bam@yahoo.com
http://www.solhiran.persianblog

---

15 October 2003

When I heard the roaring crowd chanting in one voice 'Free all political prisoners!' ... I burst into tears ... This morning our office caretaker wanted to know when she [Ebadi] was coming ... 'Why do you want to know?' I asked ... he replied that he and his wife were going to the airport to welcome Shirin back to Iran ... I knew then that I would not be alone tonight ...
   Mrs Ebadi spoke to us briefly: 'This prize belongs to all of the people'.. She could not control her tears either and wept too ... I'm exhausted and will post the photos tomorrow ...
   There was a small group with their black placard ... people kept teasing them and they just grinned back. When everyone in one voice booed them! They had nothing to offer but silence ...

What a night ...

Email: shabah@shabah.org
http://www.shabah.org

16 October 2003

We had all come to see our lady of peace ... old men and women, students, human rights and women groups ... Jafar Panahi [a filmmaker] was there, as was Ali Daeii [the captain of the Iranian football team] ...

Balloons, accordions, drums, music, songs and slogans. On the way back I saw so many abandoned cars on the motorway that it looked like a huge car park ... The main slogan was: 'Free political prisoners!'

By Havoc

Photo © Roshan

A FEMALE PROTESTER IN THE CROWD AT TEHRAN AIRPORT AWAITING SHIRIN EBADI'S ARRIVAL. HER BANNER READS: 'WE ARE AGAINST CAPITAL PUNISHMENT.'

The sheer delight expressed at the news of Ebadi's Nobel Prize was in no way confined to the Iranian blogosphere. Nasser Zarafshan, a writer, translator and lawyer, is serving a five-year prison term for criticizing the official investigation into the murders of several writers in the late 1990s. He wrote to Ebadi from prison: 'News of your Nobel Prize has filled all the jailed journalists, lawyers, and political prisoners at Evin Prison with joy ... We are convinced that the present era of decline and undemocratic conditions in Iran will come to end. On behalf of myself and my fellow prisoners, I congratulate you and all those who revere freedom and justice, wishing you and all enlightened social forces, victory and pride.'

Photo © Roshan

SHIRIN EBADI RECEPTION AT TEHRAN AIRPORT, 14 OCTOBER 2003

14 October 2003

I went to see Shirin Ebadi, a truly once in a lifetime experience; there were about 25,000 people there ... She said: 'This prize does not belong to me. It belongs to the people of Iran and is proof that we are a peace-loving people.'

Tonight I was proud to be an Iranian woman and I felt proud to share this soil with Shirin Ebadi ...

I am now sure that there will be an end to this dark night and our dawn will come ... Liberty for Iran and Iranians!

Email: foroogh_payizi@hotmail.com
http://www.froogh.blogspot.com

10 October 2003

Shirin Ebadi today, after winning her Nobel Peace Prize, has said: 'There is no contradiction between my being a Muslim and also fighting for democracy'! It's as if being a Muslim is a fatal disease!

But I guess with prominent Muslims like Ben-laden and Ayatollah Hassani respectively representing Sunni and Shia Islam, you can't really blame them for seeing us as a fatal disease.

Email: hamed@hamedyou.com
http://weblog.hamedyou.com

15 October 2003

It was an extraordinary evening ... even though not many people knew about the arrival of our 'lady of peace', a big crowd had turned out despite the news blackout ... I left the house around 7.30 and on the way to the airport I went to see my friend at his shop ... as he's had the honour of spending two months in jail after the last demonstrations ... I thought it would be good to have a chat and pick up a few pointers ... just in case I get arrested tonight ...

Anyway, we arranged to meet outside terminal 2 at 10 o'clock ... I got a taxi, but the motorway was so jam-packed I jumped out near the airport, with a flower in one hand and a book in the other (I forgot to say that I popped into a bookshop on the way and bought Gabriel Marcus's Lonely Days – it was on sale ... but that was a big mistake as I had to lug it around till the end of the night).

From the edges of the motorway all the way to the airport you could see the huge crowds … I got to terminal 2 at around 10, but found out that our 'lady of peace' was now coming out of terminal 3. So I ran the marathon all the way to terminal 3 (by this time I had put Marcus down my trousers – very uncomfortable) …

There were about four mullahs in a car probably coming back from a trip somewhere and as soon as the crowd noticed them they started booing. One of the mullahs put his hand out of the car and gave us 'the finger'. For me it really symbolized the finger that this bunch of mullahs have been giving us all these years.

Once in a while you could spot the occasional agent who had shaved off his beard for the night, filming with their government cameras … These Hezbollahi's, no matter how hard they try there is an evil in their faces that makes them stand out … some were even chanting along with the crowd …

Thank God there was no tear-gas or electric batons tonight, even though on the way back we saw anti-riot police stationed in Azadi Avenue.

By Santiago

---

10 October 2003

Once I heard someone say that because Switzerland is a neutral and peaceful nation it has given the world clocks and delicious chocolate. But a country like Italy, in turmoil throughout its history, gave us great men such as Leonardo da Vinci. I don't want to analyse this to see whether there is any truth in the statement or not … I just want to say that perhaps things may turn out all right for us in the end …

Congratulations Mrs Ebadi! I believe you deserve even higher accolades … But you brought true happiness to our hearts today. Stay strong and resolute as ever … and again, thank you.

By Lady

Photo © Roshan

SHIRIN EBADI RECEPTION AT TEHRAN AIRPORT, 14 OCTOBER 2003

15 October 2003

'[President] Khatami, shame on you!' – for me, that was the best
slogan of the night ...

    After deciding to go, I was only worried about how my wife
would react ... that she might again raise concerns about my safety
... but I had nothing to worry about as she said she was coming too
... so all we had to do was to find someone to baby-sit.

Email: bamdadz@yahoo.com
http://bamdad.blogspot.com

17 October 2003

I was not taken aback by the enormous crowd at her reception ...
Yet I am still stunned by the confidence and the power I witnessed
in people's eyes ... an inexhaustible power was released that night

... A new start ...

Email: zahrkhand@yahoo.com

http://ostorlab.persianblog.com

There was eventually some coverage of Shirin Ebadi's Nobel Prize in the hard-line press. They called it an 'anti-Islamic American conspiracy'. *Yasaratal-Hussein*, an official Hezbollah publication, referred to her as an 'apostate' and 'enemy of God' (in Iran apostasy carries the automatic death penalty). Its editorial went on:

> Don't think that by getting that $1.1 million prize, like the pro-democracy spinster of Burma, you are now invulnerable. We are more certain than ever before that our stance against people like you has been right all along, and our certainty in dealing with the enemies of God (and we consider you to be among them) will be a hundredfold strengthened. Insh'Allah.[6]

15 October 2003

As I didn't want to leave any thing to chance ... I got to the airport at two in the afternoon ... I ended up drinking so many cups of tea and juice that every so often I had to go to the toilet and pee on Agha's [Ayatollah Khomeini's] grave! From around four it felt like the airport was getting busy ...

It was around six that you could see the crowd ... and I was really aware of the plain-clothes security guys buzzing around ... talking in frenzied fashion to their colleagues ...

It was a memorable night even though I'm tired. I will never forget tonight for as long as I live. I am happy that even though I am living at the height of oppression and cruelty, I saw scenes of humanity and support for peace.

Freedom is near friends.

By Shima

---

14 October 2003

I hardly heard a thing Shirin Ebadi said, but my friend mockingly said don't worry we'll see it in on the television news when we get home ... It was a long time since I've seen so many people, so happy.

Email: z8unak@z8un.com
http://www.z8un.com

Islamic Republic of Iran Broadcasting (IRIB) and the 'Cultural Invasion'

The unelected clergy control most of the levers of power, including the Islamic Republic of Iran Broadcasting (IRIB), whose chief is appointed by the country's supreme leader, Ayatollah Ali Khamenei.

The tight state control of Iran's broadcast media undoubtedly raised the profile of alternative media outlets. Satellite television, a mix of popular and political programmes, provides one of the few diversions openly available to Iranians. It is a welcome relief from the religious fare offered on state-run channels. Several foreign broadcasters target radio listeners in Iran, including the Washington-backed Voice of America (VOA) with its nightly Persian-language TV programmes. Also satellite TV stations maintained by Iranian exiles in the United States are said to have played a role in student protests in 2003. Most of the media outlets controlled by opponents of the regime are based in America. Although officially banned, these foreign broadcasts have a sizeable audience in Iran, where many people have satellite dishes.

During a continuous week of protests in June 2003, the regime was reported to have stepped up the jamming of foreign Farsi-language radio and TV broadcasts so as to contain what it always describes as a 'cultural invasion'. The Intelligence Minister Ali Younessi maintained that 'events outside the campus and the general discontent of the population are being guided by the foreign media and satellite stations'. The Iranian authorities have over the years accused the United States of paying these news media outlets to destabilize the Islamic regime.

As the journalist Tim Judah noted in a report in the *Observer*:

> One area where the authorities have already lost control is television. Increasingly uninterested by the staple fare of prayers, domestic dramas and news about the Palestinian uprising, millions are tuned in to satellite television, which is, of course, strictly illegal. Climb a high building and the evidence is stunning. Mushroom-like clusters of satellite dishes have sprouted across Tehran.[7]

---

30 June 2002

Do you watch television? Unbelievably stupid ... I try not to watch ...but two or three times a day when I'm having tea, coffee or some fruit, I sit for a few minutes in front of the set ...

It's so moronic ... even if you ignore the worthless subject matter, the poor production and performances ... The worst bit is the absurd propaganda ... You can tell the good guys and bad guys from their names (the good guys have Islamic names and the bad guys Persian names*) and their appearance ... good guys are always bearded, usually of a dirty variety and the bad guys clean-shaven! Vomit inducing ...

Email: wwaaaaah@yahoo.com
http://aaab.blogspot.com

* After the 1979 Islamic Revolution, the ruling clerics banned the registration of Persian names such as Cyrus or Darius in a symbolic strike at Iran's pre-Islamic history.

---

30 November 2003

Whenever I turn on the television these days ... I just want to vomit ... For heaven's sake! What girl these days gets all flustered at a proposal of marriage?! No one has marriage as his or her ultimate dream any more! They're not insane! Not even a retard would lower her gaze these days when talking to a person of the opposite sex!

People are not so shallow or naive as to fall for your made-up religious fables …I feel physically sick at the sight of these beards on television … Do you understand? At least for the sake of variety show someone with a trimmed beard!

I do not want to listen to the speeches or the cautionary guidance of any clergy or chador-wearing woman! I don't want to make lace or artificial flowers! Or to make candles or follow your revolting burger recipes! Damn you!

I don't want to know about Palestine or Iraq! I don't ever again want to hear about the crimes of the United States! I don't want to see your concocted television series that show women grabbing their chadors and covering up as they go to the door … why don't you impostors show real people?

Don't you ever want to introduce the contemporary art of the world to this country? Art isn't just the architectural features of a mosque you know … You are so stingy that you have even cut back on showing the [David Attenborough] natural history programmes that we used to get a few years ago …

Damn you brainless charlatans who control our only national broadcasting organization! All you achieve is to waste our time while making us want to vomit …damn you!

Email: rere_reera@yahoo.com
http://abovethewall.blogspot.com

13 November 2002

Does anyone watch the daytime programme Return Home?

Today a lady surgeon was talking about breast cancer and ways of detecting it early. During a segment of the programme she attempted to describe how to examine yourself. The poor doctor tried and tried, but none of it made any sense. In frustration she kept repeating: 'Move three fingers like this!!! Like this ...'

In the end she suddenly grabbed the plate full of fruit in front of her, emptied it and turned it upside down and started demonstrating on the plate ...

Now you tell me what resemblance, if any, has an overturned plate with our breasts?

Email: avemaria_mm@yahoo.com
http://golekaghazi.blogspot.com

8 A Quarter of a Century Later

A quarter of a century ago they overthrew Iran's last monarch. In the bygone days of the Cold War they introduced the world to a new radical Islam and the modern world's first theocratic state. The Revolution began as a pro-democracy movement, but it evolved into something that was no more democratic than the monarchy it replaced.

In recent years Iran has been hailed as having the most dynamic movement for democratic change in the Islamic world. Since 1997 a clear desire for change has led to three landslide election victories for the reformists. As we have seen, 80 per cent of Iranians wanted change. The elections were billed as a showdown between reformists demanding social and political change, and conservative hardliners supporting strict Islamic rule. But despite huge election victories for the reformists, eight years under ex-President Muhammad Khatami had done little to shake the monopoly on power of the unelected Islamic hardliners.

THE CHICKEN FARMER PRESIDENT

In reality, Iran's political system only makes a show of being democratic. In practice, unelected institutions such as the Guardian Council intervene to oversee and reject potential presidential and parliamentary candidates. In the 1997

© Amirali Ghasemi amiralighasemi.com

MASH'HAD AIRPORT

elections the Guardian Council approved only four presidential candidates out of a total of 200. In the face of such blatant corruption, however, whenever an election is called, hundreds of people put themselves forward as possible candidates in an almost surreal show of optimism.

During the 2001 presidential elections (when yet again, hundreds of candidates rushed to sign up as presidential hopefuls) Ayatollah Jannati, a member of the Guardian Council responsible for vetting candidates, grumpily stated that 'some candidates register for the elections merely to create trouble and to generate problems for people, government and officials' (9 June 2004, IRNA).

The regime naturally finds the whole spectacle of mass candidacies an embarrassment. According to a report by the Iranian Student's News Agency (ISNA), 'officials at the Interior Ministry did their best to keep foreign journalists away from most of the presidential candidates' (8 June 2001). Nevertheless, ISNA – one of Iran's most active and reputable nationwide news agencies, run by experienced journalists and student reporters – released numerous reports that day about these presidential hopefuls.

One of them was an office manager at Talesh magazine. He asked an ISNA reporter: 'If King Shah'pour the First was ordained Shah of Persia while still in his mother's womb, why can't I be the next president at the age of 28?' His first priority once elected President was to resume ties with the United States. Another candidate was a clergyman accompanied by his wife. Reading the Koran he had come across a verse that had inspired him to run for office and serve his country. One 68-year-old labourer, a political veteran (who had taken part in the last eight presidential elections), described in detail three vivid dreams that had persuaded him to take part. His ultimate aim once elected as President of Iran was to bring about world peace.

Those who know Iran and Iranians will understand these mass presidential candidacies. Iranians in general are not the most subservient people in the world and no matter what their circumstances they feel that they are as good as the next man. Iran is a society in which even a common labourer feels he has every right to be President.

A lorry driver from Yaft-Abad, an impoverished area of South Tehran, described a life-changing vision to an ISNA reporter. In his dream he had been told that hidden treasure was to be found in Yaft-Abad and that it belonged to all Iranians. Also in the race that year was a 22-year-old farmer with shoulder-length hair. He described himself as a 'spiritual Sufi philosopher' and his main objective was to deal with the problems that faced the youth of Iran. When asked about his long hair he replied: 'My hair is irrelevant. The whole point for me is to be a candidate for the Presidency of Iran and not for anyone to approve of me. We all know that they will not approve anyone.'

According to ISNA reports on 8 June 2001, other candidates included a chicken farmer, an unemployed youth, a man who made his living selling socks, an 82-year-old man with a desire to serve the people; a woman who gave out flowers to journalists and another who hid her face behind her veil and was too shy to be photographed; and a man who adamantly refused to discuss his background, but barked back at the reporter: 'In America people address me as "Professor"!' Yet despite the obvious hurdles, the Iranians' show of optimism has gone on unabated. According to the interior ministry a record 1,010 people registered to run in Iran's presidential election in June 2005.

At election time there are always genuine political veterans who stand, knowing full well they will get nowhere. For instance, on 8 March 2005 Ebrahim Yazdi (accompanied by his Nobel Prize-winning lawyer, Shirin Ebadi) announced that he would be standing as a presidential candidate on the condition that the Guardian Council 'resigns' and all political prisoners are freed. Yazdi is head of the Iran Freedom Movement (IFM) founded by the late Mehdi Bazargan, who was deputy Prime Minster to Dr Mossadegh in the 1950s. In 2001 about 40 of his elderly liberal colleagues were arrested on charges of plotting to overthrow the Islamic regime and he is also facing similar charges. Yet at the age of 73 Yazdi is still making a stand for democracy.

---

10 March 2005

Ebrahim Yazdi has become a candidate. Obviously it is just to put the regime under pressure. One of my friends told me Yazdi had said in a gathering: 'Well, I know I won't be allowed to stand, but at least then they can't turn around and say they conducted a free election.'

Email: hamedyou@gmail.com
http://weblog.hamedyou.com

---

9 March 2005

Politics is a bit like playing poker, you have to taunt your opponent or at least raise the stakes for them by entering the game. Basically that is why I think the announcement by Ebrahim Yazdi and his pre-conditions to run for the Iran Freedom Movement are totally right. As we know, taking an active part in these elections won't solve anything, but simply boycotting them is a hundred times worse.

http://omidvaar.blogspot.com

---

13 March 2004

The entry of Yazdi to the presidential race was in itself a beautiful thing and he carried it out with style. If they reject him they have to answer to world opinion and if they confirm him as a candidate it means there is no longer a Guardian Council veto in existence in the Islamic Republic. You have to admire him and we have to support him in any way we can.

Email: alpr_ir2002@yahoo.com
http://alpr.30morgh.org

The previous blogger, a political journalist in Iran, is perhaps rather naive to believe that the Iranian government cares a fig about 'world opinion'. He also ignores the fact that outside Iran barely anyone knows who Yazdi is. Nor would the silencing of a veteran liberal politician in Iran matter much to Western governments or their constituents.

FREE AND FAIR ELECTIONS

For a quarter of a century a small group of nepotistic revolutionaries has taken it in turns to rule Iran. Election after election, Iranians have got used to seeing the same people in top ministerial and governmental posts. Yet in the last decade a group of reformists has risen out of this inner circle. People like Khatami, who feel that the regime needs to change in order to survive. The reformist Parliament has unanimously passed more than 100 progressive laws: a ban on torture, a Free Press Bill, the raising of the legal marriage age, improved divorce legislation and the expansion of trial by jury. All of these laws have been endorsed by Parliament – but vetoed by the Guardian Council. On 12 August 2003 Parliament unanimously voted in favour of joining the UN Convention on the Elimination of All Forms of Discrimination Against Women (CEDAW). Iran's conservative Guardian Council vetoed the adoption of the convention, saying that it violated Iranian and Islamic Sharia law.

9 September 2003

The CEDAW was naturally vetoed. Anyway it's not too bad: at least we know where we stand ... and we can see the hypocrisy of those

we elected when they speak of enlightenment, modernism and
equality ...

Anyway, why is it up to a bunch of men who subjugate us to
bestow rights that are rightfully ours? Iranian women are like tiny
little silk worms and for generations have spent a lifetime weaving
cocoons dreaming of a flight that never happens.

The Songstress

Let down by the system, people had turned away from the ballot box. By March
2003, council elections in Iran were seen by many as a test for ex-President
Khatami, and for reform within the system. Returns showed a historically low
national turnout of just 10 to 12 per cent in the major cities. Mostafa Tajzadeh, a
former deputy Interior Minister under President Khatami, said the polls showed
that 'people have lost hope of seeking democratic change through the ballot'.

27 February 2003

I am sick of their fake promises, their nauseating fake smiles, the
hypocrisy and lies ... so many election posters all over Tehran ... I
want to vomit and there isn't anywhere you can pour out ... I want
to pour, break, explode! When my eyes fell on that poster, I was on
the verge of a nervous breakdown ... I wanted to throw off my veil
and stick it on the hair and beard of the guy in the poster ... so that
you could only see its face and then smear my lipstick on it till it ran
out ... batter it against its head ...

Instead I walked into the café across the street and poured so
much sugar in my cup of coffee that it started to spill out ... I didn't
leave the house for two days after that.

Email: at_857@hotmail.com
http://atash3.blogspot.com

© Amirali Ghasemi www.amiralighasemi.com

Coffee shop in Fereshteh Street, Tehran

By 2003 many felt that their President had been in office but not in power. Parliament had become a place where powerless people complained about things. Parliament's inability to stand up to the unelected clerics lost its respect and its staunchest supporters.

Tahkim Vahdat, Iran's largest student union, had wholeheartedly supported the reformists in two previous presidential elections. Now it publicly withdrew its support from the parliamentary reform movement, announcing in February 2003 that the last seven years of struggle for reform within the constitution had proved that a theocratic democracy was unworkable. It has since called for a national referendum and constitutional reform. The idea of holding a referendum unites many pro-democracy groups in Iran as their last means of achieving non-violent change.

A quarter of a century ago, on 1 February 1979, Ayatollah Khomeini flew home from exile in Paris. In 2004, on the twenty-fifth anniversary of this date, 134 out of 290 parliamentary deputies resigned. A few weeks later a further 607 candidates who had been qualified to stand withdrew in protest from the elections. The reformists had gained 21 million votes in the previous general election, yet just six members of an unelected constitutional body had barred 3,600 candidates, including 87 elected MPs.

Many of those disbarred were accused by the constitutional watchdog of 'lacking loyalty to Islam and the constitution'. The disqualified list included the likes of Reza Khatami, brother of the President, and Reza's wife, the grand-daughter of Ayatollah Khomeini. These candidates were a part of the State's small, nepotistic inner circle, but even they were prevented from standing. If even the conservative, chador-wearing granddaughter of the founder of the Islamic regime is officially deemed as 'lacking loyalty to Islam and the constitu-tion', where does that leave the rest of the population?

---

14 February 2004

Free Elections!

Dear Sirs,

What moron out there dares to think our elections are not free?!

When for each constituency, on average, there are 19 candidates ...

and then you have the nerve to say that we do not have free

elections!? For instance in our village! We don't need more than one

elected candidate, do we?!

You can vote for Hajji Aghah. God forbid you don't think he is

suitable. His daughter is also standing in the elections! Well, there is

no difference between men and women?! Is there?!

Now listen, you dog eaters! You don't like her?! His son is also a

candidate. All the more his uncle and his sister-in-law and ... all are

candidates! How could an election be more free than this?!

Email: hamedyou@gmail.com

http://weblog.hamedyou.com

On 1 February 2004, 134 parliamentary deputies read out their resignation state-ments during a fiery parliamentary session. They accused the powerful, unelected clergy of seeking to impose a 'Taliban-style' religious dictatorship.

We cannot continue to be present in a Parliament that is not capable of defending the rights of the people and which is unable to prevent elections in which the people cannot choose their representatives.

---

4 February 2004

This is not the defeat of the reformist candidates in Parliament ... It's the collapse of the ideology of a religious democracy.

Email: blindphilosopher@hotmail.com

http://iranmehr.blogspot.com

---

2 February 2004

Parliamentarians today started handing in their resignation letters ... If only they had woken up earlier ... if only people still believed them.

Email: dr_salardr@yahoo.com

http://www.doctoractor.persianblog.com

A few weeks later the reformist majority was replaced with hardliners. The reformist parliamentarians used this time to attack the elections as rigged and accuse hardliners of imposing a rule similar to that of Afghanistan's ousted Taliban.

Parliamentarians such as Ali-Akbar Mussavi-Khoeniha openly dared to criticize the legitimacy of Iran's Supreme Leader, 'God's representative on earth'. On 7 March 2004 Mussavi-Khoeniha said in a speech that was broadcast on the radio throughout Iran: 'We have witnessed a parliamentary coup ... no longer will there be letters of protest, or voices that reveal the forbidden truth concerning those that have been terrorized or voices that highlight the killings of free-thinkers or the onslaught of the Army against the students or the solitary confinement of students, journalists and political activists.' The new hardline parliamentarians, he said, 'will do as the regime commands and say what the regime likes to hear ... Let's not forget,' he added, 'that in the last year of his rule Saddam had elections when more than 98 per cent voted for his regime, but such endorsements did not strengthen in any way the legitimacy or the validity of his regime ... nothing but genuine reform from within will keep this regime alive.'

---

8 March 2004

[By recently exiled Sina Motalebi, a journalist imprisoned in 2003 because of the content of his blog]

For Ali-Akbar Mussavi-Khoeniha and his courage

Kings are slain in Parliament
We have heard many times that the 'Supreme Leader' is the red line of the regime. Even prominent reformists have not dared cross this line ...

Perhaps leaders in the free world do not regard criticism in Parliament as a matter for anxiety or dread ... But the nature of the oppressor is such that the harder they rule, the more mouths they sew up and the more they imprison ... In turn, it is easier for them to feel fear and the more they shudder ...

When Ali-Akbar Mussavi-Khoeniha stated that the conduct of the Supreme Leader was not consistent with 'honesty, prudence and justice' he knew what fiery ground he was stepping on. May his life be safe and his name honoured!

http://www.rooznegar.com

Having watched for seven years as the so-called reformists struggled to overturn hardline opposition, their disillusioned supporters merely watched from the sidelines as they were removed from Parliament. Had the reformists been unable or unwilling to confront the ruling clerics? Whatever the reason, those who sought political change in Iran were still being attacked and the people who had backed the reformers were more discontented than ever – especially the pro-democracy activists, writers, journalists and students who were still being brutally suppressed by the regime. Nevertheless, there seemed to be a new voice of opposition coming from inside the regime itself. It started to look more and more like a power struggle between two factions within the Establishment.

---

3 February 2004

On the twenty-fifth anniversary of Khomeini's return to Iran, his followers and heirs are experiencing unprecedented turmoil …

Yet this time, it is not the official opposition, but the elected members of the regime that with one voice have hailed their rule over Iran as illegitimate.

Email: arshinirani@yahoo.com

http://gharibeyeirani.persianblog.com

---

5 February 2004

An interesting mood is rising in Iran … everyone is publicly swearing at the Supreme Leader and the heads of the regime … In taxis, bazaars, universities … A remarkable thing today was that I even witnessed a friend (who due to the nature of his job has always had right-wing inclinations) so irritated that he was openly swearing at the Supreme Leader.

By Doctor

---

21 January 2004

One of my colleagues (a diehard supporter of the Supreme Leader) has become a candidate for the seventh Parliament. He can barely string a sentence together, but to my amazement the Guardian Council has endorsed his candidacy. He brought the despicable letter of his endorsement to the office!!

Everyone is teasing this wretched candidate of ours. One of my colleagues said to him: 'Pay me 200,000 tomans [approx. $229] and

I will vote for you' ... Another says: 'Take me out for a nice meal and
you have my vote.'

He finally came over to me yesterday and said: 'I know you're not
into bribery, so how about voting for me?'

I said: 'Only if you promise that if you get elected ... you will
stand in the balcony of Parliament, pull down your trousers and
urinate on the whole of that Parliament!!'

He was furious!!

Email: bamdadz@yahoo.com
http://bamdad.blogspot.com

A disillusioned electorate was refusing to vote, the regime was mobilizing its
diehard supporters, and thousands of candidates were barred from standing for
election: a hardline monopoly on elected office was virtually guaranteed. On 21
February 2004 Iran saw the lowest turnout for elections since the conception of
the regime.

On the eve of the 2004 election, Ayatollah Jannati, a member of the powerful
Guardian Council had branded abstainers as 'traitors' to the regime. Yet there
were 'traitors' to be found even among the senior Shia clergy. The cleric Nasser
Ghavami, head of the reformist Judicial Parliamentary watchdog, announced
soon after the election that in the holy city of Qom, out of a dozen or so grand
ayatollahs, only three voted in the elections. It was a damning indictment: the
regime had even lost its legitimacy among the majority of the senior Shia clerics.
Meanwhile, 70 per cent of people in Iran's biggest cities had not voted. In the
aftermath of the elections Grand Ayatollah Montazeri, one of the most senior-
ranking religious figures in Shia Islam, announced that the Iranian people did
not go through a revolution in order to 'substitute absolutist rule by the crown
with one under the turban'.

---

19 February 2004

Yesterday I was eavesdropping on a conversation of a couple of
middle-aged women. The older woman was saying: 'I have to vote

Friday, as I'm a pensioner ... I'm anxious that if my birth certificate doesn't get an election stamp, they'll cut off my pension and my daughter is a university student. I'm afraid for her too if she doesn't vote.' ...

Albeit this time round even the religious teachers at schools are appealing to their students to ask their parents not to vote ... people are now less scared ... especially after the earthquake in Bam.

Email: z8unak@z8un.com

http://z8un.com

20 February 2004

Today all of the soldiers at our base were given the day off ... we were all told to come back with an election stamp on our birth certificates.

http://sobhaneh.net

During voting all birth certificates are stamped, so far from being a sign of apathy, not voting is a radical statement. Most of the country's industrial sector is owned by the State – all state employees, civil servants, members of the armed forces, teachers, factory workers and students could face harassment if they do not take part in the elections.

There were accusations of vote rigging and squabbles over the exact number of Iranians that voted, but figures show the regime was endorsed by fewer than 15 per cent of the electorate – exactly the same percentage that had voted for hardliners in the previous elections. In 2004, however, the Iranian regime had consolidated its absolutist rule and had rid itself of a Parliament that was powerless anyway – powerless but at times far too brazen in its futile demands for change. Iran's hard-line leadership had maintained considerable unity in the face of these reformist challengers, but now, with the reformists out of the way, the in-fighting had begun between various factions.

Mostafa Tajzadeh, President Khatami's former deputy Interior Minister, summed up the situation in a speech at Tehran University (9 March 2004):

> Currently, a 15 per cent minority have conquered two thirds of the seats in Parliament. This means that the majority in Parliament represents the minority in Iranian society. There is a huge gap opening up between the manifestation of democracy, Parliament and the citizens.

---

21 February 2004

'I saw the lava of a dawning ... flowing from the highest mountain.' ... Today was a really good day, a day of solidarity ... not voting was not because we didn't care or that we had lost hope ... It was an unmistakable decision not to vote, based on knowledge and hope ... We were brave enough to say no, with hope that things will change.

Email: z8unak@z8un.com
http://z8un.com

---

20 February 2004

The most astonishing event today – which even surprised those in charge of the polling station and the Hezbollahis of _____ [a village in central Iran] – was the arrival of a group of people who were bussed in to the village. After half an hour of wandering around like fools, they voted and left ... With such dirty tricks going on, it won't be surprising if extraordinary election results are reported by the state media.

http://sobhaneh.net

---

21 February 2004

During the last month our TV programmes have been dominated by round-the-clock propaganda, with channels repeatedly transmitting calls for everyone to go out and vote ... yet every time a programme about the elections came on ... my wife would grab

the remote control and immediately change the channel, saying:
'Well, we're not voting!' ...

The problem we have now is that every time my son wants to
change the TV channels he points the remote at the TV and says
'Well, we're not voting!' ...

Soon he's going to be starting school and if we don't get him to
stop saying this, we are going to be in some trouble.

Email: bamdadz@yahoo.com
http://bamdad.blogspot.com

---

20 February 2004

We were crushed ... we people who didn't vote and those who have
struggled for democracy, we were defeated ... the fascists are
entering Parliament ...

I feel that danger is near ... They called in one of the guys for
questioning yesterday ... and my name had come up too ... I feel so
stressed out ... I nearly had an accident - twice ... I'm not too well
... God, why have you abandoned me?

25 February 2004

Tragically we have no newspapers, otherwise we could publicize the
circumstances of this fraudulent election. Documenting the details,
backed up with evidence, so that everyone would know what a sham
it was and how they were elected ...

Even so, for those who resisted and took on the potential stigma
of not having an election stamp on their birth certificates ... despite
our stand we feel a sense of failure ...

There are now significant numbers of the population without
representatives or any outlets for their opinions and we are all
experiencing a mass sense of failure ... I am certain that this
concealed force will soon manifest itself somewhere.

By Digit

The Ever More Exclusive Elite

In the 2005 presidential elections the electorate was drawn to the ballot box by promises of radical change. Yet one possible legacy of the parliamentary reform movement was that in 2005 all candidates professed to be staunch reformists and pledged more than Khatami had ever dared to. Mostafa Moin, the candidate of Iran's main reformist party the Islamic Iran Participation Front, went further than most by standing on an issue that no mainstream politician had been willing to confront since the conception of the regime over a quarter of a century ago. His daring campaign pledge was that if elected he would contest the supreme leader's 'ruling decree' (hokme hokomati). In August 2000 the supreme leader had used such a decree to block a Free Press Bill and in 2001 Ayatollah Mesbah-e-Yazdi, a member of the Guardian council, had warned the ardent reformists in parliament who had been pushing for change that in 'special situations' the Supreme Leader could rule by decree, even replacing Parliament.

Mostafa Moin's campaign pledge to contest this decree was essentially a stand against what many see as the regime's primary problem: that all power rests in the hands of an unelected supreme leader who can rule against parliament at a whim. In a byzantine move that one blogger dubbed the 'Revenge of the Sheikh', Moin was initially disqualified by the Guardian council. Yet after an intervention by the supreme leader, which was overtly heralded by the conservative press and members of the Guardian council as a 'ruling decree', Moin was later reinstated. Moin's decision to stand following the supreme leader's intervention made a total mockery of his subversive stance and neutered his chances with the majority of the electorate who once again saw reformists as all talk and no action.

---

25 May 2005

I've been paying attention to the graffiti in the office toilet recently:
  Death to the Mullah's ass lickers, Death to the Mullah pimps,
Death to fake Muslim wolves dressed in sheep's clothing
  Well, the 'brothers' who support to regime have not left it at that:

Death to Monarchist, Death to anti-revolutionaries (communists, infidels ...)

The interesting thing is that these two groups use different tools. The dissidents resort to hacking their graffiti on the wall so that it can't be wiped away, while the 'brothers' use the official office-supply stationary felt-tips. The latest piece of graffiti hacked into the wall:

Oi! Useless reformists, take a dump on the 'ruling decree' if you dare.

bamdadz@yahoo.com
http://bamdad.blogspot.com

Yet through the magic of Iranian blogosphere barriers were coming down. Most presidential candidates had set up their own websites or, in the case of Moin, a personal blog. Bloggers were able to confront a presidential candidate directly and, in another unprecedented move in Iran, thousands of vetted comments – nevertheless including many that were critical of Moin and the regime – were published in his weblog:

May 2005

: I say to you that the Islamic republic cannot be reformed.

: I heard about your disqualification on the news, it upset me as unlike the children of the ruling clerics I don't have the financial means to emigrate and live in a free country ...

: To accept the 'ruling decree' is to tear down your campaign pledge ... I plead with you not to accept. It can be a chance for a democratic struggle. Be certain that your support base will spread out amongst the population.

http://drmoeen.ir

Only time will tell if Iranian blogs are merely a place for the beleaguered to let off steam or a modern day Gutenberg press that would usher in the age of Democracy. Yet having watched for eight years as the so-called reformists struggled to overturn hardline opposition, many bloggers openly stated that they had lost hope of bringing change through the ballot box.

---

27 May 2005

I had asked Mr Moin a question and I still don't really know his answer.... He says that the seventh parliament [after the mass disqualification of elected reformists in 2004] is illegal. If he gets elected he will have to work with that parliament for three years ... All we hear are slogans ... How will they implement what they promise?

By Eclipse

---

28 May 2005

The weather is heating up with the talk of elections; what difference does it make whose turn it is to be President next or that you will wake up every day in disbelief at who you have as president ...

For a lot of people it makes no difference: for those that have been in solitary confinement and are just getting used to the damp walls of their prison cells ... for those that not so long ago became ladders [for politicians on their way to the top] and today are wounded and ineffective and can sense the bitter taste of being forgotten ... for the boys huddled at the street corner right now, who only dream of jobs ...

It makes no difference, as we have realised 'all roads lead back to Rome'.

By Stone

While a reformist candidate was making promises people felt he could not keep, the hardline candidate Mahmood Ahmadi'nejad was promoted as the man of the people. By presenting himself as taking a stand against corruption and cronyism Ahmadi'nejad tapped into a vein of popular anger, and appealed to the minds and hearts of jobless youth and underpaid workers with promises of food and housing subsidies for the poor. According to Behzad Nabavi, acting Chairman of parliament during Khatami's era, the modest-looking Mayor of Tehran backed by the establishment 'was promoted as an anti-establishment figure'. At one stage during his campaign Ahmadi'nejad even falsely complained that the 'establishment' had cut off the electricity supplies in large areas of Iran so that his campaign speeches promising a fight against corruption could not be heard by the ordinary people.

In May 2005, a group of more than 600 Iranian political activists called for the boycott of presidential elections, among them a number of former recent MPs and leaders of The Office to Consolidate Unity, Iran's largest student organization. This resulted in a fractional boycott and a degree of voter apathy that may well have further thwarted the hopes of the moderates.

With the victory of Revolutionary Guards veteran Mahmood Ahmadi'nejad as President in the 2005 election, hardline rule was further extended to the executive branch of the regime. The election result was announced amid accusations of foul play by many observers including three of the candidates. Cleric and former parliament speaker Mehdi Karoubi stated that, 'there has been bizarre interference. Money has changed hands'. In a statement to the press, Mr Rafsanjani, another candidate and the head of the powerful expediency council, claimed that: 'All the means of the regime were used in an organized and illegal way to intervene in the election.' And Elaheh Koulai, spokeswoman for the main reformist candidate Mostafa Moin, told a news conference that 300,000 members of Islamist militias had taken part in an operation (costing some $15.5 million) to influence the vote. 'Take seriously the danger of fascism,' Moin said in a statement. 'Such creeping and complex attempts will eventually lead to militarism, authoritarianism as well as social and political suffocation in the country.'

Once more the regime's inner circle was becoming more exclusive. President

Ahmadi'nejad even promised to 'cut the hands off the mafias' that controlled the oil industry and to share out Iran's oil wealth more fairly.

Yet there is a painful irony in the fact that Ahmadi'nejad comes from and is endorsed by the hardline core of the regime that has ultimately controlled power in Iran since the revolution. The possibility that Ahmadi'nejad will be unable to keep his campaign promises over the next four years will present a critical challenge to the heart of Iran's revolutionary elite. As Martin Woollacott writing for the Guardian (June 27, 2005) put it, 'What is both worrying and hopeful for Iranians is that this consolidation of power has a last-ditch aspect about it. Khamenei has increased control, but the regime has lost flexibility and much of whatever legitimacy remained.'

June 26 2005

I want to congratulate Mr Ahmadi'nejad and remind him that I voted for him because of his esteemed goals of social justice and the fight against poverty.

samir19031@yahoo.com
http://sadegh56.blogfa.com

June 26 2005

I don't regret not voting. I only wish that circumstances were different and my choice hadn't been one between bad and worst ... If Ahmadi'nejad can keep only a few of his promises [such as the fight against poverty] then I will be happy that I didn't vote for Rafsanjani ... They [the poor] are hungry and tired ... and only want financial security

foroogh_bahari@yahoo.com
http://foroogh.malakut.org

June 23 2005

For the boycotters ... our dear human rights friends abroad ... for how long are we to be bait in your traps so that you can chant your slogans, show off that you have not been idle and that you are a social activists, fighters, you are politically aware ... while your fellow countrymen ... that is I ... we are being crushed ... by a minority that can take the whole of this nation towards slavery ...

By Varseh

June 26 2005

Do not worry or become alarmed. Nothing much has happened, except that we can see what has been up to now hidden, a fresh force outside the power structure has not been empowered ... the force that during the last eight years held the real power is now come to the forefront and has only made itself visible.

shabah@shabah.org
http://www.shabah.org

June 26 2005

They have built him [President Ahmadi'nejad] up as an opposition figure to the regime or as he puts it, to return rule to the people ... No one will expel the Taliban from our homes. To reach democracy perhaps there is no other way but to tame this tribe ... It is not simple and those who have naively taken such promises [of redistribution of wealth] to their hearts have to realise that justice will not prevail with such talk and only poverty can be fairly and speedily distributed.

By Even Now

June 25 2005

Our community of pseudo-intellectuals is like the Laos soccer team.

They always lose ten to one and at the end of the game say: Failure
is the start of Victory!

mollaincanada_2@hotmail.com
http://mollah.blogspot.com

CONCEALED FORCE

Once the hardliners had secured their monopoly on Parliament, the Iranian
Government intensified its campaign of torture, arbitrary arrests and deten-
tions. A Human Rights Watch report (7 June 2004) stated that:

> Faced with increasing political pressure for reform in the past four years,
> the Government has intensified its campaign against dissent. As of June,
> the Government has closed virtually all independent newspapers, several
> key journalists and writers have fled the country, many prominent writers
> and activists have been imprisoned, and scores of student activists have
> been intimidated into ending their involvement in peaceful political
> activity.

10 July 2003

I was still a student during the student riots of July 2000. I
remember I was at the dorm in Shiraz preparing for a chemistry
exam when Ali suddenly came in and told us they had attacked the
students in Tehran. I ran out to a newspaper kiosk but everything
had sold out. I sat in front of the TV news that night, but other than
a story about a cat and a dog in Thailand that had decided to live
together there was nothing else happening in the world!

I rang up Tehran and soon found out what was going on. Hamid,
who lives in Amir-Abad [near Tehran University], told me about the
violent assault against the students at the dorm. I was furious.

My mum and dad kept constantly calling up [from Tehran] and saying: 'Isn't it enough that you got a beating last year? Don't be so stupid as to come down here!' But experience has shown that I am always stupid!

A group of us planned to go in the next day dressed in black as a sign of mourning. I think we managed to get together a good crowd, considering a lot of people were oblivious as to what had gone on and were busy with revising. There were a lot of us there that day dressed in black. But wearing black just wasn't enough and soon we were chanting: 'Murderers! Psychopaths!'

Soon our protests spread to the streets. I heard that it was even worse in Tehran. My exams were finally over and I really wanted to go there. Ali had got hold of a bus to take a group of us to Tehran. But I found out about it too late and it left without me.

So I got on another bus. But the highway police saw me and I was arrested and taken down the station.

'Where are you going?'

'Tehran?'

'An agitator?'

'No! I'm going home!'

'Why now?'

'Because my exams have finished.'

They took me and four others in a security van (one of those vans they use for carrying cash) back to Shiraz. At that stage I really felt I was done for; especially as I'd been filmed in the earlier protests.

I was taken blindfolded to another room and interrogated by someone standing behind me. The interrogator didn't seem like such a bad person. His questions kept going back to my history at the student union. They had found my student union membership card in one of my pockets.

He asked his questions very calmly. Until, that is, he said: 'Do you know that if we arrest you in the demonstrations you will be put away for ten years?'

And I said: 'Do you think these people will be around for another ten years?'

Suddenly he got really angry and said: 'You son of a bitch! Do you want me to empty this gun in your head, so then you'll realize who'll be around for another ten years?'

I said, 'No, I'm sorry,' and started grovelling.

The cold metal gun against my head gave me a feeling of utter helplessness. I knew I could do nothing. If he hadn't had a gun I would've shown him. After about 15 hours they let me go. Their only aim was to really frighten me.

I had a lump in my throat the whole way home [to Tehran], but I refused to cry. Well, men don't cry.

The next day in Tehran I asked my father: 'Father, why did you have children? Why did you demonstrate against the Shah? I'll never forgive you for sending me to university.'

The only thing he could say was: 'If you don't want to feel ashamed in front of your children, keep your eyes open and start thinking who you want to replace this lot.'

Email: soheil_topol@yahoo.com
http://nimpahlavi.persianblog.com

It is worth remembering that the generation that gave birth to a revolution twenty-five years ago was made up of ideological factions and political groups ranging from dogmatic armed Maoists to diehard Islamists calling for a holy war.

As for the next generation, they have been accused by some of lacking leaders and offering no new ideology. If the commentaries by young Iranian bloggers are anything to go by, it seems that ideals have replaced ideology. They want accountability, pluralism and democracy and have shed the dogmatic ideologies of the past.

Masoud Behnoud has been a leading author, journalist and social commentator in Iran for four decades, struggling to produce a faithful body of work under two autocratic regimes. His efforts have led to imprisonment and more recently to exile. Here is his analysis of the current situation.

---

15 April 2004

Each day as I open and look at the websites and blogs by young Iranians, I am filled with a new spirit. I say to myself how gratifying it is that our youth now possess an outlet for their beliefs ...

They value freedom and do not sell out to fanaticism. Their blogs are reflections of the unveiled and candid views of our youth and future generations of Iran ...

In our day, everyone was looking for an opportunity to shout, and the louder their voices the more attention they would get. But today's generation is not like that. If they want freedom it is so that they can coexist in this society and build a better world for the whole of humanity.

Email: masoud@behnoudonline.dot.com
http://behnoudonline.com

Iran's new generation no longer sees political radicalism as the way forward. The failure of parliamentary reform has not led them to give up on changing Iran for the better, especially the country's students. Today young people make up 70 per cent of the population and lead the way in calling for a secular democracy. This impressive majority will ultimately determine the future of Iran.

Iran's students have shown a remarkable amount of resilience. Ali Afshari, who once headed the largest nationwide student union Tahkim Vahdat, was released after three years in prison, most of that time spent in solitary confinement. On 26 April 2004, within days of his release, he was addressing a packed gathering at his old university. 'The failure of political reforms do not mean the end of our desire for democracy or a progressive society,' he said. 'The reform movement in its present form has reached a dead-end, but it offers us other opportunities.' True to form, he even threw in a jibe at the Islamic hardliners, whose campaign pledge was to turn Iran into the 'Islamic Japan'. 'Knowing their track record as we do,' he said, 'we'll be lucky if they don't turn us into the new Ethiopia.'

---

11 May 2003

Two days ago the Supreme Leader Khamenei honoured Shaheed Beheshti University 'students' with a visit ... before the Leader's arrival, large numbers of buses and minibuses carrying young Basij Militia supporters arrived at the campus ... There were in reality only a handful of actual students present and even then some were expelled from the hall for making fun and mimicking the warm-up guys ...

www.parizi.blogspot.com

In the early days of the Revolution it was Ayatollah Khomeini who had regular gatherings with the country's 'students', but it has been many years since his successor has met up with 'real' students. And when President Muhammad Khatami visited Tehran University in December 2004 to mark Student's Day, a thousand students showed their frustration by booing and chanting 'Shame on you!'

---

13 January 2005

What happened to Khatami showed that we have come a long way ... these regime reformists did not realize that today the children of Iran are entirely of their own era – and at a time of their own choosing they will speak in their own language.

Email: saeededigar@gmail.com
http://saeededigar.blogspot.com

The annual gathering to mark Iran's National Youth Day 2004 proved another flashpoint. Some 150 representatives of the country's youth groups met with the

President and all were allocated three-minute slots to put their questions to him.[1]

Traditionally on such occasions, representatives of different youth groups gather and, rather than actually asking questions, they praise the Supreme Leader and the good deeds of the President. But Youth Day 2004 was a very different affair: the President got a 'severe grilling' from many of those present. One young girl demanded: 'Mr President, look me in the eye when I ask my question.' She went on to say: 'Mr Khatami, you were unfaithful to us all.' Another asked: 'Do you sleep well at night?' A revolt was brewing.

The bold language of these student representatives was unprecedented. As a generation they see themselves as citizens with rights struggling for a civil society – and they greatly outnumber the soldiers of the ideological state.

The President was 'astonished', but he was further taken aback when Samieh Touhidlo, another student representative, stepped up to him. She began by saying:

> I have consulted many friends as to what I should say to you ... I am sorry, very sorry that a lot of my friends agreed with me ... when I suggested that today I should stand in front of you and hold three minutes of silence ... Dear Mr Khatami, Do you remember the student dormitory [attacks]? That day, in addition to the brutal injustice we endured ... instead of our attackers, our fellow students were imprisoned. You were silent and told us to be silent too. Everything started then ... everything started when all at once 16 publications were closed down, and you were silent and taught us to be silent too ... When they condemned our professors to death you were silent ... from then on, one by one, our classmates en masse were sent off to jail and you were silent, and taught us to be silent. What we endure today, this bitter silence, is your legacy ... Mr Khatami, you did nothing for our youth. Your ultimate achievement was to destroy a tidal wave of hope – my generation voted for a reformist agenda in two consecutive elections ... I say today, with conviction, that you are the guilty party.

This bold and damning speech won Samieh Touhidlo three minutes of fervent applause from the crowd. Perhaps the greatest legacy of the Islamic Republic is its children – educated young women like Samieh Touhidlo, who bravely stand up for democracy in Iran.

---

8 January 2005

We have a long way to go to convince the reformists that reform is not the logical continuation of the Revolution. We want reform because we regret the Revolution ... When are these supporters of Khomeini going to realize that the world has moved on and we are left behind and what a long journey we have ahead of us to get our deserved share of this world?

Well, some might say that at least we must be grateful for these reformists, as there are others who still want a united Islamic world ... What an unfortunate youth we are that we have to tolerate such people.

By Digit

CHALLENGING THE REVOLUTION'S LEGITIMACY

The ruling clerics might have removed the reformists from government, but they have failed to prove they are capable of taking Iran into the twenty-first century.

Twenty-five years after the Revolution, Iran's economy (supported by one of the world's largest oil reserves) is crippled by corruption and negligence. The regime has not produced employment and prosperity. Even if promises of reform have not borne fruit, the underlying desire for change is as strong as ever. Today the Islamic Republic of Iran confronts the greatest challenge to its legitimacy ever seen. Its ideology of political Islam has been rejected by its own religious leaders and MPs; it has seriously mismanaged what should have been a booming economy; and on top of that it must answer to the demands of Iran's educated and politicized young people who make up a massive 75 per cent of the nation.

23 February 2004

Now that the totalitarian regime has uniformly pulled together ...
And the lines have been drawn ... A total split between the
population and its rulers will be soon revealed ... The biggest
struggle for us today is to dissuade Western powers from
supporting the regime ... In the meantime we have to publicize
through the Internet the protests that are taking place around the
country and all anti-government gatherings ...

Start the spread of anti-government slogans on every available
wall space and even on our websites. If every single one of us writes
an anti-regime slogan in our neighbourhoods, the Islamic Republic
will start to look so pathetic that it won't be able to wipe the shame
from its facade.

Email: fozoolak@hotmail.com
http://fozool.blogspot.com

9 March 2004

[by an Iranian journalist based in Tehran]
I've just heard that The Teacher's Pen, a teacher's union newspaper,
has been closed down. This is the same organization that has been
printing news of teachers' complaints and strikes. Today pensioners
and staff at the medical sciences universities have also joined the
strikes* ...

These incidences prove that the absolutists are being faced
sooner than imagined with a wave of social protests.

Another piece of exclusive news ... in a recent meeting Morteza
Haji, the Minister of Education, announced that he was pleased that
the level of school closures have come down to 500 in Isfahan [a
major provincial capital in southern Iran], especially as 800 schools
in Isfahan were shut on the first day of the strike.

* The national teachers' strike in March 2004. 'No figures for the number of

strikers were given, but one paper said at least 400 schools in Tehran had been hit.

Work stoppages were also taking place in the cities of Isfahan, Kermanshah,

Hamedan, Yazd and Ardebil.' (AFP 9 March 2004)

By Journalist

It is not only secular liberals or student groups that challenge the legitimacy of the regime. Mohsen Sazegara was a former Islamist revolutionary and one of Ayatollah Khomeini's attendants in exile in Paris. Later he facilitated the creation of the Revolutionary Guard, but in May 2004 he had this to say about the regime.

> Twenty-five years ago we forced our religion into a marriage with a
> revolution that assaulted it and taught it aggression, while politicians
> swindled and tormented our faith. It's time for a divorce of this unholy
> alliance. Religion has to be returned to its personal parameters ... It's
> time for a divorce, and our society is now ready for this ... As far as society
> is concerned, the revolutionary paradigm has come to an end ... and
> whether anyone likes it or not, society has already given birth to a liberal
> paradigm.'

Today Sazegara is a member of a pro-referendum committee that includes major student groups, leading writers, academics, human rights lawyers and politically diverse activists both inside and outside Iran. It is busy collecting the names of Iranians who support a national referendum on the future of Iran. A website set up by this committee collected 20,000 names in a matter of days, before access to it from inside Iran was blocked by the authorities. Meanwhile, many of Iran's leading student groups are still collecting signatures and passing out the e-mail address of the site for potential petitioners to send their support. Many diverse political groups from monarchists to left-wing socialists have pledged their support for a referendum. Their aim is to enlist the support of Western democracies, including America, to support this movement through international bodies such as the United Nations.

12 October 2004

The only help America can give the Iranian people
In reality, if the United States supported the cause of democracy in
Iran (which I doubt), instead of stressing Iraq and nuclear power, it
would push through the United Nations for a national referendum
about the future of Iran by the people. This would sort out America's
dilemma and our problem too.

yourmail@yourserver.com
http://noshin.blogspot.com

THE DIEHARDS

Nobody denies that the regime has some diehard supporters: the 10 to 15 per
cent of the electorate who religiously turn out to rallies to denounce the traditional enemies of Israel and the United States. These people also dutifully vote
for the candidates endorsed by the authorities. The regime's hardline Islamic
militiamen and women are financially well looked after, and now that conservatives control Parliament, funding has greatly increased for militia groups and
strongholds of hardliners like the armed forces, as well as state television and
radio and the judiciary.

Perhaps because their opinions are well catered for by the state media, blogs
kept by staunch supporters of the regime are rare. The following Iranian
blogger, a young photojournalist, works for a number of hardline publications.
He echoes the concerns of many hardliners that Islamic principles are being
eroded. From his perspective, a great injustice is taking place within Iranian
society: the righteous are being marginalized and mocked by a majority that has
been corrupted by the West.

21 August 2003

I am tired of being force-fed their pseudo-intellectual ideals. We are
getting to a point where if we object to anything contrary to their
beliefs, then these so-called libertarians shout us down ... All you
have to do is disagree with them and you're the 'oppressors' or
'allied with the Taliban or al-Qaida' ...

   Throughout history the righteous have always been in the
minority.

http://vizor.persianblog.com

The next blogger, Muhammed Sarshar, is the literary critic of *Hareem*, one of the
most sinister hardline youth publications in Iran. *Hareem* regularly calls for the
religious killings of pro-democracy figures whom it labels as apostates. In his
blog, Sarshar has complained that he has a problem getting 'liberal' writers to
discuss their work in *Hareem*. (Among the radical Islamists, the word 'liberal' is
used in much the same derogatory manner as words like 'fascist' or 'terrorist' are
in the West.) As an example of the 'fanaticism' of 'liberals', he posts a reply by a literary agent of an Iranian author.

13 June 2003

Judge for yourself from this reply I received from Ms Parva:
'I know the newspaper game, especially the kinds of games played
by publications such as *Hareem* ... My answer to you is that Mr
Shajoai does not need your kind of attention! Anyway what
percentage of the readers of *Hareem* are interested in modern
literature or actually read it?'

23 August 2003

Having just checked, I have a total of 46 messages:
Personal Messages: 9 ... Messages from the Opposition: 31 ...

including 14 curses, 3 of which are directed at female members of my family! Therefore, 67 per cent of messages are from the opposition: (45 per cent civil; 55 per cent discourteous) … Sorry, no time to analyse the data.

Email: mim_sarshar@yahoo.com
http://mdidevar.persianblog.com

Mojtabah Mir'ehsan is a clergyman based in the holy city of Qom. His blog usually contains sermons on the significance of Islamic edicts, but on rare occasions he discusses his day-to-day life. In the following post he is annoyed by the appearance of the children of the Revolution.

31 January 2003

Please, control yourselves
Instead of 'Salaam' he said 'S'aam' … six feet tall, he stood by the doorway … Yet he bore no resemblance to the Maysam I once knew … His hair was covered in goo … However hard I tried to see in his eyes the likeness of someone I knew – all I could see was my own reflection in his dark glasses … A tight black shirt with an upturned collar … a discoloured pair of trousers, eight sizes too big and shoes that looked like powerboats …

I asked him to sit down and offered him some tea.

'Tea is too high-voltage,' he said, 'and it gives me no satisfaction.'

Perhaps some fruit?

'No, I have excess vitamin C in my blood. If you don't mind I'd rather smoke.'

'No problem,' I said. 'Feel free.'

He took out a cigarette and lit it with a Zippo lighter … the first puff made him cough. It was obvious he was a novice smoker … the thing that upset me most about Maysam, though, was his pretentious beard: a very thin line around his jaw.

I had grown up with Maysam's father and his uncle Davoud. But I couldn't control myself ... the way he looked really made me angry ...

I quickly gave him the book he had come to borrow for his father and sent him on his way. But seeing him really took me back to my own youth and memories of growing up in the old neighbourhood ... Davoud and I and Maysam's father used to really look up to this man in our neighbourhood called Mr Naderi ... we used to want to dress and even walk and talk like him ... The fashion in those days was called 'hippy' ... and our idols were the stars of the cinema ... we were what my father used to call 'misguided youth' ...

But we started changing; we read and grew up ... We exchanged our jeans for combat gear and our idol became Khomeini ... we were prepared to die for him ... We no longer had any time for the likes of Mr Naderi ... We used terms and had an outlook that my father couldn't even understand ... and he still called us 'misguided youth' ... Not long after that Davoud was martyred in the war and three years later Maysam's father lost his leg to a landmine ... and I ...

When we were young we used to dress and speak in a way that used to make our elders cross with us, but enlightenment came to us through Imam Khomeini ... I am trying to practise patience, so that the appearance of the likes of Maysam don't make me angry ... as it has been proved to me many a time that appearance has no correlation with the way someone really is ... the youth will always do their own individual thing ...

But I think the time has come that you and I stop getting mad at these new thin beards, the jelled hair and the faded trousers ... not to get angry or at least to control ourselves.

Email: mojtaba110@noavar.com
http://mojtaba11.persianblog.com

© Nafise Motlagh

Mir'ehsan would like the 'devout' to be more indulgent and understanding of young people who no longer resemble their revolutionary predecessors. It is a view that even appears to be shared by the ruling clerics. Not that they haven't tried to crack down, but with a young population on the rise it has not been easy.

In the last decade, as we have seen, St Valentine's Day has become a huge national event, much to the chagrin of Iran's unelected rulers. Year after year the Morality Police have padlocked the shops and printing houses that produce Valentine's Day cards, while the clerics have preached furiously against this profane trend. But on Valentine's Day 2005 there were no significant reports of shops being closed or young lovers being arrested and flogged in public. Has the regime finally accepted the fact that the new generation wants to adopt its own traditions?

---

1 October 2003

As a nation we all have dual personalities … At home we are as free as can be … we have fun, drink, have parties … and pay no attention to the religious dictates of the Supreme Leader. But in public we are forced to act devout and show support for the regime ...

This has destroyed our culture and has turned us into the worst kind of hypocrites ... and as a society we are rotting from the inside.

Email: fozoolak@hotmail.com
http://fozool.blogspot.com

Alcohol is banned in Iran, except for religious minorities such as Armenian and Assyrian Christians who are allowed to brew alcoholic drinks for personal consumption. In September 2003 Reuters reported that 'alarmed by soaring sales of medicinal spirits, Iranian authorities had begun seizing large quantities of the

© Amirali Ghasemi 2005, amiralighasemi.com

ONE NIGHT IN TEHRAN

liquid, which Tehran black marketeers say has fast become a favourite tipple in the officially "dry" country.' The Health Ministry also ordered pharmacies not to sell alcohol without prescriptions and closed down a handful of pharmacies in Tehran that had flouted the new regulations.

Home brewing is very common and in June 2004 the AFP reported the death of 17 people in the southern Iranian city of Shiraz due to alcohol they had bought on the black market. The report added that '60 others were admitted to hospital after drinking a locally-made alcohol that doctors suspect was laced with methanol, a highly poisonous industrial alcohol'.[3]

In November 2003 Iran's hardline judiciary discreetly introduced the first ever fine for drink driving. (It was hidden away in a list of 171 other driving offences.) The fine was 10,000 tomans [approx $11] and not the customary punishment of public flogging and imprisonment. For the first time since its conception, the regime was ignoring its own strict Sharia dictates, though it continued to call pro-democracy activists 'enemies of God', a crime punishable by death.

Photos © Maziar Zand www.mzand.com

WOMEN AT AN OUT-OF-TOWN TRADE EXPO
THESE WOMEN ARE CONSERVATIVELY DRESSED BY WESTERN STANDARDS, BUT ONLY A FEW YEARS AGO THEY COULD ALL HAVE BEEN ROUNDED UP BY THE MORALITY POLICE AND PUNISHED, FOR MERELY SHOWING TOO MUCH WRIST OR HAIR OR, GOD FORBID, AN ANKLE. A FEW YEARS AGO ANYONE HAVING A WEDDING THAT WAS NOT SEGREGATED OR DRIVING WITH A MEMBER OF THE OPPOSITE SEX OR JUST WEARING MAKE-UP WAS PUNISHED BY JAIL OR A LASHING. THESE ACTIVITIES ARE STILL CRIMES, BUT IN RECENT YEARS THE AUTHORITIES HAVE BEGUN TO TURN A BLIND EYE.

Photos © Maziar Zand www.mzand.com

IRAN, 2003

---

10 February 2004

I remember a time when our television reporters covering, for
instance, the anniversary of the Revolution ... would only approach
the obvious types for interviews (men with beards or stubble,
dressed in combat gear, some with Palestinian shawls draped round
their necks ... or women totally enveloped in black chadors with
only the tip of their noses showing), basically the types that
everyone calls Hezbollahi ... In our everyday life we see them
coming out of mosques during Friday prayers or around the bases
of the Basij or in the remote housing compounds for the
Revolutionary Guards ...

Well it seems that they have finally cottoned on that ordinary
viewers watching these public hate figures (symbols of oppression
and backwardness) are going to feel even more hostile ... Today you
never see the reporters on TV interviewing such individuals ... now

we get the interviewees in T-shirts, clean-shaven, dark glasses, jeans and gelled hair ... women with hair tumbling out of their headscarves and full make-up and what not ...

But more interestingly you get these same people praising the regime ... It's so incredibly funny that they really think of us as a herd of cattle.

Email: sharymahak@yahoo.com
http://www.sandiego.persianblog.com

---

30 January 2005

An Illegal existence

Have you noticed that everything that Iranians do is considered illegal and is banned by the regime? In reality, everything is outlawed, in a way. Listening to music or watching a film. The clothes you wear, what you drink, the games you play, the conversations you have and what you discuss. What you read and write. What you do on the Internet, keeping a blog or joining ORKUT* are all illegal.

In total everything that Iranians do on a daily basis is outlawed and the way people live their lives is illegal. Perhaps there is no other country in the world where there is such a cultural gulf between the people and its rulers.

I think this is the biggest mistake of the Islamic Rrepublic. If they tried to reduce this gulf it would in turn make people less and less interested in politics. But by widening the gulf, the tension between the people and the Government can only increase.

* ORKUT is a popular online forum that connects people through a network of friends.

Email: youness@gmail.com
http://www.younessa.com

© Noushin Najafi

A YOUNG GORL OUT FOR A WALK WITHOUT THE
MANDATORY MANTEAU

ACCESS DENIED

On the subject of Iran, a report by the Committee to Protect Journalists (CPJ)
entitled 'Attacks on the Press in 2004' noted that:

> In an effort to counter the growing influence of Internet journalists and
> news bloggers, whose popularity has grown as sources of dissident news
> and opinion, Iranian officials imposed new constraints on Internet use,
> blocked Web content, and arrested a number of on-line journalists.
>
> With the reformist press nearly gutted and broadcast media firmly
> under the control of conservative political elements, many banned
> newspapers and pro-reform journalists migrated to the Web. A lively
> culture of news blogging captivated young readers, as evidenced by a 2004
> survey suggesting that many Iranians trust the Internet more than other
> media, the Iranian Students News Agency reported. Bloggers also proved
> somewhat resistant to government censorship. In an on-line protest
> during several days in September, bloggers renamed their sites after
> government-banned newspapers and ran outlawed articles. The bloggers –
> some trained journalists but many simply young, involved Iranians – are
> not formally organized, but their loose affiliation and common pursuit of
> free expression enabled them to become a collective force in 2004.

On 29 June 2004 Judge Saeed Mortazavi, head prosecutor of Tehran's revolutionary court proudly announced to (ISNA) reporters that 40 per cent of all sites

deemed illegal by the State had either been shut down or filtered. He added that those responsible for these illegal websites would be vigorously pursued through the courts. Judge Mortazavi can be credited with the closure of more than 120 publications and the harassment and imprisonment of many writers and political activists in recent years. It was only a matter of time before the Internet – a last refuge for Iran's liberal journalists and independent bloggers – would come under his scrutiny. In the early days of 2005 Iran's hardline judiciary launched an unprecedented assault on the Iranian blogosphere and on-line journalists. There was blanket filtering of websites and many bloggers were arrested.

In February 2005 a young cleric and blogger, Mojtaba Lotfi, was sentenced to three years and ten months for posting 'lies' on his website (www.naqshineh.com). Based in the holy city of Qom, Lotfi and a group of young theologians at the Qom seminaries had dared to grapple with such thorny notions as the need for Islamic reform, twenty-first century Islamic jurisprudence and human rights abuses by state clerics, as well as how to deal with social problems such as the use of ecstasy and the spread of AIDS. Yet it was an article entitled 'Respect for human rights in cases involving the clergy' that earned Lotfi a prison sentence. One thing Iran's state clerics are rather sensitive about is being accused of being unjust and un-Islamic by other clerics.

As usual the judiciary has not been idle in dishing out its own peculiar justice. The blogger and human rights activist Najme Omidparvar, pregnant with her first child, was arrested in March 2005. A month earlier, the Iranian blogger Arash Sigarchi was jailed for 14 years.

---

26 February 2005

The heavy sentence for a journalist [Arash Sigarchi] is the last desperate symbol of the prehistoric regime of mullahs showing its teeth and claws ...

Email: saeededigar@gmail.com
http://saeededigar.blogspot.com

Omidparvar and Sigarchi had written blogs using their own names, but more and more bloggers are forced to write under a pseudonym.

---

8 March 2005

I don't want to end up in a 2 x 1m prison cell ... to be imprisoned for one, two, three, six months. I don't want to be beaten and tortured. I don't want to repent and sell out my old friends. I don't want to wear prison clothes ... I want to be free and stay that way ... I want to write freely. I want to sit on the sofa eating crisps and watch Scarlet O'Hara. To stay free to be able to watch Scarlet O'Hara I have to hide my real name from the torturers.

This is my right and if it is cowardly and undesirable, then I am not at fault here. Blame a regime that in the most vicious way tries to oppress anyone who dares to think and write.

fmsokhan@gmail.com
http://www.fmsokhan.com

A LOGO POSTED ON COUNTLESS BLOGS ASKING FOR THE FREEDOM OF YET ANOTHER BLOGGER, MOJTABA SAMIE'NEJAD. ON 12 MARCH 2005 HE WAS OFFICIALLY CHARGED WITH APOSTASY, WHICH CARRIES THE DEATH PENALTY.

---

15 March 2005

A blogger has been accused of apostasy. As we know, if he is convicted he will hang. Who is he? A 26 year old who sometimes writes a blog ... What has he done? Perhaps he has written something against religion or perhaps he has been critical of our self-appointed gods?

If you say 'I don't worship God, but I like positive energy; I like hope and I like the life you say God has created' … they can easily kill you, for simply uttering that first sentence …

Until we can break our mental taboos, no progress or creativity will come from within our culture … If Galileo had allowed himself to think like his forefathers … the earth would still be at the centre of the universe …

Young people can't help but have doubts and ask questions … They have to break their mental taboos … When they come to realize that the greatest barrier to creativity is the forced beliefs of their forefathers … the first thing they will do is shed that religion … Faith in itself is worthy of respect … but when it goes as far as forcing punishments by death … it loses all esteem or integrity.

Activists should use this tragedy to unify in calling for the most basic of human rights … a unified call against the penalty for apostasy …

Even if it is merely to make people around the world realize that we Iranians do not wish anyone's death … and will not kill someone for his thoughts or for turning against the viewpoints of his forefathers.

Let's all shout: 'Hey world, believe us! We are humans too!'

Email: baba@eparizi.com
www.baba.eparizi.com

On 10 November 2004 Amnesty International observed that 'the arbitrary arrest of about 25 Internet journalists and civil society activists in recent weeks marks an alarming rise in human rights violations in Iran'. Among the detainees was Freshteh Ghazi, a young journalist who wrote on women's issues. Ghazi had tried to highlight the case of Afsaneh Norouzi, the woman condemned to death for killing her would-be rapist (see page 189), and had bravely written an impassioned open letter to the leaders of Iran and the judiciary, protesting against Norouzi's sentence and publicizing the details of this shadowy case. Now that the story was out in the open, Ayatollah Shahrodi, the head of Iran's judiciary, had to make a statement saying that due to 'irregularities in the case', Norouzi's sentence would be suspended and there would be a retrial.

It has since transpired from forensic evidence and court testimonies that Norouzi and her family were invited to Kish Island by the head of the Islamic Republic Police Intelligence to stay at his house. Then he had sent Norouzi's husband on an urgent business errand to Tehran. He was found stark naked stabbed to death in Norouzi's bedroom after trying to rape her. Her children witnessed the attack. After eight years in jail, Norouzi was eventually freed soon after Judge Sajadi, the head of the Kish Island courts, announced to the press in January 2005 that she had 'legitimately defended her honour'.

However, Ghazi, the journalist who exposed the 'irregularities' in Norouzi's case, was now being held in an undisclosed location accused of a number of crimes, including adultery. According to Reporters Sans Frontierès, five other imprisoned on-line journalists were forced to sign confessions stating that they had had sex with her. Adultery carries the sentence of death by stoning. For this reason Ghazi was the only one of the detainees who refused to sign a confession, yet reportedly she had to be hospitalized immediately after her release from prison in December 2004. According to Reporters Sans Frontierès, 'the seven journalists imprisoned between October and December 2004 had been beaten, humiliated and sometimes threatened with rape by their jailers. Most of them had been accused of moral crimes, that is, having sexual relations outside marriage, a pretext often used in Iran to attack political dissidents ... They also received daily threats by phone. One police officer suggested to one of the journalists that he "watch out for cars, because a lot of pedestrians get run over in this country".' (6 January 2005)

Released from jail, Ghazi continues to write her blog. Today, however, many Iranian blogs are filtered, so that only the most technologically savvy surfers can read them. Blogs that once had a few hundred readers every day suddenly had only a handful, if any.

26 January 2005

Now that I am relatively free, sitting here writing, how many
people are in jail in those dark and dingy cells for the crime
of writing? You try to keep your hopes and fears from the
interrogators ... ...

Being lazy, I did not take the upkeep of my blog very seriously.
But prison taught me that you have to write in newspapers, in blogs
and on websites, on walls and anywhere you can. I remember the
time when Larijanai Vison [state-controlled television] had banned
the songs of Hossein Zaman. He said: 'Let them ban my songs. I
will sing them in the streets and alleyways.'

Email: fereshteh_ghazi@yahoo.com
http://fereshteh.blogfa.com

9 January 2005

Mr Mortazavi, we know that you are aware of the spreading power
and influence of the Internet among the youth. Otherwise we would
not now be witnessing this unprecedented widespread filtering. We
warn you that if you make any move against Rozbeh Mir Ebrahimi,
Omid Memarian, Freshteh Ghazi, Seyed Muhammad Ali Abtahi or
their families, in a unified and widespread action we will tell the
world of your illegal and iniquitous deeds.

Email: hoder@hoder.com
http://www.i.hoder.com

Freshteh Ghazi is not alone in refusing to be silenced. Nearly all of her fellow
detainees have continued writing after their release. Despite the regime's
extreme measures against the use of the Internet, the determination of Iranians
to break their isolation is strong. Only time will tell whether they can reclaim
their right to free speech, yet many of those struggling against the totalitarian

regime are just as resolute as their tormentors. Here is a post by a journalist on the *Siah Sepid* group-blog in response to death threats.

---

26 October 2003

In the name of God.
I commence with the name of a supreme God, the God of Zarathustra, Moses, Jesus and Muhammad, the God of life itself. On the eve of the holy month of Ramadan when we are all the guests of God, the stench of fear, terror and revenge is in the air.

This air is the air of the Middle Ages when the tyrant clergy in the name of holy dictates and the protection of their faith would burn the bodies of worthy men and women ... What is this Islam of yours, that through its fight for righteousness has filled the world's atmosphere with the stench of decomposing corpses? ... When with his mad dogs quenching their thirst with the blood of our youth, Khamenei [Iran's Supreme Leader] is supposedly the only orphan child of Zahra [the prophet Muhammad's daughter] ... I tell you that the Shia are purely the followers of one God and no one else.

Your protestations are that you will safeguard the honour of the blood that was shed in our 'sacred defence' [the eight-year war with Iraq]. No Iranian can forget those years which are a testament to the bravery of our youth ... They did not die for your contrived Islam but for the defence of their homeland and you are not the same breed as those blessed men ...

If my pen and my literary activities are so harrowing to you that you want to kill me and now threaten me with a bullet ... If my pen is the menace, I will resort to writing in my own blood: long live freedom, equality, peace and democracy, long live Iran and Iranians! What higher honour than to die for my country?

Your worship of the Supreme Leader is worthless, and as for your threats, I am not 'a willow that will quiver at such breezes'.

Email: weblog@SiahSepid.net
http://www.siahsepid.com/weblog

Hossein Derakhshan sent thousands of other Iranians into the blogosphere following his simple how-to-blog guide in Persian. Ever since, he has been one of the most active supporters of Iranian bloggers.

---

6 January 2005

Friends in Iran, journalists and technicians, are saying that judiciary officials have ordered all major ISPs [Internet Service Providers] to filter all blogging services, including PersianBlog, BlogSpot, Blogger, BlogSky and even Blog Rolling.

They have also ordered them to filter Orkut, Yahoo Personals and some other popular dating and social networking websites.

5 November 2004

A hot topic of the last couple of weeks in the Persian blogosphere has been a blog called 'Islamic Army' ... They have picked particular posts from my Persian blog, in which they think I've insulted God and other sacred concepts of Islam and therefore, quoting from a Koranic verse, I deserve to be killed.

It seems they have a serious message this time, and when I add this to the recent mentions of my name in the radical Islamic newspapers such as Jomhouri-e Eslami and Kayhan, it doesn't look very good.

So, even though it still may be only a childish game, I guess I have to inform Canadian police and contact Google to see whether they can trace them, especially via their e-mails in their Gmail account: islamicarmy@gmail.com.

What do you think?

Email: hoder@hoder.com
http://hoder.com/weblog

The Iranian blogosphere could not have wished for a more nurturing parent than Derakhshan. He was a popular young tech-journalist in Iran before he emigrated to Canada in 2000. Today a student at the University of Toronto, he tirelessly promotes the cause of Iranian bloggers at every given opportunity, speaking at conferences and alerting the media of the arrest and harassment of bloggers in Iran.

Taking part in the 'Internet and Society' conference at Harvard University on 9 December 2004, Derakhshan described Iranian blogs as either 'bridges', 'cafés' or 'windows'. 'Bridges' connect the young and the old, men and women, politicians and the people, Iranians and the world. 'Cafés' are cyber-sanctuaries for authentic public debate. 'Windows' provide an important view inside Iran, a view that challenges the stereotypes of Westerners, as well as any illusions Iran's rulers might have about the general public.

© Hossein Derakhshan

THE GODFATHER OF IRANIAN BLOGOSPHERE HOSSEIN DERAKHSHAN

Derakhshan was one of the first Iranian bloggers to introduce his readers to the technicalities of web addresses or proxy servers which help users see filtered pages; he passed on the addresses of these pages and showed how to set up new ones when the old ones are shut down. As well as maintaining his own personal blog, he has also set up several very popular group blogs, with contributors posting the latest news and their reactions.

During the 2004 parliamentary elections Derakhshan organized bloggers to send up-to-the-minute reports on polling day from all over Iran. Another one of his websites (www.stop.censoring.us) provides reliable 'official and unofficial accounts on Internet censorship in Iran so that International observers and activists have a better picture about the situation of freedom of information in the Islamic Republic of Iran'.

In December 2003 he encouraged bloggers in Iran to post their complaints on-line on the UN digital summit website in the hope of reaching key summit delegates. Iranians swamped the Daily Summit blog with posts on Internet censorship. It led to some tough questions on censorship being posed to the Iranian President at a press conference.

---

12 December 2003

[Speaking in Geneva on 12 December 2003 at the UN's digital summit, Iran's President:] Muhammad Khatami has insisted that the Iranian government has only blocked access to 'pornographic and immoral' websites ... He said the ban only applies to sites that are incompatible with Islam; with Mr Moatamadi [a government official] adding, 'All political sites are free' ...

What he did not explain, though, is that in a theocratic regime the amount of subject matter deemed incompatible with Islam is vast.

Email: weblog@ksajadi.com
http://www.ksajadi.com/fblog

In 2005 Derakhshan even launched Radio Hoder, a 'podcast' (amateur radio programme) that can be downloaded on to a computer or an MP3 player. Once again, he was a pioneer in introducing and explaining the technology of 'podcasting' to Iranians and encouraging them to try it themselves. Here he is trying to get his fellow Iranian bloggers to write in English.

---

16 June 2004

If news isn't in English ... it never happened
The European community has been pressurizing Iran to improve it's human rights record for two years now, and in return they have promised improved economic ties with Iran.

If more people really knew what went on in Iran ... European leaders, fearful of public opinion, would no longer tolerate the charade presented to them by the mullahs.

If a news item isn't written or printed in English ... it has never happened ... and if we keep the frightening details of human rights abuses locked away in our hearts we will never be able to show the realities of Iran to outsiders.

Email: hoder@hoder.com
http://editormyself.com

Iranian bloggers have become increasingly resourceful and defiant in the last few years, but at the same time more and more blogs, especially the politically sensitive ones, have been shut down. Bloggers regularly receive threatening e-mails from people claiming to be security agents and are forced to close and resurface under a new name. Here is a familiar notice from persianblog.com.

وبلاگ مورد نظر شما هب علت رعایت توافقنامه کردن توافقنامه پرشین بلاگ ، مسدود می باشد.

'THE REQUESTED WEBLOG HAS BEEN DISABLED DUE TO A TERMS OF SERVICE VIOLATION'

15 July 2003

The closure of political blogs:
The management of Persianblog have closed so many political
blogs recently that I think it's time we started using alternative
venues ... even if it means having to write in English.

Email: arshinirani@yahoo.com
http://gharibeyeirani.persianblog.com

3 March 2004

Let's not forget that terror always starts with language ... Iranian
history is a testament to this ... Censoring words has always led to
the censoring of our identity and ultimately to our oppression.

By Hope

In response to the State's sudden campaign against blogs, various petitions
have been set up by Iranian bloggers, such as the following (from www.
home.tiscali.no/anjoman):

We, the undersigned, hereby express our condemnation of the
forthcoming legislation to implement blanket filtering of Internet traffic
in Iran.

The Iranian Government has systematically and methodically denied
Iranians the ability to speak freely and communicate with each other and
with people outside the country, through suppression of the national
press, television, telephone calls and now the Internet. The free
expression of ideas and opinions is cherished by Iranians, and we hold
this to be a fundamental human right. We condemn all efforts by
governments and telecommunication firms both within Iran and outside
the country to implement restrictions on the free exchange of speech and
ideas.

We respectfully request that you put pressure on both your local and

the Iranian governments to reinstate free speech and communication on
the Internet, and limit the censorship of traffic to material that is
universally, unanimously and internationally condemned.

June 2004

Petition to Human Rights Watch, International PEN, Reporters Sans
Frontières

A BANNER POSTED ON MANY
IRANIAN BLOGS

Recent reports suggest that the Iranian authorities want to implement a
national Intranet, which would separate Iran from the World Wide Web.
However, the rate of change of technology might well be working in favour of
free speech, as even the Chinese authorities have not been fully able to contain
the free flow of information. According to Reporters Sans Frontières:

> The Iranian regime censors thousands of websites that it considers 'non-
> Islamic' and harasses and imprisons on-line journalists. Internet filtering
> was increased in the run-up to the February 2004 parliamentary elections,
> in which the hardliners strengthened their grip on the country. But
> despite this, the Internet is flourishing, with fierce debate and weblogs
> ('blogs') sprouting up all the time. The Internet has grown faster in Iran
> than in any other Middle Eastern country since 2000, and it has become
> an important medium, providing fairly independent news and an arena
> for vigorous political discussion.[4]

A TOUGH NEIGHBOURHOOD

By all accounts Iran's rulers have a much bigger fight on their hands than taking
on a few bloggers. For more than a quarter of a century the United States has

been the regime's hated nemesis. Since 11 September 2001 and the consequent 'war on terror' in neighbouring Afghanistan and Iraq, Iran's leaders have watched the gradual encirclement of their country's borders by hundreds of thousands of enemy soldiers.

---

4 February 2005

God invented war so that Americans can learn geography!

Email: shakhsari@hotmail.com
http://farangeopolis.blogspot.com

Images courtesy of Kevin Tracy at ktracy.com

Merchandise from The Kevin Tracy Store by a 'Republican Artist'
Above, Organic Cotton T-Shirt ($20.99), Invade Iran Next Bib ($8.99)

On 29 January 2002, US President George W. Bush described Iran in his State of the Union address as part of an 'axis of evil'. In another State of the Union address three years later, he said:

> Today, Iran remains the world's primary state sponsor of terror –
> pursuing nuclear weapons while depriving its people of the freedom they
> seek and deserve. We are working with European allies to make clear to

the Iranian regime that it must give up its uranium enrichment program and any plutonium reprocessing, and end its support for terror ... To the Iranian people, I say tonight: As you stand for your own liberty, America stands with you. (3 February 2005)

There are US soldiers on Iran's doorstep and Washington is using the sort of rhetoric it used in the build-up to the war in Iraq ... Many Iranians think the chances of conflict are high. Only time will tell whether this stand-off between the United States and Iran will be resolved through diplomatic channels or by another war in the region. However dissatisfied they might be with their unelected rulers, Iranians are not in favour of aggression. As the seasoned commentator on Iran Dan De Luce has pointed out:

> One sure way to derail the cause of democracy would be a heavy-handed US action. Iranians retain a deep sense of national pride, and a clumsy covert operation or a stray bomb from the United States would be a gift to the mullahs. Air raids or other intervention of this kind would turn the focus away from the regime's failures and revive the idea of America as the villainous imperial meddler. The troubled American-led occupation of Iraq next door has already given the regime a rationale for cracking down on dissent at home and painting its critics as traitors.[5]

---

30 January 2005

America says you are terrorists. It says you are endangering the security of the region. It says you are part of the axis of evil. There is no democracy in your country. In your county human rights are not observed. And on top of all this you are trying to build an atom bomb.

Now what is our solution? Should we disqualify everyone who wants to stand in the elections? Kill a Canadian journalist in one of our prisons? Chuck a few bloggers in jail? Close down all newspapers overnight? Filter all political websites and then go and build a nuclear reactor and keep shouting that for God's sake, deep down we are really sweet people?

Or is the solution for us to gradually move towards democracy? Keep the atmosphere free from tension and leave the people alone so that the nation doesn't reach a point when they pray for our [the regime's] demise?

Which is the right way? If Iran's regime at least had the backing of the majority of people, would George Bush dare talk about attacking?

By Blunder

1 February 2005

I hate war. I hate the liberating soldiers that trample your soil, home, young and old under their boots. Believe me I love freedom. But I believe that you have to make yourself free. No one else can free you.

Email: ghasedak17@hotmail.com
http://shargi.blogspot.com

17 January 2005

Today I was reading on the BBC news website about a tragic train fire in India last year that killed 60 Hindus. These peace-loving Hindus who would not knowingly step on an insect for fear of being reincarnated as one, blamed Muslims for the fire. So they went on the rampage and according to the BBC killed nearly 1,000 Muslims. Today an official enquiry by the Indian government has conclusively found that the fire was started accidentally on the train, probably by someone cooking in one of the carriages.

Now that is the story of us Muslims since 9/11. Now they are looking for any excuse to kill us. Those people that blew up the Twin Towers had no nation or religion. They were simply a group of insane murderers. So why call every lunatic a Muslim? Maybe we should start doing the same. If there are reports of an axe-murderer who goes crazy and kills 20 ex-schoolfriends in the West, we should not just say a crazy person killed 20 people. We should do as they do in the West and say a Christian or Jew killed 20 people.

In the Rwandan genocide, 800,000 were killed and 7,000 Muslims were massacred at Srebrenica. In both cases Christian priests were the key instigators. Does anyone call them Christian terrorists?

Would someone out there please do a body count and tell me how many Muslims have been killed at the hands of these liberators since 9/11? I bet it's a similar ratio of the 60 Hindus and 1,000 Muslims massacred in India.

And now it's our turn to die. They want to kill us. And it is even more tragic than the Indian train fire. Because we are to pay for the actions of our rulers, whom we despise. Even though they are clerics, again like those people that blew up the Twin Towers, they have no nation or religion. But we the ordinary people will have to pay.

By School Friend

---

30 January 2005

I can see a war on the horizon ... In the depth of my heart I want the people of Iraq and Afghanistan to reach peace and freedom, but it might mean that America will find even stronger reasons to attack Iran ... I'm scared. I feel incredibly helpless.

Email: sanaz5674@yahoo.com
http://khojaste.persianblog.com

---

30 January 2005

If we want to get rid of this terror we have [of an American attack]. If we want to do something to stop American politicians attacking us. We have only one way.

We have to take our destiny and our country in our own hands.

Wars are there to advance the goals of dictators and the only losers are ordinary people. Everyone should know that no war is a good war and there is no such thing as a bad peace.

Standing up to the Americans and their allies is not the only way out. It is not just about deterring our external enemies, but standing up to our enemies within. The regime must understand that the people will not fight to defend it and that they are despondent and oppressed and just waiting to hear the noise of American planes. They are waiting to pull down the statues of dictators.

Email: kooche@Gmail.com

http://weblog.kooche.net

---

15 March 2005

Iranian Foreign Minister Kharazi, in answer to America's recent offer*: 'Concessions are not enough. Lift sanctions.' BBC [Persian service 15 March 2005]

How greedy! Well why don't you first of all free all political prisoners and recognize the rights of women and minority groups? Get rid of the Supreme Religious Guide and the Guardian Council and all these unfair organs that preside over the people and the nation. Recognize the freedom of political parties and allow all such parties that you have barred and banned to become active. Run a referendum and free elections so that then sanctions may be lifted.

How wearisome, that a group of people who for 26 years have had full control, ultimately still possess the same political methods as hostage takers.

* 'Iran has urged the US to offer it further incentives to resolve the dispute over its nuclear programme.' BBC, 13 March 2005.

By Scandal

---

17 February 2005

Tips on how to liberate Iran!

Seymour Hersh has told us that some GIs are creeping around
the deserts south of the Zahedan preparing for W.'s next war. I do
not subscribe to the New Yorker, but I tend to listen when Mr
Hersh speaks. He seems to know what's cooking way ahead of
time. So I would like to make some suggestions to the GIs, in
case they actually do make it to Tehran and decide (God forbid)
to 'obliterate' ... oops. Sorry. I mean, 'liberate' us ... Falluja
style.

Tehran Traffic: If your Central Intelligence Agency has been
telling you that Tehran has a functioning traffic system, well they've
been somewhat mendacious again. Over there, not even a Daisy
Cutter is going to help you. Just sit down in your Humvee, plug in
that iPod 40G and pop a Prozac ... extra strength.

Café Naderi*: Please ... please ... please pay a bit of attention
when carpet bombing the city with your 'precision' bombs. We are
already shocked and awed by your re-election of W. last
November, so there is no further need to stun us. The only place
that truly will be missed if levelled will be our beloved Café Naderi.
The waiters are primordial, the food is so-so and the Turkish
coffee is dreadful, but it has a slightly dowdy fin-de-siècle feel to it
and is much loved.

The Pollution: Those wily Israelis keep saying Iran is 'five years'
from obtaining the bomb, albeit those elusive 'five years' started in
1977 and we are apparently still 'five years' away, but do not be
disenchanted. The air in Tehran is the true WMD you have been
searching for so desperately. Those scheming Eyerainians have
managed to manufacture it right under the nose of IAEA. Put on
those chemical warfare jumpsuits you've been gingerly saving since
Baghdad, and be sure to wear them as you go to downtown Tehran,
where the sky has a bluish hue to it.

Body Counts: Never mind them, so long as you reinstall our silly little exiles à la the 1953 coup, all will be forgotten. Well, at least that's what they'll tell you.

The Current President: I say keep the fellow. After all is said and done: new hospitals, refineries and bridges need to be inaugurated. Red ribbons need to be cut. Foreign diplomats' credentials need to be accepted in colourful receptions. This chap is a skilled master of ceremonies, and not much else (he has had eight years of practice).

Tehran Drivers: The guy with a beat-up RD trying to squeeze in between your 8 x 8 light armoured vehicles, while throwing insults and waving his middle finger at you is not an insurgent. Trust me. He is just trying to make maximum usage of the road by turning a three-lane highway into six lanes. Put it down to a cultural difference.

Esteghlal Football Club: Feel free, absolutely free, to disband this terror cell. Take naked photos of its players for your viewing pleasures, and Gitmo the managers. As a diehard Persepolis fan, I can see no harm in any of it.

P.S. Iranians loathe the Bahraini national football squad and equally abhor the *National Geographic Magazine* for branding our beloved Gulf as 'Arabian'. So if you could drop a few of your 'precisions' on the Bahraini training ground and keep the current ban on that inflammatory publication, you will certainly win all the hearts and minds in the streets of Tehran.

In closing, remember that Alexander (no ... not Colin Farrell), the Arabs, the Mongols and even the British did us in a few times here and there along our long treacherous history. But along the way, they all became a bit Iranian themselves. So if many years from now you find yourself a bit superficial, slightly superstitious and a believer in conspiracy theories (commonly involving the British) you will finally realize that the Iranian insurgency is in full swing.

* Café Naderi in central Tehran has been a famous haunt of artists and writers since the 1930s.

Email: snmafi@hotmail.com

http://peaceiran.blogspot.com

THE HUMAN RIGHTS TRADE

Iranian-born Farzaneh Milani is the director of Women and Gender Studies at the University of Virginia. After a recent visit to Iran she wrote that a 'bloodless and non-violent revolution is reorganizing Iran's cultural and political landscape'.[6]

According to Shirin Ebadi, the human rights activist and 2003 Nobel Peace Prize-winner, 'Attacking Iran would bring disaster, not freedom'. She argues that the best way of supporting Iran's 'vigorous' human rights groups would be to demand that the regime 'adhere to the international human rights laws'.[7]

In 2004, while the regime was busily discarding any pretence at democracy and reasserting full control over the State, European nations such as France and Britain declared themselves satisfied that Iran's ruling clerics showed signs of moderation, because they had agreed to stricter inspections of Iran's nuclear programme. Some people obviously feel that the question of human rights in Iran can be left on the back burner for now and that the emphasis should be on EU negotiations with Iran over nuclear issues. The Europeans are so eager to persuade Iran to halt its nuclear activities that they are happy to compromise on the human rights issue for the time being.

A letter written on 29 January 2004 by Iran's national student union to the EU's foreign policy chief Javier Solana perhaps best echoes such concerns. The students wrote that 'We who represent 47 nationwide student union groups and whose leaders have been elected directly by the votes of the students of this country implore the European Union not to officially recognise, and negotiate with dictators just because they hold power.'

The students referred to Hassan Rohani, a leading unelected hardliner and the Supreme Leader's representative on a bipartisan body called the Supreme National Security Council (SNSC). Rohani had recently made a state visit to France to meet President Chirac. 'It is regrettable that France, considered the cradle of democracy and the Enlightenment in the modern world, sees fit to be a host to the representative of an autocrat,' they wrote. Rohani also led Iran's negotiations with the International Atomic Energy Agency and had made state visits to France, Brussels and Moscow.

The students went on to give the example of Saddam Hussein and the long-term outcomes of the West's associations with despots. 'Whatever they concede to the West, at home the leaders of the Islamic Republic oppress us,' they said. Western governments eager to befriend the regime should also listen very carefully to worrying public announcements by many of Iran's leading hardliners that Iran should pursue a 'Chinese model' of governance. This would mean liberalizing the economy and making peace with Europe and the United States – while maintaining political repression.

---

5 February 2004

Parliament is in the hands of the ruling clerics ... and now Iran's UN ambassador Zarif is in negotiation with members of the American congress! Then there is Iran's preordained future President Rohani's state visit to France!

There is a putrid stench of appeasement coming from the European Parliament as they make deals with the tyrants! And our rulers drastically need to do deals with the West, while they rule with an iron fist at home!

It's as if every 50 years they have to instigate a coup and stop us from ever realizing our dreams of a democratic Iran ... 1906 ... 1953 ... 2004 ...

Email: black_mak82@yahoo.com
http://blackmak.blogspot.com

There is a remarkable tendency among many Iranian bloggers to dwell with an almost tedious obsession on their historical past. It is also a prominent characteristic of Iran's political activists. A major student conference entitled 'The Defence of Republicanism' (3 February 2004) was held at Teheran's Amir Kabir University and attended by many leading pro-democracy speakers. The students involved likened what is happening today to the Constitutional Revolution of 1906, when hopes of democracy were dashed and authoritarian rule was implemented with the help of foreign powers.

Similarly inspired by Iran's recent past, the following blogger has chosen 19 March as a day on which to make a stand against international aggression. It is the anniversary of the nationalization of Iran's oil. Many believe this step led to the CIA coup which overthrew the democratically elected government of Mossadegh.

---

15 March 2005

19 March: Hands Off Iran!

We are three days away from 19 March (the day we stood up to the rest of the world and nationalized our oil industry!).

I had previously suggested that on the anniversary of this day we all change the titles of our blogs to a slogan that would show the world that we (Iranians) still stand by our sovereignty and are still committed to the same noble principles that made us fight for our rights 54 years ago.

Many people have come up with great suggestions for the slogan. My favourite is 'Hands Off Iran!' I think it is simple and has a good ring to it.

Of course, everyone is free to add other words to this slogan if they want to, but I suggest that we keep 'Hands off Iran!' as the common denominator.

We just have three days left, so I encourage everyone to promote the campaign on their blogs and invite others to join.

Email: rezanasri@gmail.com
http://rezansr.blogspot.com

IRAN'S VICIOUS CIRCLE

Fourteen thousand pro-democracy activists spent the long hot summer of 1906 in a mass protest in Tehran, living in tents and eating fresh baked bread and Aash (soup) prepared in enormous cauldrons. A climactic moment in Iran's struggle for democracy came in a joint declaration: 'The law is what Parliament decides ... No one is to block the laws of Parliament.'

On 29 October 1925, when the power of Parliament was threatened, Mossadegh held up the Koran and told his fellow parliamentarians that to leave total power in the hands of a single individual would usher in 'pure tyranny'. 'Was it to realize absolute rule that our people bled their lives away in the Constitutional Revolution?' he asked.

Iranians have been grappling with this unresolved impasse for at least 100 years. They are painfully aware that democracy and human rights are not abstractions, but affect their everyday lives.

Throughout Iran's recent history, each subsequent generation has endeavoured to bring about political change. In the last 150 years, Iran's absolutist monarchs were either ousted by the people or forced to flee and die in exile – with the exception of Mozzafar'addin Shah, who gave in to pro-democracy activists and agreed to create a Parliament and hold elections. He even signed Iran's constitution in 1906. Iranians do not give in to brute rule. However, in the 1920s a dictatorial monarchy, with Britain's assistance, brought to an end Iran's constitutional government.

A generation later, the democratically elected government of Mossadegh was finished off in a coup backed by the United States and Britain.

In the Post-Mossadegh era some of Iran's new generation, having witnessed the failure of non-violent protests, chose the path of armed rebellion against the dictatorial monarchy. Like most Islamic countries, the absence of democracy created a void that only the Islamic militants were able to fill. While governments brutally suppressed the meetings of dissident groups, radical Islam was spared because it enjoyed the use of the sanctified space of the mosque. Come the Revolution, this new breed of mutant Islamists was well equipped to take control.

© Nafise Motlagh

PROTESTERS AT TEHRAN UNIVERSITY 2002

In the early days of the Revolution a range of political groups – from the far Left to the far Right, from secular to ultra-Islamic – jostled for political power, pushing their rival agendas. The Revolution that had begun as a pro-democracy movement, developed into something worse. Its leader Ayatollah Khomeini spoke of freedom and independence but very soon Iran was an ideological state governed by Islamic revolutionary law. Khomeini was established as Supreme Leader – 'God's representative on earth' – and as such accountable only to God. Iranians had traded one unaccountable regime for another.

The former US President Bill Clinton recently referred to the case of Iran in an extensive interview during the 2005 World Economic Forum at Davos.

> … It's a sad story that really began in the 1950s when the United States
> deposed Mr Mossadegh, who was an elected parliamentary democrat, and

brought the Shah back in [the interviewer says 'CIA'] and then he was overturned by the Ayatollah Khomeini, driving us into the arms of one Saddam Hussein. Most of the terrible things Saddam Hussein did in the 1980s he did with the full, knowing support of the United States government, because he was in Iran, and Iran was what it was because we got rid of the parliamentary democracy back in the fifties. At least, that is my belief.

Iran is the most perplexing problem … we face, for the following reasons: it is the only country in the world with two governments, and the only country in the world that has now had six elections since the first election of President Khatami. [It is] the only one with elections – including the United States, including Israel, including you name it – where the liberals or the progressives have won two-thirds to 70 per cent of the vote in six elections: two for President; two for the Parliament, the Majlis; two for the mayoralties. In every single election, the guys I identify with got two-thirds to 70 per cent of the vote. There is no other country in the world I can say that about – certainly not my own.[8]

---

2 March 2004

According to many of our social commentators, religion has ceased to be a unifying force among our people … the conduct of our rulers has pushed religion out of its sacred dimensions and have turned religion into something anti-social. No one can deny that after all these years if anyone admits to being religious or having faith … in the view of most people they are lined up alongside liars, hypocrites and even tyrants … Believe me, any solutions that are put forward within a religious framework will not make any difference to how the new generation views religion.

It was this religion that took away the people's right to vote … and has taken away from them the right to be modern and resourceful, and denies them the basic pleasures of life … equality and freedom …

I believe that if the older generation today still hold strong religious values, it is because they did not grow up under a meddlesome religious regime ... The older generation can never comprehend the level of humiliation, slander and insult that this totalitarian regime has poured down our throats under the guise of religious values ...

If this society does not explode due to a lack of democracy or the denial of our right to vote, be assured that the young will bring about a monumental eruption that will destroy everything, even themselves, due to a lack of the basic pleasures of life, for the young have no place of their own in this society.

Email: baba@eparizi.com
http://baba.eparizi.com

15 February 2004

Islamic rule has brought so much misery upon us that supporters of the monarchy use our present predicament as an excuse to call the Shah's period the era of civilization ... but our people's memories are not so bad that they've forgotten that swamp or the fact that this Islamic Revolution grew out of that swamp ...

In our country all forms of oppressive rule have been tested out ... But this time everyone is primarily concerned with democracy and freedom. The Iranian Revolution is alive and eternal and is ongoing ... Long live the Iranian Revolution!

Email: gashtal@hotmail.com
http://siprisk.blogspot.com

It is a long and complicated journey towards democracy, which cannot be imposed but must come from within a culture and its people. Iran's recent modern history shows that each subsequent generation's efforts to win freedom alas proved futile, either through ineptitude or foreign interference. Iran's long struggle for democracy appears to be caught in a vicious circle. Here is Emadeddin Baghi, a leading democracy advocate based in Iran, on the subject:

> Society itself, not the Government, creates change. And there are deep
> transformations occurring in Iran. Out of sight of much of the world,
> Iran is inching its way towards democracy.[9]

Iranian blogs offer a unique glimpse of the changing consciousness of Iran's younger generation. It is nothing less than a revolution within the Revolution. Since the tragedy of 9/11, political movements in the Islamic world have taken centre stage. It seems possible that Iran, which a quarter of a century ago introduced a bemused world to radical Islam, may yet surprise the world all over again.

NOTES

CHAPTER 1

1 The NITLE program crawls through the web using statistical analyses, with an algorithm that identifies blogs and their languages.
2 'Cyberdissent: The Internet in Revolutionary Iran' (MERIA, September 2003).
3 'The Unrest Is Growing', interview with Jürgen Habermas, Frankfurter Allgemeine Zeitung (18 June 2002).

CHAPTER 2

1 See All the Shah's Men: An American Coup and the Roots of Middle East Terror (John Wiley, 2003).
2 'The Iranian.com: Iran's American Martyr', Robert D. Burgener (31 August 1998).
3 Ali Ansari, Modern Iran Since 1921 (Longman, 2003).
4 All the Shah's Men: An American Coup and the Roots of Middle East Terror (John Wiley, 2003).
5 In 'The State, Civil Society, and the Prospects of Islamic Fundamentalism' in Comparative Studies of South Asia, Africa and the Middle East (Autumn, 1996).
6 Tortured Confessions, Prisons and Public Recantations in Modern Iran, Ervand Abrahamian (University of California Press, 1999).
7 Translated from 'Lettre ouverte à Mehdi Bazargan', Le Nouvel Observateur, n° 753, p.46 (14–20 April 1979).
8 See 'Officers Say US Aided Iraq In War Despite Use Of Gas', Patrick E. Tyler in the New York Times (18 August 2002).
9 Kenneth Pollack, The Threatening Storm (Random House, 2002).

10 'Officers Say US Aided Iraq In War Despite Use Of Gas', Patrick E. Tyler, New York Times (18 August 2002).
11 'Letter from Tehran: Shadow Land', Joe Klein, The New Yorker (18 February 2002).
12 Jahangir Amuzegar AxisofLogic.com (19 February 2004).

CHAPTER 4

1 Stephen Kinzer, All the Shah's Men: an American Coup and the Roots of Middle East Terror (John Wiley, 2003).
2 Paul Klebnikov, 'Millionaire Mullahs', Forbes Magazine (21 July 2003).

CHAPTER 5

1 Morgan Shuster, The Strangling of Persia (1912); (Ibex Publishing, 1990).
2 Janet Afary, The Iranian Constitutional Revolution (Columbia University Press, 1996).
3 Nikki Keddie, Iran: Understanding the Enigma (MERIA, September 1998).
4 Elaine Sciolino, Persian Mirrors: The Elusive Face of Iran (The Free Press, 2000).
5 WAF [Women Against Fundamentalism], 1994.

CHAPTER 6

1 Nicholas Kristof, New York Times (15 May 2004).

CHAPTER 7

1 Reporters Sans Frontières, 'Internet Under Surveillance Report 2004'.
2 Hooshang Amirahmadi (Payvand.com, 29 March 2004).
3 Dan De Luce, Guardian (24 May 2004).
4 IRNA [Islamic Republic News Agency] (1 June 2004).
5 Roya Hakakian, Journey From the Land of No: A Girlhood Caught in Revolutionary Iran (Crown, 2004).
6 Yasaratal-Hussein (19 October 2003).
7 Tim Judah, Observer (25 August 2002).

CHAPTER 8

1 As reported by AFP [Agence France–Presse], and in greater detail by an Iranian independent newspaper Vaghaye Etefaghiyeh, which was shut down soon afterwards (27 April 2004).
2 Mohsen Sazegara, interview with the BBC Persian Service (10 May 2004).
3 AFP, 14 June 2004.
4 Reporters Sans Frontières, 'Internet Under Surveillance Report 2004'.

5 Dan De Luce, 'Not Much of an Opening in the Mullahs' Robes', *Washington Post* (21 November 2004).

6 Farzaneh Milani, *Washington Post* (12 March 2005).

7 Shirin Ebadi, *Independent* (19 February 2005).

8 Bill Clinton at the 2005 Economic Forum at Davos. Interview conducted by American journalist Charlie Rose on 26 January 2005. Quoted in *Executive Intelligence Review* (11 February 2005).

9 Emadeddin Baghi, 'Hope for Democracy in Iran' the *Washington Post* (25 October 2004).